THE LIFE OF REPENTANCE AND PURITY

Coptic Studies Series

The Coptic Studies Series at St Vladimir's Seminary Press
was conceived with a two-fold purpose: to increase the accessibility
of the many treasures of Coptic Orthodox Christianity to a wider
English-speaking audience; and to cross-pollinate the spiritual minds
of Coptic Orthodox Christians and their Eastern Orthodox
brethren with the knowledge of a common faith in the incarnate
Word of God—who is the true source of all wisdom and knowledge.

Series Editors:
Bishop Suriel and John Behr

BOOK I
The Life of Repentance and Purity
Pope Shenouda III

The Life of Repentance and Purity

His Holiness

POPE SHENOUDA III

117th Pope of Alexandria and
Patriarch of the See of Saint Mark

Second English Edition

Translated by His Grace Bishop Suriel
Bishop of Melbourne
Dean of Saint Athanasius Coptic Orthodox Theological College
Melbourne, Australia

ST VLADIMIR'S SEMINARY PRESS

YONKERS, NEW YORK

2016

Library of Congress Cataloging-in-Publication Data

Names: Shanūdah III, Coptic Patriarch of Alexandria, 1923–2012, author. | Behr, John,
    editor. | Suriel, Coptic Bishop of Melbourne, 1963– translator.
Title: The life of repentance and purity / His Holiness Pope Shenouda III 117th Pope of
    Alexandria and Patriarch of the See of Saint Mark ; co-editors, Archpriest John Behr &
    Bishop Suriel ; translated by His Grace Bishop Suriel, Bishop of Melbourne.
Other titles: Hayāt al-tawbah wa-al-naqāwah. English
Description: Second English edition. | Yonkers : St. Vladimir's Seminary Press, 2016. |
    Series: Coptic studies series ; book 1 | In English; translated from Arabic.
Identifiers: LCCN 2016001131 | ISBN 9780881415322 (paper) | ISBN 9780881415339
    (electronic)
Subjects: LCSH: Repentance. | Christian life—Coptic Church authors.
Classification: LCC BT800 .S536 2016 | DDC 248.4/8172—dc23
LC record available at http://lccn.loc.gov/2016001131

Edited by the Translation Committee of
Saint Antonious & Saint Mina Coptic Orthodox Church in East Rutherford, NJ

First edition published in Arabic in 1983
by the Coptic Orthodox Theological Seminary in Cairo, Egypt

First translated edition published in English in 1990
by Coptic Orthodox Publication and Translation in Sydney, Australia

SAC PRESS
ST ATHANASIUS COLLEGE PRESS

COPYRIGHT © 2016 BY
St Athanasius Coptic Orthodox Theological College

SVS PRESS

ST VLADIMIR'S SEMINARY PRESS
575 Scarsdale Road, Yonkers, NY 10707
1-800-204-BOOK (2665)
www.svspress.com

ISBN 978-088141-532-2 (paper)
ISBN 978-088141-533-9 (electronic)

PRINTED IN THE UNITED STATES OF AMERICA

Contents

Introduction to the Second English Edition

On 17 MARCH, 2016 we commemorated the fourth anniversary of the falling asleep of a giant of modern Coptic history: His Holiness Pope Shenouda III, the 117th Pope of Alexandria and Patriarch of the See of Saint Mark. Egyptian newspapers called his funeral "the funeral of the century." Such was His Holiness's influence on all Egyptians, both Muslim and Christian.

His Holiness Pope Shenouda III was born Nazeer Gayed in 1923, in the village of Salam, near Assiut. He graduated with a B.A. in history from the Faculty of Literature of Cairo University in 1947. He worked as a history and English teacher while attending evening classes at the Coptic Orthodox Theological Seminary in Cairo. In 1949, he was appointed to the faculty of the seminary by the recently canonized saint, Archdeacon Habib Girgis. In 1954, he entered Saint Mary's Monastery, known as Deir al-Syrian, in the Western Desert. From 1956 to 1962, he led the life of a monastic hermit in a desert cave about seven kilometers from the monastery. He was later ordained a priest with the name Father Antonius Al-Syriaany, and served as the secretary of His Holiness Pope Cyril (Kyrillos) VI, the 116th pope, who has also been recently canonized a saint in our Church. His Holiness Pope Kyrillos eventually consecrated him a bishop and assigned to him the position of bishop of theological education. Under the leadership of Bishop Shenouda, the number of students at the Coptic Theological Seminary increased threefold.

After his consecration, Bishop Shenouda started weekly public lectures to extend theological education to all of the congregation, not just those who could attend seminary. He delivered lectures on Fridays in Cairo and in Alexandria on Sundays. When he was ordained pope in 1971, after the falling asleep of His Holiness Pope Kyrillos VI, Pope Shenouda III started the weekly Wednesday sermons that he continued to deliver until his last days.

In 1981, His Holiness Pope Shenouda III was banished to the monastery of Saint Bishoy for forty months by the late Egyptian President Anwar Sadat during Sadat's crackdown on anyone who spoke against him. During that house arrest His Holiness completed this book, and wrote several others. He returned to his papal see on January 6, 1985. His Holiness continued to write prolifically throughout his papacy, publishing over 100 books and an even larger number of magazine and newspaper articles.

His Holiness demonstrated a strong commitment to Christian unity, visiting the various sister Orthodox Churches and their patriarchs, such as those of Constantinople, Moscow, Romania, and Antioch. In 1973, His Holiness became the first Coptic Orthodox pope to visit the Vatican in over 1500 years. There was also dialogue with various Protestant Churches worldwide. Under his leadership, the Coptic Orthodox Church became a founding member of the Middle East Council of Churches and a member of the All-African Council of Churches, the National Council of the Churches of Christ in the USA, the Canadian Council of Churches, and the Australian Council of Churches.

During his forty-year papacy, the Coptic Orthodox Church saw major expansion in the diaspora. In 1971, there were only four churches in North America. Today, there are over 150. Pope Shenouda established mission churches in Bermuda, St. Kitts, and the U.S. Virgin Islands. Moreover, he founded the first Coptic Orthodox Church in South America in Sao Paolo, Brazil, and another in Bolivia. In Australia and New Zealand, there are currently fifty churches; there are over fifty churches in Europe; sub-Saharan Africa has over 100 churches in ten countries (including Sudan), and the number continues to grow.

Pope Shenouda was keen to travel abroad to meet with priests and bishops and offer his pastoral care. In every visit to the churches of the diaspora, among his first questions was how many young persons a church had, and how many children attended Sunday school in each grade. Sometimes he would have discussions directly with the youth to learn the progress of their youth groups and Sunday Schools, often saying, "A church without youth is a church without a future."

The gifts and talents that the Lord bestowed upon him are too numerous to mention. For my part, I remember him as a true man of God. Even his voice was godly; when I heard it, I felt sanctified and at peace. This was the effect he had on millions of people. He lived the true life of an ascetic, and yet had a deep love for his people, both young and old.

We will never forget his beautiful smile, his sense of humor, his powerful sermons and teachings, and even his poems, full of spirituality. We will never forget his joyfulness, which clearly sprang from a heart full of God's love. He had an excellent mind, committing much of the Bible to memory, as well as many sayings of the Desert and Church Fathers, quoting them verbatim in his weekly sermons. An avid reader, he turned his monastic cell into a scholarly library.

To serve his expanding flock around the world, His Holiness's writings were quickly translated from Arabic into many different languages and disseminated to the churches. They now deserve a closer look, as well as translations that do His Holiness's original writings justice, so that a wider audience of people who wish to strengthen their faith, deepen their spirituality, and draw closer to Christ in their walk with Him, can do so with the help of these texts.

Pope Shenouda's *The Life of Repentance and Purity* is one of the best examples of his teachings and personality. It is at once spiritual, poetic, biblical, patristic, comprehensive, and practical. Not many teachers or writers can accomplish this all at once in the way His Holiness does in this book.

I first translated *The Life of Repentance and Purity* from Arabic into English in 1989, when I was still a layperson living in Australia and contemplating the monastic life. For eight months, I would come home from teaching at a secondary school and spend four or five hours translating, using El-Mawrid's Arabic-English dictionary when needed. I wanted to publish the English translation when His Holiness arrived for his first visit to Australia in December 1989. We were able to give him a copy of the translation on this first visit, and then we gave him the published version in 1991, when he came back for the Seventh Assembly of the World Council of Churches in Canberra. In March of that same year, I left for the monastery.

This book strengthened my resolve toward a monastic vocation, and became a spiritual and ascetical guide during my monastic journey. His Holiness Pope Shenouda III was truly an inspiration to me, not only through his words of wisdom, but also through his life and the monastic ideal that he followed. Merely seeing him was sufficient to fill my heart and soul with joy, hope, and peace at the same time.

The Life of Repentance and Purity is one of His Holiness's first published books. He wrote it while still a monk, but then unfortunately he lost the original manuscript and had to rewrite it in the early years of his papacy. He completed it while under house arrest at Saint Bishoy Monastery, Scetis, in the early 1980s. The book has been a source of repentance for many people, especially the youth. His Holiness managed to communicate these deep spiritual concepts and practices to a large audience that includes monks and nuns as well as laypeople who are living in the world but struggling to live a pure life—it is, in other words, a book for all Christians.

This second edition of the English translation has been reviewed and edited carefully by a committee dedicated to translation under the guidance of the Very Reverend Fr Athanasius Farag and the Reverend Fr Bishoy Mikhail at Saint Antonious and Saint Mina Coptic Orthodox Church in East Rutherford, New Jersey. The contributors to this edited translation include:

- Phoebe Farag Mikhail, Writer and Writing Instructor (thoroughly edited English translation, authored some explanatory notes, researched references for liturgical and patristic quotes in the text)

- Mary Morgan, United Nations Translator (retired) (reviewed edited version against the original Arabic)

- Omneya Amir Risk El-Far, reviewer (reviewed edited version against the original Arabic, researched some references for patristic quotes in the text)

- Sola Armanious, English as a Second Language Instructor (reviewed edited sections against the original Arabic)

This effort has spanned several years, and has been a labor of love for all participants. It is my hope that all who read this book will grow in God's grace and truly experience the joy that the life of repentance and purity bring to all who live in it.

Suriel
Bishop of Melbourne
Dean of Saint Athanasius Coptic Orthodox Theological College

A Note to Readers from the Translation Committee

IN THE ORIGINAL ARABIC EDITION, as well as in the first English edition of *The Life of Repentance and Purity* by His Holiness Pope Shenouda III, there are many footnotes by the author. These notes referred to sermons, lectures, and related material in his other books.

Because much of this book was originally delivered as lectures and sermons, His Holiness Pope Shenouda III quoted from memory many sayings and anecdotes of the fathers and mothers of the Church, especially monastic fathers and mothers. The original print edition of the book did not provide the sources for these quotes.

To help the reader locate the quotations and sayings, we have provided the sources for as many of these quotations as possible. The specific editions that His Holiness used for his quotations, however, were not available to us. Some were monastery manuscripts, while others were Arabic or other translations of the texts, as His Holiness was multilingual. Where references were found, we have indicated the source without specifying the edition or translation. However, there were some quotations we were unable to locate. If any reader can locate those sources, we will include those reference in the next edition.[1]

Other notes, marked as "editor's notes," serve as explanations of terms and liturgical practices in the Coptic Orthodox Church.

---

[1]Please send notes to: director@sacpress.com.au.

Foreword to the First Arabic Edition

REPENTANCE, MY BRETHREN, is not only for those beginning their lives with God but for everyone, even the saints. It is part of our daily prayers. Every person needs repentance, no matter how great his position or his spiritual progress. We are all in need of repentance, in need of it every day, since we sin every day. "For there is no person without sin, even if his life were one day on earth."[1] With repentance we prepare our hearts for the dwelling of God, and with purity, we will see God (Matthew 5.8). Repentance is the beginning of the path toward God. It is a friend along the path until the end.

Repentance is therefore one of the fundamental topics about which I have lectured frequently since the beginning of my work as Bishop of Christian Education, approximately twenty years ago. I delivered many lectures on repentance in Saint Mark's Hall at the Monastery of Anba Rewais, at youth meetings and for university groups. During the years between 1965 and 1969, I presented other condensed lectures at the Church of the Angels in Damanhour, at Saint George's Church in Al-Mahala Al-Kobra, and in other cities.

It had been my wish for many years to publish a book on the life of repentance. I actually compiled the lectures for it and presented them to the printers in August of 1971. Three sections of it were published. However, the responsibilities of the Patriarchate preoccupied me, keeping me from the book (and from publishing any other) for a long time. The workload was great during these years and did not give me a chance to write. The time then came, after twelve years, when God willed for the book to be published.

Because of the delay in publishing *The Life of Repentance*, many of my beloved friends chastened me gently, saying, "Our repentance has been slowed by the delay in publishing the book. Shall we assume you will take this responsibility for this delay before God?" I regularly answered them with these words: "Pray that the Lord may give me time." The Lord then

[1]*Editor's note:* Job 14.4–5 (the Coptic Orthodox Litany for the Departed).

gave me time, and I presented the book for printing. Here it is, finally, in your hands. Its delay was an opportunity to add to it other lectures that I presented later in the Great Cathedral during the seventies. After all, do you think I had collected all of what was said about repentance? This is clearly not the case. The topic of repentance is a large one with many branches. It is interrelated with many other topics from the spiritual life; it arises with contemplation on the psalms and the sections of the *Agpeya*,[2] the book of Revelation, the book of the Song of Songs, Romans 12, the characters of the Bible, and in various lectures on salvation.

We have published other small books, besides this one, under the heading *A Series on the Life of Repentance and Purity*. From this series came the books *The Spiritual Awakening*, *The Spiritual Vigil*, *Returning to God*, and the book *The Fear of God*, which is on the way to being printed.

To complete this series, I will shortly publish a book called *The Spiritual Wars*.[3] This will likely first appear as a series of small books to be collected later in general into a large book. It will cover spiritual warfare, and then the combat with each sin that delays repentance individually.

It only remains for me to say that the topic of repentance and purity is open. It is life itself. . . .

SHENOUDA III
Coptic Orthodox Patriarchate
Pope of Alexandria and Patriarch of the See of Saint Mark

---

[2] *Editor's note:* The *Agpeya* is the Coptic Orthodox Book of the Seven Daily Canonical Hours (Divine Offices). For more information, see Archbishop Basilios, "Canonical Hours, Book of," *The Coptic Encyclopedia* 2, (1991 edition), http://ccdl.libraries.claremont.edu/cdm/singleitem/collection/cce/id/413/rec/2

[3] *Editor's note:* His Holiness's books were mainly published by the Coptic Orthodox Theological Seminary in Cairo.

PART ONE

WHAT IS REPENTANCE?

CHAPTER I

What Is Repentance?

IF SIN IS SEPARATION FROM GOD, then repentance is returning to God.[1] God says: "Return to me and I will return to you" (Malachi 3.8). When the prodigal son repented, he returned to his father (Luke 15.18–20). True repentance is a human longing for the origin from which we were taken. It is the desire of a heart that strayed from God, and finally felt it could go no further away.

For just as sin is conflict with God, so repentance is reconciliation with God. This is what our teacher Saint Paul stated about his apostolic work, saying: "Therefore we are ambassadors for Christ, as though God were pleading by us: we implore you on Christ's behalf, be reconciled to God" (2 Corinthians 5.20). But repentance is not confined to reconciliation. Through repentance, God returns and dwells in the human heart, transforming it into a heaven. As for the unrepentant, how can God dwell in their hearts while the sin is dwelling therein? As the Bible says: "What communion has light with darkness?" (2 Corinthians 6.14).

Repentance is also a spiritual awakening. The sinful person is unaware of his state. The Bible says to him "that now it is high time to awake out of sleep" (Romans 13.11). In this context, repentance is the return of a person to himself. Or, put another way, it is the return of a person to his or her original sensitivity, the return of the heart to its fervor, and the return of the conscience to its work. It is justly said about the prodigal son upon his repentance: "He came to himself" (Luke 15.17). He returned to alertness, to correct thinking, and to a spiritual understanding.

For as sin is regarded as spiritual death; the Bible says about sinners that they are "dead in trespasses" (Ephesians 2.5). Repentance, then, is a transfer from death to life, according to the expression of Saint John the Evangelist

[1]See my books, *Return to God* and *The Spiritual Awakening*, which are focused on returning to God and reconciliation with God.

(1 John 3.14). Saint Paul the Apostle says about this: "Awake, you who sleep; arise from the dead, and Christ will give you light" (Ephesians 5.14). Saint James the Apostle confirms the same interpretation when he says: "He who turns a sinner from the error of his way will save a soul from death and cover a multitude of sins" (James 5.20).

Repentance is resurrection for the spirit, because the death of the spirit is separation from God. As Saint Augustine said: "Repentance is a new pure heart, which God gives to the sinners to love Him with." It is a divine act performed by God inside the person, according to His divine promise: "I shall sprinkle clean water on you, and you will be cleansed from all your uncleanness. . . . I shall give you a new heart and put a new spirit within you. . . . I shall . . . cause you to walk in My statutes, and you will keep My judgments and do them" (Ezekiel 36.25–27).

Repentance is freedom from the slavery of sin and the devil. It is also freedom from the most sinful habits and from running after lusts. It is impossible for us to partake of this freedom without the work of the Lord in us. Therefore the Bible says: "If the Son makes you free, you shall be free indeed" (John 8.36). It is true freedom, because "whoever commits sin is a slave of sin" (John 8.34). We receive this freedom if, by repentance, we stand firm in the truth—we do not receive it through vanity. "And the truth shall make you free" (John 8.32).

Not every forsaking of sin is considered repentance. Repentance is the forsaking of sin because of the love of God and the love of righteousness. Other reasons for forsaking sin include fear, embarrassment, inability, pre-occupation (with the remainder of love for this sin in the heart), or the consequences of unsuitable situations. These reasons are not considered repentance. True repentance is the discarding of sin practically, mentally, and from the heart, which springs out of love for God, His commandments, and His kingdom, and the care of the repentant person for his or her lot in eternity.

True repentance is forsaking sin without return. This has been the story of many saints who have repented, including Saint Augustine, Saint Moses the Black, Saint Mary of Egypt, Pelagia, Thais,[2] and Sarah. Repentance is

---

[2]*Editor's note:* For more information on Saint Mary of Egypt, Pelagia, and Thais, see Benedicta Ward, *Harlots of the Desert* (Kalamazoo: Cistercian Publications, 1987).

found in the lives of all these and others. It is a turning toward God, continued throughout life, without a return to sin. This reminds us of the saying of Saint Bishoy: "I do not remember that the devil has tempted me into the same sin twice." It is possible that the first sin was as a result of ignorance, negligence, weakness, or lack of awareness of the tricks of the devil, or lack of cautiousness. But after repentance and awakening, there is strictness in living and a caution of sin. The person who discards sin and then returns to it—therefore sometimes leaving it, and sometimes returning—has not yet repented. This is only an attempt toward repentance. Every time the sinner arises from his sin, sin drags him lower. If his freedom is struck down, he will not repent.

Repentance is a cry from the conscience and a revolt against the past. It is repulsion from sin, great regret, and rejection of the old state with embarrassment and shame. Hence, repentance is often called "a daring judge."

Repentance is a complete change in a person's life, not a temporary emotion. It is a real and fundamental change felt by the person, as well as by everyone that deals with him. His thoughts change, as well as his principles and values, his outlook on life and his manner of speech, his habits and dealings with people, and most importantly, his dealings with God. The person also changes from within, with a heart refusing the once-beloved sins. The love of God enters his heart and he becomes spiritually revived, in a state of spiritual ecstasy.

Thus, it is perfectly accurate to describe repentance as the exchange of one lust for another. The lust to live with God replaces sinful and bodily lust. Along with the contrarian act, which is forsaking sin and its love, repentance has also a positive side, which leads a person to the love of God, His kingdom, and His ways. It is a warm feeling, making the person desire a pure life.

Repentance is renewal for the mind. The renewal of one's *nature* occurs in baptism (Romans 6.4), but the renewal of the *mind* occurs in repentance. As the apostle says: "Be transformed by the renewing of your mind, that you may prove what is that good and acceptable and perfect will of God" (Romans 12.2).

Repentance is the golden key that opens the door to the kingdom of heaven. Or rather it is the true door that leads to heaven, because without repentance, God does not reign in our hearts. Repentance is the oil in the lampstands of the virgins, granting them the right to enter into the wedding feast (Matthew 25).

Repentance is the channel that delivers the justification of the blood from the cross. This is the only way for our sins to be removed after baptism, and so some have called it "a second baptism." Repentance is a strong rebuke to Satan. It is a dissolution of the communion between the sinner and the devil, that the sinner might enter into communion with the Holy Spirit (2 Corinthians 13.14).

Repentance is a fire, taken by the seraphim from the top of the altar. With it he eliminates the iniquity of the sinner, while saying to him: "Your iniquity is taken away, and your sin purged" (Isaiah 6.7). It is the only way to erase our sins from the book of judgment. How beautiful are the Lord's words, "Their sin I will remember no more" (Jeremiah 31.34). The importance of repentance for receiving forgiveness is reflected in the Lord's saying: "Unless you repent you will all likewise perish" (Luke 13.3).

Repentance is the way of escaping from the coming anger. Of course, this is under the condition that it is true repentance and is appropriate to the seriousness of the sin. The repentance of the people of Nineveh made God relent from the disaster that He had said He would bring upon them (Jonah 3.10). Other judgments of God were similar (Jeremiah 26.13; Exodus 18.22). A lovely saying of one of the saints is: "God will not ask you, 'why did you sin?' But He will ask you, 'why did you not repent?'"

Repentance is therefore God's way of preserving you and His pardon of your sin. God, from the depths of His love, has given everyone the chance for salvation, no matter how great his sins are. God does not take anyone in sin before first giving him a chance to repent. Repentance is a divine privilege that God has given sinners to purify them and pacify their consciences, giving them inner peace and ensuring their return to their original nature before the first sin.

Repentance is God's outstretched hand, seeking reconciliation with you. It is a chance to turn a new page, which God opens in His relationship with you by forgiving you for the past. He shall wash you, and you shall be whiter than snow (Psalm 50 [51]).[3] It is a chance to build up hope and rid yourself

[3]*Editor's note:* Psalm numbers are according to the Septuagint and Coptic number-

of despair. It has been said about repentance that it is the door of mercy, forgiveness, and life, a bridge linking heaven and earth.

The previous points describe God's role in forgiveness. The following presents the human role.

Repentance is a reply from mankind to God's invitation. It is the reply of the conscience to God's voice. It is a reply from the will to the work of grace. It is non-resistance to the Spirit, which works in us for our salvation (Acts 7.51). It is neither grieving nor quenching the Spirit (Ephesians 4.30; 1 Thessalonians 5.19).

When Saint Isaac [the Syrian] was asked about repentance, he said: "It is a contrite heart."[4] It is the contrite heart returning to God. It is the bent knee, the weeping eye, and the broken heart. It is the mother of tears, contrition, and humility, because repentance gives birth to all of these. It breaks the sinner's pride, softening his hard heart and leading him into the life of humility. Saint Isaac also said: "The sacrifice of repentance that we present to God is the heart which has repented contritely, and has been broken by the tears of prayer before God, asking forgiveness for his weak nature."[5] As said in Psalm 50 (51), the psalm of repentance: "The sacrifices of God are a broken spirit, a broken and a contrite heart—these, O God, you will not despise."

Saint John Saba [of Dalyatha] said: "Repentance is a great torment to the devil, who tries to stop it."[6] It saves and releases those whom the devil has captured with his evil. Many years of the devil's hard work are lost in one hour of repentance. All the thorns he has planted in our land and nurtured with great care over many years get burned up in one day. Our land is purified. Repentance makes virgins of adulterers.

---

ing. Psalm 50 (51) is prayed during the introductory prayer for each of the seven hours of the *Agpeya*. Hereafter, Psalms quoted from the Coptic Orthodox liturgical books will be indicated with the Septuagint numbering, sometimes followed by the Hebrew numbering in parentheses. Citations to the rest of the Old Testament Scriptures are to the standard Hebrew numbering, except that the books of 1 and 2 Samuel and 1 and 2 Kings are all referred to as 1–4 Kingdoms.

[4]Isaac the Syrian, *Ascetical Homilies* LXIV.
[5]Ibid., LIV.
[6]John of Dalyatha, *Letters*.

Who does not love you, O repentance, O you who carry all the blessings, except the devil, from whom you have captured all his riches and wasted all his possessions? O Mother of forgiveness! The Father who is filled with mercy will not be angered by your pleadings, since He granted you to be an intercessor for the sinners, and He gave you the key to His kingdom.

After Saint John Climacus visited the penitents' monastery and saw the contrition of their souls, the intensity of their struggle, and the fervor of their prayers, he said: "I blessed those who sinned and repented weeping, more than those who did not fall and did not weep for their souls."[7] Repentance is joy in heaven and on earth. It is written, "There will be joy in heaven over one sinner who repents" (Luke 15.7, 10). So if you wish to make heaven joyous, repent. It is joy on earth also: joy for the penitent, the pastor, and all the Church. Repentance is joy, as it is an invitation to liberty for the captives (Isaiah 61.1). It is joy for the freedom from the slavery of Satan and sin, joy in the new pure life, and joy in forgiveness. It is a joy, for repentance is the life of victory and the song of the victorious. The penitent offer praise with David: "Blessed is the Lord, who did not give us as prey to their teeth. Our soul was delivered like a sparrow from the snare of the hunters; the snare was broken, and we were delivered" (Psalm 123.6–7).

However, repentance is not the objective of the spiritual life, but merely the beginning of a long journey toward the life of purity. Repentance is the beginning of the relationship with God. It is the beginning of a long path whose aim is holiness and perfection. One may therefore ask how the person who has not begun to repent until now can reach the end. How will the person who delays the first step until his elderly years, or until the hour of death, achieve the Lord's saying: "You shall be perfect, just as your Father in heaven is perfect" (Matthew 5.48)?

[7]John Climacus, *The Ladder of Divine Ascent* V.26.

CHAPTER 2

Repentance: Its Progression and Perfection

A PERSON PROGRESSES AND ADVANCES in repentance just as in any other virtue. He keeps progressing until he reaches its perfection. So then, what is the starting point of repentance? Is it leaving sin in the fear of God? There is a point before leaving sin, and that is the desire for repentance.

Many do not want to repent because they enjoy sin and wish to remain in it. Their character is beautiful in their own eyes and they do not want to change. So the simple *desire* to repent is a good starting point. God's grace accepts this desire and asks: "Do you wish to be healed?" The desire to be healed begins the work of His grace in the person. The next step, then, is actually leaving sin.

More important than leaving sin is abandoning it in the heart and mind. A person may leave sin practically, but the love of sin is still in his heart. He yearns for it and regrets certain opportunities when he could have sinned, but did not. Such a person has left sin for the sake of God's command-ments, not because he hates sin. He should progress in repentance until sin is removed from his heart.

The perfection of repentance is the hatred of sin. That means a person hates sin with all his heart, is disgusted by it, and does not need any effort to overcome it since it no longer agrees with his nature. Here the person reaches the edge of purity. Purity of heart is a profound topic, so we will set aside Part Four ("The Signs of Repentance") and Part Five ("The Purity of Heart") to discuss it.

Leaving the most prominent sin in one's life and hating it comes after the next upward step. That next step is leaving the sins that are revealed through spiritual progression. Thanks to God's compassion for us, He does not reveal our every sin and weakness to us all at once, so that we do not feel worthless. Each time we hear spiritual sermons and read God's book and other spiritual books, our weaknesses and shortcomings—which need treatment, struggle, and repentance—are revealed to us. Here we enter into a process of cleansing and purification that continues throughout life.

Because the devil leaves one battleground and fights in another, we should be ready for him in every battlefield. Even the sin of which we have been relieved for a period may tempt us again. In this way repentance will remain with us throughout life.

Repentance is not only for resisting sin. There is also repentance for shortcomings in spiritual progression. The penitent should bear fruit worthy of repentance (Matthew 3.8); with this he will enter into the fruit of the Spirit (Galatians 5.22). If he does not bear fruit, then he needs repentance for the sin of not bearing fruit, as the Bible says: "To him who knows to do good and does not do it, to him it is sin" (James 4.17).

Repentance, then, is not merely a stage which passes; it remains with us. There is no one without sin, not even if he lived only one day on earth. For we all sin and need repentance. Therefore, repentance becomes a daily activity. "If we say that we have no sin, we deceive ourselves, and the truth is not in us" (1 John 1.8).

There is a difference between the repentance of sinners and the repentance of saints. Sinners repent of the sins that are an obvious breach of the commandments, the sins which show their lack of love for God. As for the saints, they repent of minor shortcomings, which are caused by human weaknesses. Because of their desire for the life of perfection, they see before them stages to be overcome before they are perfected. During all of this, their hearts are protected in the love of God.

The Church has laid down for us daily prayers during which we can ask for repentance. In the petitions[1] and psalms of the *Agpeya*, we note the following prayers:

i. The confessing of sin and the worthiness of punishment, in Psalm 6 (in the First Hour) and Psalm 50 (51) (in the introduction to every hour) and in the petitions of the Sunset Prayer (the Eleventh Hour).

---

[1] *Editor's note:* The petitions are prayers prayed after the Gospel reading in each of the seven hours of the *Agpeya*.

ii. The request for forgiveness, such as in the petitions and absolution of the Sixth Hour, and in the rest of the prayers.

iii. Asking the Lord to save the person who is praying from sin itself, such as in the absolution of the Third Hour.

iv. Asking for guidance for forgiveness along the path, as in Psalm 118, which is prayed in the Midnight Prayer, and the petition, "Lord, by Your grace, protect us this night from sin," which is prayed during the Twelfth Hour.

v. Blaming oneself and rebuking one's soul for its falling and carelessness, as in the petitions of the Prayer Before Sleeping (the Twelfth Hour).

vi. Awakening the soul to repentance, reminding it about death, the Judgment, and Christ's Second Coming, as in the petitions of the Prayer Before Sleeping and in the Gospels and petitions of the Midnight Prayer.

This demonstrates that we ask for repentance every day and at every hour. Here are some examples. The person praying prays in the petitions of the Prayer Before Sleeping (the Twelfth Hour): "Behold, I am about to stand before the Just Judge in fear because of my numerous sins. . . . Repent, therefore, O my soul, so long as you dwell on earth. . . . What answer would you then give? You are lying on the bed of sin and slow to control the body." In the Sunset Prayer (the Eleventh Hour): "If the righteous through toil are saved, where shall I, a sinner, appear?" In the Midnight Prayer: "Give me, Lord, fountains of tears as You did in the past to the sinful woman." In the Sixth Hour: "Break the bonds of our sins, Lord Christ, and save us." In the Third Hour: "Purify us from the iniquities of the body and soul, lead us to a spiritual life so that we may proceed in the Spirit and not fulfill the desire of the flesh."

More time is required to enter into the details concerning repentance in the prayers of the *Agpeya*; in fact, this would require a separate book. With all of this daily prayer, would anyone have the courage to say that repentance was a stage through which he had passed, and that he was now entered into a state of heavenliness in which he could ask for virtues and miracles?

He who thinks that he has passed the stage of repentance has not examined himself well. In other words, he has not examined himself in the light of the commandments and with the spirit of humility. For example, who among us truly loves his enemies (Matthew 5.44)? Who among us enjoys reading the law of the Lord day and night (Psalm 1)? Who among us prays at all times without losing heart (Luke 18.1)? The commandments are many, and we have not fulfilled any of them.

I am embarrassed to go into further detail, since some people might fall into humiliation. Silence is better. Suffice it to say that repentance is a must for all of us, in every day of our lives. If only we would all read and contemplate the spiritual stages that were reached by the saints. Then we would know that we are sinners! Amazingly, the saints who reached these stages used to say that *they* were sinners who required repentance, and they wept over their sins. What, then, should we do?

CHAPTER 3

An Invitation to Repentance

THE LORD, WHO LOVES MANKIND, urged by His love for His children, calls them to repentance. This is because "He desires all men to be saved" (1 Timothy 2.4). It is not His will that any should perish, but that all should come to repentance (2 Peter 3.9). For the sake of mankind's salvation, He is prepared to overlook our times of ignorance (Acts 17.30). He says in His amazing love, "Happiness does not occur at the death of the wicked . . . but at his return to life" (Ezekiel 33.11). He loves us, and through repentance He wants us to enjoy His love.

He wants, through repentance, to share His kingdom with us and to satisfy us with His love. It is not simply a matter of orders that God gives through the tongue of His prophets and saints, but an invitation of love for salvation. "Repent therefore and be converted, that your sins may be blotted out" (Acts 3.19). "He who turns a sinner from the error of his way will save a soul from death and cover a multitude of sins" (James 5.20). So this commandment is for our sake and for our salvation. It is for our sake and for our salvation that He became incarnate and suffered for us. We cannot partake of this without repentance. So we can see His love in His invitation to us to repent.

He says: "Return to Me and I will return to you" (Malachi 3.7); "Repent and return" (Ezekiel 14.6); "Turn to Me with all your heart. . . . Return to the Lord your God" (Joel 2.12–13). He also says, in His love, with the tongue of Jeremiah the Prophet: "I will put My law in their minds, and write it on their hearts, and I will be their God, and they shall be My people . . . For I will forgive their iniquity, and their sin I will remember no more" (Jeremiah 31.33–34).

In His invitation to repentance, He promised us washing and purification. He says: "'Wash yourselves, make yourselves clean. Put away the evils from your souls. . . . Come now, and let us reason together,' says the Lord, 'although your sins are like crimson, I shall make them white like snow'" (Isaiah 1.16–18). He also said: "I shall sprinkle clean water on you, and you will be cleansed from all your uncleanness, and I will also cleanse you from all your idols. I shall give you a new heart" (Ezekiel 36.25–26).

He calls us to repentance because we are in need of it. "For I did not come to judge the world, but to save the world" (John 12.47). He says, "Those who are well have no need of a physician, but those who are sick. I did not come to call the righteous, but sinners, to repentance" (Mark 2.17). Indeed, "the Son of Man has come to save that which was lost" (Matthew 18.11).

Repentance, then, is for our own good; it is not an order forced upon us. We have the complete freedom to choose. God calls us to repentance and says: "If you are willing and obedient, you shall eat the good things of the land. But if you are unwilling and disobedient, you shall be devoured by the sword" (Isaiah 1.19–20). So it is better for us to listen, act, and be happy with God for the sake of our purity and lot in eternity. Saint Paul the Apostle calls His invitation to us "a service of reconciliation" and says: "Be reconciled to God" (2 Corinthians 5.18, 20). Why do we then refuse to be reconciled to God? Is it in our best interest to refuse reconciliation?

Repentance is useful however it is achieved, whether through leniency or harshness. Saint Jude the Apostle says: "On some have compassion, making a distinction; but others save them with fear, pulling them out of the fire, hating even the garment defiled by the flesh" (Jude 22–23). Saint John the Baptist was strong in his call to repentance (Matthew 3.8–10). Saint Paul the Apostle says to the people of Corinth: "Now I rejoice, not that you were made sorry, but that your sorrow led to repentance" (2 Corinthians 7.9). That is why the sermons of some of the saints made the people weep. This was useful to them. The Church's punishments were also in the service of repentance and salvation.

Hence, the invitation to repentance is the most important topic in the Bible, that the people might be purified and saved. When repentance became necessary for salvation, the Lord Jesus Christ sent before him John the Baptist to prepare the path to repentance. Saint John called for repentance, saying: "Repent, for the kingdom of heaven is at hand" (Matthew 3.2). This kingdom cannot be gained except through repentance. He then presented the baptism of repentance to the people.

So the work of repentance preceded the work of redemption, as the Baptist preceded the Messiah. The Lord Jesus Himself called the people to repentance. "From that time, Jesus began to preach and to say, Repent, for the kingdom of heaven is at hand'" (Matthew 4.17). He said: "The time is fulfilled, and the kingdom of God is at hand. Repent, and believe in the gospel" (Mark 1.15). Then He sent out the twelve. "So they went out and preached that people should repent"(Mark 6.12). Before His Ascension, He commanded "that repentance and remission of sins should be preached in His name to all nations, beginning at Jerusalem" (Luke 24.47).

The first to preach repentance was Noah. Many other prophets joined him in this: for example, Isaiah (Isaiah 1), Ezekiel (Ezekiel 18), Jonah (Jonah 3), Joel (Joel 2), and Jeremiah (Jeremiah 31). It is completely clear in the books of the New Testament. The invitation to repentance is the work of every shepherd, teacher, preacher, priest, and spiritual advisor. It is also clear in the sayings of the fathers.

The fathers were very much concerned with the invitation to repentance. Saint Antony said: "Ask for repentance during every moment." Saint Basil the Great said:

It is good that you do not sin. If you do sin, then it is good that you do not delay repentance. If you repent, then it is good that you do not return to sin. If you do not return, then it is good that you know this is with God's help. If you know, then it is good that you thank Him for the state that you are in.[1]

Saint Isaac said: "At all times during the twenty-four hours of the day, we are in need of repentance."[2] He also said: "Every day that you do not sit for one hour with yourself and think about the day's sins and your shortcomings to help yourself up again, then do not count the day as part of your life." So the invitation to repentance is a must for every person.

We should also pay attention to the fact that the invitation to repentance was directed to the angels of the seven Churches. The Lord says to the angel of the Church of Ephesus: "Remember therefore from where you have fallen; repent" (Revelation 2.5). The word "repent" is also said to the angel

[1]Basil the Great, *Bustān al-Ruhbān* (*Paradise of the Fathers*, Arabic version).
[2]Isaac the Syrian, *Ascetical Homilies* LXX.

of the Churches of Pergamum (Revelation 2.16), Sardis (Revelation 3.3), and Laodicea (Revelation 3.19). He also sent Nathan the Prophet to call to repentance David the Prophet, the anointed one of the Lord.

God's invitation to repentance carries His feelings of compassion for His children. He wishes for all who have strayed to return to Him, so that they may share in the kingdom, in the inheritance of the saints, and in the fellowship of the Church. Walking in darkness keeps us from fellowship with God (1 John 1.6) and prevents our fellowship with one another. "But if we walk in the light as He is in the light, we have fellowship with one another, and the blood of Jesus Christ His Son cleanses us from all sin" (1 John 1.7).

God accepts sinners. There are many examples of this in the Bible. The prodigal son was accepted in his poor state (Luke 15). The Samaritan woman, who had more than five husbands, was accepted (John 4). The thief on the right was accepted on the cross (Luke 23.43). Jesus prayed for the forgiveness of the sins of His crucifiers (Luke 23.34). Zacchaeus, the chief tax collector, was accepted (Luke 19.9), and the Lord gave him and his household salvation. Matthew the tax collector was accepted, and Jesus made him one of the twelve apostles (Matthew 10.3).

The following saying of the Lord is enough: "The one who comes to Me, I will by no means cast out" (John 6.37). But even more than this, we must recall that it is the Lord who stands at the door knocking, waiting for whoever opens (Revelation 3.20). Likewise, Jesus hurriedly opens to whoever knocks on the doors of His divine mercy. With regards to God's mercy toward sinners, it is true what is said, that God's mercy is mightier than all blemishes of sin. The worst and greatest sin, in comparison to God's mercy, is like a speck of dirt we throw into the sea. It does not discolor the sea, but the sea takes it and spreads it into its depth and gives us pure water. God's acceptance of repentance shows the depth of His divine love.

We should not then think that our numerous sins are too much for the power of His Blood. We should not value our sins above His great love and mercy. One of the elderly saints said: "There is no sin which defeats God's love to mankind." It is He who justifies the ungodly (Romans 4.5). I say this so that when sinners look at their sins, they will not lose hope.

CHAPTER 4

Do Not Despair

At this point, I remember a letter that I received from a youth twenty-two years ago. When I read it, I was deeply affected by it, to the degree that I wept. I replied to his letter, saying to him, "I have received your letter, O beloved brother, and I felt that I had read it many times before I had actually seen it. It is the picture of a life that I know, and the story of many hearts." Yes, despair is a war that tires many. Its thoughts are known and repeated in the people's confessions and spiritual questions. Here we will try to deal with and answer each of these thoughts concerning despair.

The first complaint: "I have lost hope. I am useless." Know, my brother, that every despairing thought is warfare from the devil. He wants you to despair of repentance, either from its capabilities or its acceptance, so that you feel that there is no use in struggling, and you give in to sin and remain in it until your soul perishes. So do not listen to the devil, no matter what he says to you. When you are struggling with one of the thoughts of despair, answer it with the saying of Micah the Prophet: "Do not rejoice over me, O my enemy, for though I have fallen, yet will I arise" (Micah 7.8).

Know that despairing of repentance is more dangerous than falling into sin. Through despair, Judas perished and died. Despair leads to deeper involvement in sin, and the sinner progresses from bad to worse. In despair, the devil battles with the sinner to keep him away from his confessor, from all spiritual advice, and from the entire Church, so that he will be alone with him, leaving the sinner without any help.

The prophets and saints were in constant warfare with despair. The prophet David said: "Many are those who say to my soul, 'There is no salvation for him in his God'" (Psalm 3:3). He answers this saying: "But You, O Lord, are a shield for me, My glory and the One who lifts up my head" (Psalm 3.4). David did not despair at his fall, but wept over it and repented. So God returned him to his original rank. God performed many good things for numerous people, "for the sake of My servant David" (3 Kingdoms 11.31, 33, 35). So do not despair, but remember those who have previously repented.

Even if you have lost hope in yourself, the Lord has not lost hope in your salvation. He has saved many, and you are not more difficult than all of them. When grace works in you, there is no room for despair. Enter into repentance with a courageous heart and do not belittle yourself.

The sinner says, "How can I repent while I am completely unable to arise from my fall?" Do not be afraid. God will fight for you, "for the battle is the Lord's" (1 Kingdoms 17.26). Your resistance, whether it is weak or strong, is not important. God can save with much, or with little. God is more powerful than the devil who fights you, and He can drive the devil away. So do not regard your own power, but look to the power of God. Cry out and say, "If you allow me, I will repent, for you are the Lord my God" (Jeremiah 31.18). If you are unable to lift yourself, the Lord has the power to raise you. "The Lord supports all who stumble and restores all who are broken down" (Psalm 144.14).

"My state has deteriorated immensely and I am hopeless," you may say. Is it possible that you have lost hope more than the barren woman, to whom the Lord says: "Sing, O barren one, you who have not borne" (Isaiah 54.1)? He gave her more than other women who had children. Your state seems to be hopeless from your point of view, but as for God, He has hope in you. Do not base your hope on your situation, but rather on the richness of God, who gives in abundance, and on His love and power.

You will say, "But I do not want repentance, nor do I strive for it." Of course, this is the worst part of your state. Even so, do not despair. It is enough that God is striving for your salvation. He wishes for your salvation. Many saints raise up their prayers for your sake, along with the pleadings of angels. God can make you want this repentance. Remember the saying of the apostle: "For it is God who works in you both to will and to do for His good pleasure" (Philippians 2.13). Just pray and say, "Please God, give me the desire to repent." The lost sheep was not searching for the way back, but it was its owner who searched for it and returned it to himself, not unlike the lost coin (Luke 15).

You may ask, "Is it possible for me to live the rest of my life away from sin, even though my heart loves it? If I were to repent of it, I would return to it." The error in despair is that the devil makes us think that we will live in repentance with the same heart that loves sin. On the contrary, the Lord will give you a new heart (Ezekiel 36.26). He will remove from you the love of sin, and you will not think about returning to it. On the contrary, God will make you hate sin in your repentance and be disgusted by it. Your present feelings will change.

Perhaps you will say, "Even if I repent, my thoughts will remain stained by old visions." Do not be afraid. In repentance, God will purify your thoughts. You will achieve "the renewal of mind" of which the apostle spoke (Romans 12.2). How many visions lived in the memories of Saint Augustine and Saint Mary of Egypt? The Lord erased those visions so that their minds would be sanctified by His love. Be certain that those who returned to repentance were in a more powerful state. Many of them received virtues and miracles from the Lord: for example, Jacob the Struggler, Mary the niece of Abraham, and Mary of Egypt. The love of the penitent is greater, just like the sinful woman who loved much because He forgave her much (Luke 7.47). David in his repentance also deepened his love and humility.

You will ask, "Will God forgive me? Will He accept me?" Be confident, for He says: "The one who comes to Me, I will by no means cast out" (John 6.37). David the Prophet says: "He has not dealt with us according to our sins, nor punished us according to our iniquities ... As far as the east is from the west, so far has He removed our transgressions from us ... For He knows our frame, He remembers that we are dust" (Psalm 102:10–14). Not only does He accept us, but He washes us and we become whiter than snow (Psalm 50). He does not again remember our sins (Jeremiah 31.34; Ezekiel 33.16; Hebrews 8.12). Remember that your soul is precious to God, and for its sake He became incarnate and was crucified.

You will say, "But my sins are extremely disgusting." I will answer you with this saying of the Bible: "Every sin and blasphemy will be forgiven men" (Matthew 12.31). God forgave even those who left the faith and then returned to it. Similarly, those who fell into heresies and then repented were forgiven. Peter, who denied Christ swearing, cursing, and saying, "I do not know the man," was also forgiven. Not only this, but he was returned to his rank of pastoral care and apostleship.

Even those who are in a position of leadership are forgiven, like Aaron the chief priest who shared in the making the golden calf along with the people of Israel (Exodus 32.2–5). He was forgiven when he repented. The Lord rebuked the devil for the sake of Joshua the great priest and clothed him with a new garment (Zechariah 3.1–4).

You will say, "But I have delayed too long. Is there still a chance?" Saint Augustine says in his *Confessions*: "I have delayed too long in Your love,"[1] but the Lord accepted him. He accepted the workers of the eleventh hour and gave them the same reward as those of the first hour (Matthew 20.9). He accepted the right-hand thief on the cross during the last hours of his life. As long as we are in the flesh, then there is a opportunity for repentance. We say in the prayer before sleeping, "Repent therefore, O my soul, so long as you dwell on earth," because hope in repentance will not be eliminated except in the abyss (hell). This abyss is what our father Abraham meant when he said to the rich man: "Between us and you there is a great gulf fixed" (Luke 16.26). But so long as we are in the flesh, there is an opportunity for repentance: let us take it.

You will say, "I fear that my sin might be a blasphemy against the Holy Spirit." I say to you that blasphemy against the Holy Spirit is a complete and continual refusal, throughout one's life, of all the work of the Holy Spirit in the heart, and so there will be neither repentance nor forgiveness. If you repent, then you have responded to the work of the Spirit in you, and your sin will not be a blasphemy against the Spirit.[2]

---

[1] Augustine, *Confessions* X.27.

[2] *Editor's note:* See the book, *So Many Years with the Problems of People* by His Holiness Pope Shenouda III for further discussion on this topic.

CHAPTER 5

Repentance Between Struggle and Grace

O UR WORDS ABOUT GOD'S WORK in repentance and the assistance of grace do not imply that a person may become lazy and relaxed, waiting for God to raise him. The apostle reprimands such people, saying: "You have not yet resisted to bloodshed, striving against sin" (Hebrews 12.4). It is necessary then for a person to resist—to the point of bloodshed—every thought of sin, its lusts, and its paths, to avoid stumbling blocks, and to use every spiritual means that strengthens the love of God in his heart.

A repentant person also enters into a spiritual war against the hosts of wickedness (Ephesians 6). In this war he fights and endures and does not give in to the enemy. He puts on the complete armor of God so that he may overpower the wiles of the devil (Ephesians 6.11). In all of this he is watchful for his own salvation (Ephesians 6.18). Saint Peter the Apostle says: "Be sober, be vigilant, because your adversary the devil walks about like a roaring lion, seeking whom he may devour, so resist him, steadfast in the faith" (1 Peter 5.8–9). God wants you to resist and, in your resistance, grace will support you with power. So show your love to God by your resistance to sin. Pray that the Lord will grant you power to resist it.

In this way you will cooperate with God in the work. The prodigal son did not wait for his father to come to him in the far country and take him back; rather, he came to himself, felt his terrible condition, knew the solution, carried it out, and returned to his father, who accepted him (Luke 15). The people of Nineveh fasted, were humbled, sat in the ashes, cried mightily to the Lord, and turned from their evil, so God accepted them (Jonah 3). God reminds us of our duty in repentance, saying: "Return to Me and I will return to you" (Malachi 3.7).

He says, in the words of Isaiah the Prophet: "'Wash yourselves, make yourselves clean; put away the evils from your souls. . . . Come now, and let us reason together,' says the Lord" (Isaiah 1.16, 18). In the book of Joel the

Prophet, He also says: "Turn to Me with all your heart, with fasting and wailing and with mourning; rend your heart and not your garments" (Joel 2.12–13).

Therefore, in the work of repentance, there is a duty to be done by each person. He should not be satisfied by casting himself at the feet of the Lord without inner and outer struggle. Some might say, "Your work is to simply accept the work of grace in you." Does this opinion agree with the reprimand of the apostle: "You have not yet resisted to bloodshed, striving against sin" (Hebrews 12.4)? Therefore we should struggle. However, we should not rely on ourselves, but we should ask for God's working hand to help us. With our struggle, we thus confirm our wish for repentance and our resolve in seeking it.

CHAPTER 6

The Importance of Repentance

T HE MOST IMPORTANT THING about repentance is that there is no salvation without it. The Lord says: "Unless you repent you will all likewise perish" (Luke 13.3). He "has given to the Gentiles the opportunity to repent and live" (Acts 11.18). Some say that the Lord gave us His blood for salvation and forgiveness, so why this need for repentance? Is the blood of Jesus not enough? We answer them by saying that repentance is what transforms the merits of the blood of Christ into forgiveness.

Salvation is presented to everyone, and the blood of Christ is sufficient for all, but only the penitent can receive it. Truly, the blood of Christ "purifies us from every sin." But it purifies us only from the sins of which we repent. The apostle stresses two conditions for this purity to occur: "If we walk in the light" (1 John 1.7) and also, "if we confess our sins" (1 John 1.9). These two conditions are connected to the life of repentance.

Therefore repentance precedes baptism, for in it there is forgiveness of sins. On Pentecost, Saint Peter the Apostle said to the Jews: "Repent, and let every one of you be baptized in the name of Jesus Christ for the forgiveness of sins" (Acts 2.38). The Church also, when baptizing adults, stipulates faith, repentance, and confession. The canons of the Church prohibit the baptism of unrepentant people. With respect to children, however, the rite of renouncing the devil is sufficient for repentance.[1]

One of the important points about repentance is that it either accompanies faith or precedes it. Saint Mark the Evangelist says that the Lord preached this message: "The time is fulfilled, and the kingdom of God is at hand. Repent and believe in the gospel" (Mark 1.15). Faith without repentance will not save anyone, because a person will perish without repentance (Luke 13.3).

[1] *Editor's note:* In the Coptic Orthodox baptismal liturgy, the parent of the infant being baptized holds the child in her hands and renounces the devil three times.

Repentance precedes partaking of the holy sacraments. In the Old Testament, Samuel the Prophet said: "Sanctify yourselves, and come with me to the sacrifice" (1 Kingdoms 16.5). As for the New Testament, Saint Paul the Apostle says: "Let a man examine himself, and so let him eat of the bread and drink of the cup. For he who eats and drinks in an unworthy manner eats and drinks judgment to himself, not discerning the Lord's body. . . . For if we would judge ourselves, we would not be judged" (1 Corinthians 11.28–29, 31).

Repentance precedes every holy sacrament of the Church. This is so that the person will be worthy of the work of the Holy Spirit in him. The person receives forgiveness with repentance, which will qualify him for the grace of the Holy Spirit that works in the sacraments. The repentance of the prodigal son preceded his entry into his father's house (Luke 15).

Repentance is a necessary condition for the remission of sins. Of this, Saint Peter the Apostle says: "Repent therefore and be converted, that your sins may be blotted out" (Acts 3.19). Saint Isaac has a nice saying: "There is no sin which cannot be pardoned, except the one without repentance."[2] Repentance, then, is necessary both before and after baptism: before baptism, to qualify for baptism, and after baptism, for the remission of sins that occur after baptism.

---

[2]Isaac of Nineveh, *Mystical Treatises* II.11.9.

CHAPTER 7

The Obstacles to Repentance

THERE IS NOTHING THE DEVIL FIGHTS harder than repentance, because it wastes all of his previous labor. Therefore it seems difficult, for when the person wants to repent, the devil places in front of him every stumbling block and obstruction that might prevent or delay his repentance. These stumbling blocks, whether they are temptations or opportunities which did not previously exist, weaken a person's will when they are set before him. It is also possible that the person's surroundings delay his repentance by imposing stumbling blocks and incorrect ideas.

The sinner may compare himself with people who are weak. When comparing himself to such people, he thinks that he is in a good state, which requires no repentance. He says, "All people are like this. Why should I be different?" Of course the fact that the majority are sinners is no excuse. Noah protected his righteousness in a world full of evil, as did the righteous Joseph, Moses the Prophet in the land of Egypt, and Lot in Sodom.

A weak personality allows the person to be influenced by his environment. A person should have a firm personality that is not swept along in the direction of the world. A little fish is capable of resisting the current and swimming against it because it has life, whereas a great block of timber, which is hundreds of times bigger than the fish, can be washed away with the current, since it has no will. So, have a strong personality, and this will help you to repent. The apostle says: "Do not be conformed to this world" (Romans 12.2).

Another stumbling block is delay. The devil will not fight an open war, prohibiting you from repentance, but he will tell you to delay by presenting certain temptations. Delay has its dangers. One of them is losing the opportunity for repentance. If sin continues, it assumes authority and becomes entrenched. When one delays, even the desire for repentance will no longer be present and spiritual influences will lose their effects.

Despair is the feeling that repentance is difficult and impossible. Saint John Climacus says: "The demons, before the fall, say to you that God is kind and merciful, but after the fall, they say that He is the Just Judge and they will frighten you to lose hope in the forgiveness of God and not repent."[1] Earlier, we discussed the obstacle of despair and its cure.

In the case of self-righteousness, the person does not feel that he is a sinner. Repentance is a change from one life to another. How can a person change his life when it seems beautiful in his own eyes? For if he cannot sense his bad state, then he cannot repent and change his life. Therefore he who does not reproach himself and who refuses the reproaches of others cannot repent. A person may think that he is always right, and that the words "repent and return" are directed toward another. He lets his ears listen to words of praise and believes them; he explains God's commandments as he likes, and yet he refuses the reproach of his conscience.

Repentance is easy for the meek, but difficult for those who are righteous in their own eyes. It is easy for the humble tax collector who feels his sins, but difficult for the Pharisee who boasts in his prayer: "God, I thank You that I am not like other men—extortioners, unjust, adulterers . . ." (Luke 18.11). Repentance is easy for the sinful woman who washed the feet of Jesus with her tears, but difficult for Simon the Pharisee, who thought that he was not a sinner like her. It is good, therefore, that the Lord revealed to him that both of them were debtors. He, however, does not have the same love as she, for he sees his debt to be much less (Luke 7).

Repentance is easy for those who know and confess that they are sinners. As for those who are righteous in their own eyes, for what will they repent, if they do not confess that they have sinned in anything? Truly, those who are well—that is, those who think to themselves that they are well—have no need of a physician. Even if someone accused them of a sin, these people would either deny it, explain it in a distorted manner, give responsibility to someone else, or else argue and justify themselves. They would not confess their sin, and therefore they would not repent.

It can be difficult for those who stand in front of other people as a good example to say that they are in need of repentance. It would be beneficial if these people became a good example also by confessing their wrongdoings

---

[1]John Climacus, *The Ladder of Divine Ascent* V.31.

and their need for repentance. We can also say that repentance is easy for the catechumen, but difficult for the preacher, servant, advisor, or whoever is at this level.

Another obstacle to repentance is the lack of fear of God in the heart. As Saint Isaac says: "If there is no fear, then there is no repentance also."[2] Some avoid fear in the name of love. Their remoteness from fear makes them fall into carelessness, and they fall into sin. With this sin, they prove that they do not have the love that casts out fear (1 John 4.18). The fear of God makes a person realize his sin and pushes him to repent. We will present a separate book on this topic, God willing.

---

[2] Isaac of Nineveh, *Mystical Treatises* XLIV.317.5.

CHAPTER 8

Repentance and the Church

T HE CHURCH PLAYS AN IMPORTANT ROLE in the repentance of every person. This role includes the work of teaching, giving advice, pastoral care, visiting and searching, transferring the work and gifts of the Holy Spirit for the sake of every person's salvation, along with the merits of the precious Blood. So the Church invites sinners to repentance. It performs what Saint Paul calls "the ministry of reconciliation," while "the word of reconciliation" calls sinners to "be reconciled to God" (2 Corinthians 5.18–20). This occurs through preaching the word of God to the people. Without the Church's efforts, there may be no repentance.

The Church calls for repentance in all of its pastoral ministries—by its priests and servants visiting people and solving their various problems, both spiritual and social. The priest is like a compassionate father who cares for his children, bringing them closer to the fatherhood of God. The Church is a spiritual environment which assists in the life of repentance. Separated from the world full of stumbling blocks, every penitent finds in the Church the proper surroundings wherein he can live a spiritual life. Without the Church, it is possible that every spiritual feeling that grows inside a person might be choked by the thorns of the world, wither away, and dry up.

The Church offers to the penitent the sacrament of confession and grants him absolution and forgiveness. In the sacrament of confession, the penitent opens his heart. He is relieved of his suppressed secrets in front of God; he presents all his weaknesses and failings in the presence of the priest in order to receive absolution from God by the mouth of the priest. This is through the command of authority, of which the Lord says: "If you forgive the sins of any, they are forgiven them; if you retain the sins of any, they are retained" (John 20.23). The Lord also says: "Whatever you bind on earth will be bound in heaven, and whatever you loose on earth will be loosed in heaven" (Matthew 18.18). In this way, the penitent leaves confession with a clear conscience. He has heard the word of absolution and forgiveness from the priest (God's deputy), who says it according to the authority given to him by God. Therefore the penitent feels peace in his heart and enters on a new beginning.

In the sacrament of confession, the Church offers spiritual advice, for as it says in the Bible: "Ask the priests concerning the law" (Haggai 2.11). In this way the father explains to his son in confession the right spiritual path that he should pursue. There is no one who does not need advice, for the Bible says: "There is a way which seems right to a man, but its end is the way of death" (Proverbs 14.12). Scripture also says: "Lean not on your own understanding" (Proverbs 3.5).

In the Church, the penitent encounters a heart to which he may entrust personal secrets relating to his spiritual life, as well as weaknesses that cannot be confided to just anyone. Suppressing secrets completely can be very tiring, or sometimes impossible. But with the priest one finds trust, spiritual solutions to problems, and a helping hand that guides with sincere love.

The Church offers to the penitent all the blessings of the sacrament of the Eucharist. The Lord says of this great sacrament: "He who eats My flesh and drinks My blood abides in Me, and I in him," and he "will live because of Me" (John 6.56–57). Outside the Church he will not find the blessing of this great sacrament to strengthen him in his repentance and fill him spiritually. The Lord says that the Eucharist is to be given for our salvation and for the forgiveness of sins and everlasting life for those who partake of it (John 6.54). Perhaps someone may wonder why he needs the Church, confession, Holy Communion, or absolution, since repentance grants forgiveness. My answer is this: With repentance one becomes worthy of forgiveness, and with confession and Holy Communion one receives that forgiveness.

There is a difference between being worthy of forgiveness and receiving grace. For repentance also contains confession within it. Absolution is a part of the sacrament of confession. Holy Communion is an extension of the effectiveness of the sacrifice of Christ. One might ask, "If I repent and die before the reading of the prayer of absolution, what will happen to me?" My answer is: If you die in this way, God will have mercy upon you. The prayer of absolution will be read over you during the funeral prayers.

PART TWO

THE INCENTIVES FOR REPENTANCE

CHAPTER I

If You Know Who You Are,
You Will Rise above Sin

OUR REPENTANCE NEEDS TO BE built on a sound foundation, on a true understanding of the spiritual life and our relationship with God. The most important motive for repentance is to know our own worth—for each of us to know his own capabilities and who he is. So, my brother, know yourself. Who are you?

If you know who you are, you will rise above sin. For if you know your great capabilities and your great position, then you will not allow your exalted self to come down to the level of sin. Therefore, you will not fall. So, who are you?

You are a holy breath which proceeded from the mouth of God. You, my brother, are not a scoop of dust, as some may think. You are a holy breath which proceeded from the mouth of God and descended into the dust. So you became "a living being" (Genesis 2.7). You are neither mere dust nor dirt. You should sing with joy, saying:

> I am not dirt, but in dirt I live.
> I am not dirt, but a spirit.
> From the mouth of God, I proceeded.
> I will return to God,
> To live whence I originally came.

Your presence in this dust, O blessed brother, is only a brief period of alienation, after which you will return to God and be confirmed in Him to eternity. So know your alienation and live as a spirit, rising above matter, the world, and the works of the body.

You are a son of God; you are His image and likeness. You, my brother, are the image of God. The Bible says in the story of Creation: "Then God said, 'Let us make man in Our image, according to Our likeness. . . . So God made man; in the image of God He made him" (Genesis 1.26–27). If you are the image of God and His likeness, then how can you sin? If you are defiled by sin, will you still keep your divine image? Of course not, for it is not possible for a person to see you in impurity and say, "This is the image of God."

Saint Athanasius the Great, in his book *On the Incarnation*, said that when man fell corruption occurred, and he lost his divine image. Jesus Christ came to give us back our original image. If you knew, my brother, that you are the image of God, you could not sin.

For if you know that you are a son of God, you will not sin, for the son should be like his Father. There is nothing easier than to boast wrongly that we are "children of God," even when our deeds do not show this. The Jews likewise boasted in vain that they were the children of Abraham, and the Lord deflated their pride, saying: "If you were Abraham's children, you would do the works of Abraham" (John 8.39). For if Abraham's children are required to do the work of Abraham, then what about the duties of God's children who are in His image and likeness?

Do we live as children of God in order to be called His children? How easy it is for us to call upon the Lord in our prayers, saying, "Our Father who art in heaven." And yet we do not behave as children of this heavenly Father. Remember always, my brother, that you are a son of God and walk in the life of righteousness in order to become worthy to be called the son of the Righteous One. Place before your eyes the saying of the Bible: "If you know that He is righteous, you know that everyone who practices righteousness is born of him" (1 John 2.29). For if you do not perform righteousness, then you are not worthy to be called a son of God. I am afraid that the words "children of God" could become a reproach for us, now and on the Last Day. Saint John the Apostle explains this matter to us, saying: "Little children, let no one deceive you. He who practices righteousness is righteous, just as He is righteous. He who sins is of the devil, for the devil has sinned from the beginning" (1 John 3.7–8).

He who practices sin is a son of the devil. He is of Satan and not of God. How frightening! The apostle records for us a fundamental principle: "Whoever has been born of God does not sin, for His seed remains in him;

and he cannot sin, because he has been born of God" (1 John 3.9). By this standard, my brother, you can measure yourself whenever you say that you are a son of God. The apostle concludes by saying: "In this the children of God and the children of the devil are manifest" (1 John 3.10). Your sense of being a son of God reminds you of that heavenly nature which God placed in you. This is what the apostle means by his saying about the one born of God: "His divine seed remains in him," and also "he who has been born of God keeps himself, and the wicked one does not touch him" (1 John 5.18).

Every time you sin you must feel humiliated in the depths of your soul and unworthy to be called a son of God. The holy Church makes a person say to God every day, in the Sunset Prayer: "I have sinned against You and against Heaven, I am no longer fit to be called your son" (Luke 15.21). Why am I "no longer fit to be called Your son"? Because I have sinned, and whoever has been born of God does not sin.

We must understand very well the practical meaning of being sons of God. We enter into the depths of this title. In every work we do, in every word we say, and in every thought we accept, we ask ourselves if we work, talk, and think in ways suitable to the children of God. To be a son of God is not a mere title. We should possess the true likeness of the son to the Father.

"God is Spirit" (John 4.24), "and that which is born of the Spirit is spirit" (John 3.6). If, my brother, you are living according to the flesh and not according to the Spirit, then how can you be a son of God, who is Spirit? Furthermore, how can you be born of the Spirit? He who lives in sin can by no means say that he is a son of God, nor can he say that he knows God as a mere acquaintance. This becomes clear in the frightening words of the apostle: "Whoever sins has neither seen Him nor known Him" (1 John 3.6). For "He who says, 'I know Him,' and does not keep His commandments, is a liar, and the truth is not in him" (1 John 2.4). Can you say, "I know God," while in the life of sin? Certainly not, for He will answer you and say, "Depart from Me, I do not know you, and you do not know Me."

Therefore, my brother, if you remember that you are a son of God, you will live a life that measures up to the standards God set when He called you (Ephesians 4.1). Walk like Him, in His path. "He who says he abides in Him ought himself also to walk just as He walked" (1 John 2.6). Just as

Christ lived on earth, so you should live in complete holiness, purity, and blessing, for He has given you an example to follow (John 13.15). If you live in sin, know within yourself that you are not worthy to be called a son of God, because this is not the image of God's children.

Every time you say to Him, "Our Father who art in Heaven," your conscience should reprimand you, and you should be contrite within yourself. You will say to Him, "It is because of Your humility, O Lord, and Your love, that you called me to be your son. For with my works I have demonstrated that I am not worthy to be called your son. Treat me as one of your hired servants. Your Fatherhood, though it honors me greatly, also reproaches me greatly, making me feel the great difference between what I am and what I should be."

You are the dwelling place of God, and a temple for the Holy Spirit.

You, my brother, are not only a son of God and a holy breath which proceeded from the mouth of God, but you are also a temple for God, and God dwells in you. The apostle says to us: "Do you not know that you are the temple of God and that the Spirit of God dwells in you? If anyone defiles the temple of God, God will destroy him. For the temple of God is holy, which temple you are" (1 Corinthians 3.16–17). "For you are the temple of the living God. As God has said: 'I will dwell in them and walk among them'" (2 Corinthians 6.16).

God's eternal desire is to dwell in you, to look at your heart and say: "This is My place of rest unto age of ages; here I shall dwell, for I have chosen her" (Psalm 131.14). You will say to Him, "O Lord, you have churches, temples, and altars. You dwell in heaven and the Heaven of Heavens is Your throne." He will say that He prefers to live in your heart, rather than in any of these. "My son, give me your heart" (Proverbs 23.25).

You, O blessed brother, are more important to God than a church building. If one of the churches is destroyed, it can easily be rebuilt through the collection of money. But if a person like you is destroyed, he cannot be rebuilt except through the blood of Christ. Neither angel nor archangel nor patriarch nor prophet can return you to your original rank; nothing can do so but the blood of Christ, for without it there is no salvation for you. I repeat: you, my brother, are more important to God than a church. You are a living church, more important than bricks and stones: you are a temple for the Holy Spirit.

God permitted the destruction of the temple of Solomon and did not leave one stone intact. But for your sake, God sent the apostles, prophets, and angels; He sent appointed pastors, priests, and teachers. He organized every means of grace and presented the worthiness of the great redemption, "that whoever believes in Him should not perish but have everlasting life" (John 3.16).

If you are a house for God and God dwells in you, then remember the saying of the Bible: "Holiness adorns Your house" (Psalm 92.5). Know that by sin you defile the house of God, which you are. Remember also the saying of the apostle: "You also, as living stones, are being built up a spiritual house, a holy priesthood, to offer up spiritual sacrifices acceptable to God through Jesus Christ" (1 Peter 2.5). Jesus Christ searches for a place to dwell, and that place is you. When the Lord says about Himself that He has nowhere to lay His head (Luke 9.58), He is not simply referring to material houses, but even more so to the hearts of the people.

Your heart is the place where the Lord seeks to lay His head. Truly, His delight is with the sons of men (Proverbs 8.31). He knocks at your door and waits for you to open. In His yearning for your heart, He says: "If anyone loves Me, he will keep My word; and My Father will love him, and We will come to him and make Our home with him" (John 14.23). In this way, the Father and the Son will come and live in your heart, and you will again become a temple for the Holy Spirit.

In this way, your heart becomes a dwelling for the Holy Trinity. Here I am silent in awe and reverence before this holy heart. "How awesome is this place! This is none other than the house of God, and this is the gate of heaven" (Genesis 28.17). This is the amazing divine dwelling to which God comes from afar, "leaping on the mountains and skipping over the hills" (Song of Songs 2.8). He calls to your precious soul in love: "Open to me, my sister, my companion, my dove, my perfect one; for my head is wet with dew, and my locks of hair with the drops of the night" (Song of Songs 5.2).

How long, my brother, will you wait and not open? Imagine, my brother, that the God whom neither the heavens nor the universe can contain—the God of whom David says: "The earth is the Lord's, and its fullness, the world

and all who dwell therein" (Psalm 23.1)—knocks on your door and desires
you as a dwelling for Himself. He wants to live in your heart, and for you
to live in His heart, to be confirmed in you and you in Him, and for you to
become a holy church for Him.

I remember sending a letter to one of the blessed brethren, saying to
him, "Greet the holy church which is in your heart." For I knew that in his
heart was a church from which ascends the smell of incense, and from which
proceeds hymns and praises, and in which spiritual sacrifices are raised. Does
the psalmist not say, "Let my prayer be set before You as incense, the lifting
up of my hands as the evening sacrifice" (Psalm 140.2)? If you know, my
brother, that you are a temple for the Holy Spirit, then do not sin lest you
grieve the Spirit of God which is in you, and so extinguish its fervor.

If the devil comes to you one day with a sin, say to him:

- Go far away from me, I am not for you.
- I am the house of God, I am a dwelling for God, I am a holy place
  for the Lord.
- I am the one on whose door God knocks, that I might open unto
  Him.
- I am a temple for the Holy Spirit, I am a holy church.
- I am the one to whom the Father and the Son come to make a
  dwelling place.
- I am a dwelling for the Holy Trinity.
- Am I so insignificant that the devil can defile me? No, I am a second
  heaven, a throne on which God reigns.

You my brother, are not merely these, but also a brother to the Messiah,
a companion to Christ, and an heir with Him.

It is an amazing humility for the Lord to call us His brothers. We do not
dare to call Him by this title, because we have not reached even the level of
the unprofitable servants who did everything they were commanded to do
(Luke 17.10). But since He honors us, we should measure up to the standards God set when He called us.

It is amazing what is said about the Lord God: He is "the firstborn
among many brethren" (Romans 8.29). Many brethren? How amazing! It
is also amazing that "He is not ashamed to call them brethren" (Hebrews

2.11). Yet more amazing than all of this is that "in all things He had to be made like His brethren" (Hebrews 2.17). We also see the Lord saying to the two Marys: "Go and tell My brethren to go to Galilee, and there they will see Me" (Matthew 28.10). He repeats the same expression to Mary Magdalene: "Go to My brethren and say to them. . . ." (John 20.17).

He does not say this about the apostles only, but about everyone. "For whoever does the will of My Father in heaven is My brother and sister and mother" (Matthew 12.50). Concerning the good done for the poor and needy, he says: "Assuredly, I say to you, inasmuch as you did it to one to the least of these My brethren, you did it to Me" (Matthew 25.40).

So, my brother, you are a brother to Christ and you are also an heir with Him in the promise of eternal glory. In the parable of the evil earthly vineyard tenants, He is the Heir (Matthew 21.38). We are therefore called "heirs—heirs of God and joint heirs with Christ" (Romans 8.17).

So, my brother, come to know the importance of who you are. You are a brother to Christ and an heir with Him. Not only that, but we are also partners with Him, "if we say that we have fellowship with Him" (1 John 1.6). He partook with us in flesh and blood (Hebrews 2.14). We need to be chastened, "that we may be partakers of His holiness" (Hebrews 12.10). We partake with Him in His sufferings, in order to partake in the joy of the revelation of His coming (1 Peter 4.13).

We were buried with Him in baptism in order to be raised with Him (Romans 6.4–5). We will live our lives working with Him (1 Corinthians 3.9). We will suffer with Him in order to be glorified with Him (Romans 8.17). We will come with Him on the cloud (Jude 14). We will be with Him at all times (1 Thessalonians 4.17), for wherever He is, we will be there also (John 17.24). It is a partnership for you with Christ, O blessed brother, in which you start now and continue until eternity. So protect this holy partnership, for with sin you will lose it.

You will not be able to remain as a partner to Christ if you walk in sin, for the Bible will reproach you with its saying: "What fellowship has righteousness with lawlessness? And what communion has light with darkness? And what accord has Christ with Belial?" (2 Corinthians 6.14–15). When you sin, it is as if you say to the Lord, "The partnership between me and You has been dissolved. I have searched for another partner. I am now a partner with the devil, and I will not return to be Your partner again!"

When you compare the glory we have in the path of God with our decline and fall when we are far from Him, how can you commit sin, you who are a partner with Christ, His partner in work, sufferings, and glory? It is you who put on Christ in baptism (Galatians 3.27) and live—though not you, but Christ who lives in you (Galatians 2.20).

Not only are you a partner with Christ, but you are also a partner to the Holy Spirit, a partner in the divine nature. The blessing of Saint Paul the Apostle is that "the communion of the Holy Spirit be with you all" (2 Corinthians 13.14). We also receive this blessing from the Church at the beginning of the liturgy.

You are a partner to the Holy Spirit—not in essence, but in work. He works in you, with you, and through you for the sake of your salvation and the salvation of other people, spreading the kingdom of God and building the body of Christ. You do not work alone, or else you would be relying on your human capabilities. "Unless the Lord builds the house, those who build it labor in vain" (Psalm 126.1). The Holy Spirit participates with you in the work. He does not work alone, but takes you with Him so that you may receive blessing. So you are a partner to the Holy Spirit, a partner in the divine nature, in work.

The Holy Spirit always works with you for the good. When you do evil or sin, then you are working alone, refusing your partnership with the Holy Spirit. The Bible says about the state of sin: "Do not grieve the Holy Spirit of God, by whom you were sealed" (Ephesians 4.30). It also says: "Do not quench the Spirit" (1 Thessalonians 5.19). If a person continues in the state of sin, he may experience what David the Prophet fears when he says: "Do not take Your Holy Spirit from me" (Psalm 50.11).

My brother, what could be more amazing than for it to be said of you that you are a "partaker of the divine nature" (2 Peter 1.4)? Even more amazing is that the Lord rebukes us with this saying: "I said, 'You are gods,[1] and you are

---

[1]This does not mean that we are gods of His nature, but that we are in His image and likeness; "gods" here means "masters," just as God said to Moses, "I have made you as God to Pharaoh" (Exodus 7.1), not as his creator, God forbid, but as his master.

all sons of the Most High'" (Psalm 81.6). What a great witness this is! Can we sin after this? Is it proper for a god to sin, to indulge in filth and dirt?

When you sin, are you a partner in the divine nature? Certainly not; you are a partner to Satan, for the Bible says: "He who sins is of the devil, for the devil has sinned from the beginning. . . . In this the children of God and the children of the devil are manifest" (1 John 3.8, 10). When we sin, we forget our great glory and lose our rank. For after God says to us, "You are gods," He continues: "But you die like men, and fall like one of the princes" (Psalm 81.7). Who is this prince who fell? It is Satan, who previously was an archangel!

The person who sins does not know his capabilities. It has been said that the sinner is ignorant. We are amazed that after he ate from the tree of knowledge, he became ignorant! For he sought knowledge far removed from God, knowledge which further separated him from God. So he knew neither himself nor God, nor the relationship between them. My brother, get to know yourself and who you are, so that you will not sin.

You are a member of the body of Christ, of His flesh and bones. The Church is the body of Christ, and Christ is its head; we, the congregation of believers, are the Church. So, then, we are the body of Christ (Ephesians 4.11). "We are members of His body, of His flesh and of His bones" (Ephesians 5.30). Every organ in you is a member of Christ.

Therefore, the apostle says of the sin of adultery: "Do you not know that your bodies are members of Christ? Shall I then take the members of Christ and make them members of a harlot? Certainly not!" (1 Corinthians 6.15). How can we sin, when we are the body of Christ? How can we sin when the Lord considers us exactly as Himself, so that whoever touches us, touches Him?

When rebuking Saul of Tarsus, the Lord does not ask him why he is persecuting the faithful. Instead, He says to him: "Why are you persecuting Me?" (Acts 9.4). For He considers us to be exactly as Himself. When He blesses the merciful on the last day, He will not say to them, "You fed the hungry and gave the thirsty to drink;" rather, He will say to them: "I was hungry and you gave Me food; I was thirsty and you gave Me drink" (Matthew 25.35). How can we sin against our loving Lord, who considers us as Himself, and hurt His sensitive and compassionate heart? The sinful person cuts himself off from the body of Christ. This is because the entire body of Christ is holy.

Our membership in the body of Christ is made clear when He says, "I am the vine, you are the branches" (John 15.5), for the juice of the vine ascends and flows to the branches, giving them life. Every branch in the vine will bear the image of the vine itself, since the branch and the vine are one thing.

Are you then a true branch of this divine vine? Do you produce fruit, as a live branch would? The branches of the vine should yield fruits that represent the vine, producing a vine joyful to the Lord, of which He can drink anew in the Father's kingdom (Matthew 26.29). What do you think He meant when He said to the Samaritan woman: "Give Me a drink" (John 4.7)? Do you think He wanted water from her, or did He wish to give her to drink? He was thirsty for her soul, to unite it to His kingdom. He wished to drink of the produce of the vine—from the juice which He Himself poured into this woman's heart.

Does the juice of the vine flow in you, O blessed brother? Does its juice flow in all your veins, making you produce and bring forth leaves and fruit? Do you produce a vine, or a thorn? For if you bring forth a thorn, then you are not a member of the vine, and surely the juice which flows in you is not of the vine. You should know then that the branch which does not produce fruit is worthless and useless, and is cut off and thrown into the fire (John 15.6). If one is cut off, he can no longer be a member of the vine; it is all over for him.

Therefore the person who walks in sin—he who has refused the juice of the vine—is a stubborn branch. He has refused to allow the juice to flow in his veins, and so he withered away and fell; or he was pruned and thrown into the fire. The righteous person, by contrast, opens wide his veins for the juice of the vine. In this way he produces fruit, and the Lord purifies him to produce more.

What is the product of the vine that You wish to drink from us, O Lord? Your fruits are the fruits with which I wish to be nourished, by the fruits of the Spirit in you (Galatians 5.22). This fruit is the work of God in you. It is the result of the flow of His juice in your veins. If you, then, remember always that you are branches in His vine and members of His body, then you will never sin, and moreover you will be fruitful and He will be happy with your fruit.

Do you now know, my brother, of your great position? You are not just a member of the body of Christ, but also one who partakes of the Lord's body and blood. You eat the body of Christ and drink His blood and are confirmed in Him, and the pure and holy blood of Christ runs in your veins. Who is exalted and purified like you? After receiving Holy Communion, one person wrote in his memoirs: "This holy mouth which received the body and blood of Christ, an unnecessary word will not come out of it, and no more than enough will enter into it." Remember always, my brother, that your mouth receives the body and blood of Jesus Christ, and therefore no abuses should come out of it, nor worldly songs, nor rude jokes, nor lies, nor swearing, nor anger, nor the remainder of the sins of the tongue.

Remember also that in your body dwells the body of Christ, and you will be afraid to defile this body or to make it a tool for sin. My blessed brother, do not forget yourself; remember who you are and what is suitable for you, so that you will not sin. One of the saints said, "Every sin is preceded by either negligence, or lust, or forgetfulness." Truly forgetfulness precedes sin. For we forget that we are the image of God, His resemblance and likeness, His children, His dwelling and a temple for the Holy Spirit. We forget that we are the brothers of Christ, the partners of the Holy Spirit, the partners of the divine nature. We forget that we are members of the body of Christ and that we partake of His body and His blood. This is why we sin, for if we had remembered our true state, we would not have sinned. When you sin, you have forgotten your glories; you have lost them, and lost yourself.

CHAPTER 2

If You Know What Sin Is,
You Will Flee from Sin

For a person to repent, it is not enough for him to know who he is. He must also know what sin is, its wrong nature, its punishment, its results, and the harm it causes. Therefore we say that, if you know what sin is, you will flee from sin.

Sin is death. It is true that "the wages of sin is death" (Romans 6.23), "and sin, when it is full-grown, brings forth death" (James 1.15). In addition to the punishment of sin being death, we can say that sin itself is a state of death, a moral and spiritual death.

The references to this are many. In the Parable of the Prodigal Son, the father says: "For this my son was dead and is alive again; he was lost and is found" (Luke 15.24). He describes his state of sin as "dead." The son was not alive until after his return. Saint Paul the Apostle says of the widow who lived in pleasure that she "is dead while she lives" (1 Timothy 5.6). Likewise, he says that all of us "were dead in trespasses and sins" (Ephesians 2.1). "We were dead in trespasses" (Ephesians 2.5). When the angel (pastor) of the Church of Sardis sinned, the Lord sent him a letter through the mouth of Saint John the Theologian, saying to him: "I know your works, that you have a name that you are alive, but you are dead" (Revelation 3.1).

The sinful person is a dead person because he has been separated from the true life by his separation from God, and God is life. Did the Lord Jesus not say: "I am the resurrection and the life" (John 11.25) and "I am the way, the truth, and the life" (John 14.6)? Truly, "In Him was life, and the life was the light of men" (John 1.4). For whoever is separated from Christ by sin is separated from life and considered dead, even though he is still breathing.

Saint Augustine was right in saying that "the death of the body is the separation of the spirit from the body, and the death of the spirit is the separation of the spirit from God."[1] The sinner, then, is a dead person, no matter how much he may think himself alive and enjoying life. Sinners do not understand the proper meaning of life. They think life is merely enjoying the world and its pleasures. When you discuss repentance with a sinner, he will reply, "Let me enjoy life." He considers worldly pleasure life, when it is in fact death! It is the same as what was said about the widow who lived in pleasure.

If sin, therefore, is death, then it is appropriate to ask ourselves if we are truly alive. And what is our age on earth? More than likely, we will answer this question with the same answer that our father Jacob gave to Pharaoh: "The days of the years of my sojourn are . . . few and evil . . . [and] they have not attained to the days and years of my father's sojourn in life" (Genesis 47.9). Our lives are measured only by the days which we spent with God, confirmed in His love. The periods of sin in our lives are periods of death.

Do not then say, "I am forty years old," for your life with God may be less than ten years. My brother, ask yourself whether are you alive or dead. It alarms me that the phrase which the Lord utters to the angel of the Church of Sardis could be applied to any one of us: "You have a name that you are alive, but you are dead" (Revelation 3.1). Imagine if an angel were to descend now from heaven to count the living present in the Church. Which of us would he find alive, and which of us would he find dead? What shame to know our reality. Are we truly alive, or dead by sin? In this each one of us must judge himself.

Every fruitful day in which you are confirmed in Christ is a day of living; every day you spend in sin is a day of death. In this way, you can determine your true age. So, my brother, do not allow one day of your life to be lost, dead and buried forever. For the days that have passed cannot return, but the days that count are eternal. There are moments in the life of a person which are very valuable. One moment could be worth years, or even generations. Therefore, live your life completely, abundantly, richly, and fruitfully. Imagine one hour in the life of Paul the Apostle: it could be longer than the entire life of another person.

My brother, do not boast in vain, and do not say without truth, "I am a son of God, I am His image and likeness. I am a temple for the Holy Spirit,

[1]Augustine, *City of God* XIII.12

I am a partner to the divine nature, I am a member in the body of Christ." This is not so, for if you have sinned then you are dead and you are none of these. You will say to God, "I am your son," and He will say to you, "Depart from Me, I do not know you." For sin is death. Sin is straying.

Sin is also delusion and loss. In the fifteenth chapter of the Gospel of our teacher Luke the Evangelist we find three parables explaining to us how sin is delusion, loss, and straying. They are the Parables of the Prodigal Son, the Lost Sheep, and the Lost Coin. The prodigal son was lost intentionally, with knowledge and planning, as a result of his heart's lusts. The lost sheep strayed because of ignorance and lack of knowledge and experience. And the lost coin was lost by another person, or it fell and remained without moving.

It is regrettable if God looks in His purse and does not find you. It is regrettable if God counts His coins and does not find you among them. God continues to look for you in His purse and everywhere, to see where you have fallen, but He does not find you. Finally, He declares the painful truth: "I had a coin, but now it is lost." It is lost, missing, and no longer exists in His purse. It would embarrass me if God were to count His people and find no names written in the book of life because sin had lost them.

Do you know, my brother, that if you walk in the path of sin you are lost, and no longer in the hand of God? Yes, sin is loss, delusion, and straying. The sinner is a lost person, whether he was lost by his will or ignorance, or as a result of someone else. When the prodigal son left his father's house, he thought that he had found himself, along with freedom, wealth, enjoyment, and friends. In actual fact he did not find himself, but rather lost himself. The lost sheep might have felt that he left the small, closed field for the wide-open empty spaces. In the end, though, he found that he was lost and had departed from his shepherd and his beloved. The sinner understands freedom and enjoyment in the wrong way. In the same way in which he thinks that sin is victory, it becomes a defeat for him.

Sin is defeat, not victory. Let us pretend that a person insulted you and you insulted him; you argued with him and won, silencing and quieting him. Let us pretend that he assaulted you, and so you assaulted him, or perhaps it got worse. Do you think that you won? No, you were defeated because you were stirred up and unable to control yourself. Sin defeated you.

You might say, "I defended my honor, I did not allow this person to dominate me, but I stopped him at his limit and defeated him." You might believe that you were victorious in your own eyes, but you were defeated. The sins of anger, vainglory, judgment, and fighting back have defeated you, and also lack of love and perseverance. As the Bible says in Romans 12.21, "Do not be overcome by evil, but overcome evil with good."

The sinful person is a person defeated by sin. There are many kinds of sinful people. There is a person who is defeated by the flesh, another by honor, a third by the lust of food, a fourth by money, another by anger, and another by malice, and so on. One person looks at a woman and lusts for her and commits adultery with her in his heart. He thinks that he has enjoyed himself by this vision, whereas actually he has been defeated by sin and has fallen. One look defeated him and made him fall into lust, and made the angels look from heaven at him, saying, "This person is poor and weak, and cannot withstand a single look, but fell. He sold the kingdom and lost it for the sake of one worthless look."

So the sinful person is a defeated person, no matter how he surrounds himself with the trappings of fake power. The righteous person, in his nobleness and exaltation, seems to be defeated in the eyes of the people, yet he is at the peak of his victory. There are many examples of this.

When Cain, for example, arose and killed Abel, was he victorious or defeated? He might have thought to himself at the beginning of the matter that he was victorious over his brother, for he was able to hit him, throw him to the ground, and kill him. But he was defeated. He was defeated by jealousy and zeal. He was defeated by anger and malice, and lost his love. The devil of harshness defeated him, as well as the sin of killing. This person who considered himself strong became shaken and afraid when he stood before God. Cain then said to God, "My punishment is greater than I can bear. Surely You have driven me out this day from the face of the ground; I shall be hidden from Your face; I shall be groaning and trembling on the earth. Then it will happen if anyone finds me, he will kill me" (Genesis 4.13–14). Poor Cain was a weak person defeated by sin.

Herod the King was in a similar position. When he arrested John the Baptist and put him in prison, he wanted to silence this voice crying in the wilderness, but could not. So he cut his head off. Was Herod powerful when he killed John, or was he weak in the face of his lust, boastfulness, honor, and submission to the women? The biggest indication of his weakness is that he remained frightened of John, even after the latter's death. When Jesus appeared, Herod thought that He was John, risen from the dead (Matthew 14.2).

It is similar for you when you try to dominate another by insulting, abusing, hurting, and bullying him. It seems that he is weak and despicable, unable to stand up to you. You think you have won, but no, you have been defeated by all of those sins, as well as by evil.

The sinner imagines victory when there is defeat, pleasure when there is loss, and power where there is weakness. As the Bible says: "Seeing they do not see, and hearing they do not hear, nor do they understand" (Matthew 13.13). Some looked at the cross of Christ, to whom is due glory, with this same incorrect assessment. Those who did not understand thought that His crucifixion was an indication of His weakness, defeat, and the victory of His enemies over Him, whereas it was actually the complete opposite. It was the crucifiers of Christ who were defeated. They were defeated because of their jealousy and envy of Him. They were defeated by the demons of lying, harshness, cowardice, and ingratitude.

As for the Lord Jesus Christ, He was victorious in His love. He presented salvation to us, demolished the devil's kingdom, opened Paradise, and completed the great work of redemption for those waiting. He was victorious at every step of the way in contrast to His crucifiers, some of whom returned and regretted what they had done. The judgments of the people were incorrect, and so sin is weakness and defeat. What else can we say about sin?

Sin is separation from God. "For what fellowship . . . has light with darkness? And what accord has Christ with Belial?" (2 Corinthians 6.14–15). In his sin the prodigal son, for example, left his father's house and was separated from him.

Sin is not just separation from God, but also animosity toward Him. When the world sinned, it fell into animosity toward God, which was expressed ritually by the middle veil that separated the believers from the Holy of Holies. When Christ came, however, He brought about reconciliation between us and God, and removed the middle veil. In the liturgy it is said about Him: "You reconciled the earthly with the heavenly."[2] He reconciled them because sin had caused animosity between them and God. For this reason, we pray the prayer of reconciliation before we start the liturgy. Before we receive Holy Communion, we are first reconciled with God.

Between the sinful person and God, there is animosity. He has angered God and grieved him, and become separated from Him. He left His house and priests, His Bible and commandments, His body and blood, and he also left conversing with Him, so animosity is present. When sin increases, animosity and the separation from God also increase. This animosity between God and man reached a fearful state in the days of Jeremiah the Prophet, to the degree that God says to His prophet: "Do not pray for this people. . . . Do not pray or come to me about them. I will not hear you" (Jeremiah 7.15). The animosity reached such a level that God says: "Even if Moses and Samuel stood before Me, My soul would not be favorable toward them" (Jeremiah 15.1). This animosity reached the stage where God says to the foolish virgins: "Assuredly, I say to you, I do not know you" (Matthew 25.12). He says to others: "I never knew you; depart from Me, you who practice lawlessness" (Matthew 7.23). "I tell you I do not know where you are from. Depart from Me, all you workers of iniquity" (Luke 13.27).

"I do not know you." How shameful and terrifying! God denies knowing man and His relationship with him, exonerates Himself from man and his company, and separates him from Himself. What a great pain and disgrace this is!

In animosity, sin reaches the disgusting stage of enmity with God. Saint James the Apostle says: "Do you not know that friendship with the world is enmity with God? Whoever therefore wants to be a friend of the world makes himself an enemy of God" (James 4.4). Saint John the Apostle confirms this by saying: "If anyone loves the world, the love of the Father is not in him" (1 John 2.15).

Contrary to this, the lovers of God show their love by their friendship and familiarity with Him. What a great difference there is between favor and animosity. If we knew the effect of favor between God and his beloved,

[2] *Editor's note:* From the first Prayer of Reconciliation in the Coptic Liturgy of Saint Gregory the Theologian.

we would be overcome with zeal. Our hearts would be inflamed and we would wish to be like the beloved of God.

It has been said of our father Abraham that he is the lover of God. We remember him in our prayers, saying to God in the Ninth Hour prayer: "for the sake of your beloved Abraham."[3] He is the lover of God, His friend, and between him and God there is favor. When God was going to burn Sodom, He asked: "Shall I hide from Abraham, My servant, what I am about to do?" (Genesis 18.17). How amazing it is that God did not burn Sodom before telling Abraham first and discussing the situation with him! Who is this Abraham, O Lord? Is he not a scoop of "dust and ashes" (Genesis 18.27)? No, answers the Lord. "He is My beloved and My friend, I must tell him first and take his opinion. It is not right for him to be surprised by the situation like the rest of the people."

So God told Abraham, and Abraham discussed it with God with favor. "Would You also destroy the righteous with the ungodly? . . . Far be it from You to do such a thing . . . far be it from You! Shall not the Judge of all the earth do right?" (Genesis 18:23, 25). It was not a method we would use to talk with some people, out of fear of them, but Abraham used it to talk with God with courage and favor. He continues: "Suppose there were fifty righteous within the city . . . suppose there were five less than the fifty righteous . . . suppose there should be forty found there . . . thirty . . . ten" (Genesis 18:24, 28, 29, 30, 32). God answers: "I would not destroy it for the sake of the ten" (Genesis 18.32). Abraham is friends with God. It is amazing to find people with such a friendship with God, who can communicate with God and God with them.

The same situation that occurred with Abraham and God also occurred with Moses. The Jews made a calf out of gold and worshipped it. The Lord was very angry at this betrayal, especially after the miracles He performed with them and the series of good deeds He had presented to them. God thought of destroying these people, but He sought to tell Moses first. After God explained to Moses how the people had become stiff-necked, He said: "Let Me alone, that I may . . . . consume them" (Exodus 32.9).

We stand in awe at the words "let Me alone." What is the meaning of these words, O Lord our God, who are capable of all things? Do you require

[3]*Editor's note:* Prayer from the third petition of the Ninth Hour Prayer in the *Agpeya.*

Moses to leave You, if You are to be able to take action? Is he holding You back from taking action? Is he capable of that? Our amazement increases not just from God's words, but from Moses' answer. Just as Jacob says to the Lord, while pleading with Him, "I will not let You go" (Genesis 32.26), Moses also says to the Lord in courage and loving favor: "Turn from your fierce wrath and be merciful" (Exodus 32.12). Such amazing courageous words! Who can say them to one of the leaders of the world, let alone to God? Moses made an excuse for his protest, insisting that the Egyptians might say, "He brought them out with evil intent, to kill them in the mountains" (Exodus 32:12).

The amazing thing is that God was not upset with Moses but agreed with him, and carried out for him what Moses wanted. The Bible says: "So the Lord granted mercy for the harm He said He would do" (Exodus 32.14). What is the meaning of this, O Lord? He answers, "They are my friends, they have found favor with Me." It is amazing! Who is this Moses? What is this favor between God and His beloved? If a sinner reads about it, he will feel the fervor of zeal inflaming his heart to change and follow these examples.

In another example, we read of Moses that he was on the mountain with God for "forty days and forty nights" (Exodus 34.28). Do you think that God's writing of the ten commandments on the two tablets took all that time? Does writing require a day from God, an hour, a few minutes, or only an instant?

God left Moses forty days on the mountain because he is His friend, His beloved, and His spokesman. God was happy with the presence of Moses because he is His son, and Moses was happy and enjoying the presence of the Lord. Just tell me, what mission would have taken forty days? All of the commandments that Moses received from God would not have taken more than one day. As for the rest, it was a period of favor, friendship, and love.

God has friends and loved ones. He says to them openly: "No longer do I call you servants, but I have called you friends" (John 15.15). It is said that He "loved Martha and her sister and Lazarus" (John 11.5). When He wept for Lazarus the people said: "See how He loved him" (John 11.36). Saint John the Evangelist is repeatedly called "the disciple whom Jesus loved."

God has loved ones who have great favor with Him, and in their hands He places the keys of heaven, and they can open heaven and close it as they like. For example, we hear an amazing word from Elijah the Prophet, who says: "There shall not be dew nor rain these years except at my word" (3 Kingdoms 17.1). The phrase "except at my word" is an amazing and powerful phrase. Elijah did not say, "when God wills" or "when God permits," but said confidently and firmly, "except at my word." Indeed, the heavens were closed according to his word, and remained closed three years and six months. This caused hunger and toil for all the people. However, the heavens remained closed, awaiting the word of Elijah, and when he spoke, the heavens rained.

These keys of heaven, which are in the hands of the saints, were discussed by Saint John Saba in his conversation about their prayers and their prayers' effect. He said that they are "not like those who pray, but like those who accept prayer, just like a son who was entrusted with his father's treasures, to open and give to the people." As an example of this, we hear about the reposed saint, Anba Abraam the bishop of Fayoum,[4] who when someone came to him with a problem would say, "Go, my son, you will find it has been solved," and to the childless woman he would say, "Next year you will have a child." He would say this even without praying, and what he would say would happen.

These are blessings that he distributes to the people, gifts he received from the Heavenly Father, which He gives with compassion to whoever asks. Are we not overcome by zeal when we hear of such examples of closeness to God?

God is not satisfied with giving these loved ones His gifts; He defends them and does not accept any bad word spoken against them. An example of this is Moses the Prophet. He married a Cushite woman, despite this being against the law, for the Lord did not allow marriage to alien women. Aaron, Moses' brother, and Miriam his sister were upset by this marriage, and they talked about Moses. Moses kept quiet, for he was very patient. The Lord, however, did not keep quiet, nor did He not accept bad words against His

[4]*Editor's note:* For more information, see Mirrit B. Ghali, "Abraam I," *The Coptic Encyclopedia* 1, (1991 edition) http://ccdl.libraries.claremont.edu/cdm/singleitem/collection/cce/id/22/rec/1

beloved Moses, even if the speakers were Aaron the high priest and Miriam the Prophetess, the sister of Moses and Aaron.

The Lord called all three of them and rebuked Miriam and Aaron with a great rebuke, saying to them: "If there were a prophet among you, I, the Lord, would make Myself known to him in a vision; I would speak to him in a dream. Not so with my servant Moses; he is faithful in all My house. I speak with him face to face.... Why then were you not afraid to speak against My servant Moses?" (Numbers 12.1–8). Then God struck Miriam with leprosy and she became leprous, as white as snow, and He shut her out of the camp seven days.

What is this that you do, Lord? It is as though He says, "This is Moses My servant, My beloved whom I entrusted over all of My house, I speak with him face to face. How can I allow these to insult him while I remain quiet? They must receive a punishment in order to respect him, and everyone who hears will respect him also." Perhaps now people such as these will understand the word of God to our father Abraham: "I will bless those who bless you, and curse those who curse you" (Genesis 12.3). It is an amazing honor which God gives to his beloved: not only to be blessed, but even more to be themselves a blessing (Genesis 12.2), just as Elijah was a blessing in the house of the widow, Joseph in the house of Potiphar and in the land of Egypt, and Elisha in the house of the Shunamite.

One of the amazing honors that God gives to His children is to perform miracles through their hands. These are miracles that God would have performed Himself, but instead He bestows them on His beloved, to honor them in the eyes of the people. For example, a sick person prays to God to heal him. Instead of healing him Himself, God sends one of His saints to heal him. He sends our Lady the Virgin or Saint George or Saint Demiana. The people then praise the Virgin, Saint George, and Saint Demiana, and the Lord is joyous, reciting in the ears of these saints, "Whoever honors you, honors Me. I honor those who honor Me."

We ask the Lord, "To what extent will You honor them?" He says that they "will sit on twelve thrones, judging the twelve tribes of Israel" (Matthew 19.28). We say to Him, "O Lord, how can they sit with You in Your glory, You before Whom stand the angels and archangels?" He says, "I honor those who honor Me." We ask Him, "How can they sit on the thrones of the judges in the Day of Judgment, while You are the only Judge, the Judge of all the earth, judging the living and the dead, all judgment being given to You from the Father" (John 5.22)? He answers, "My delight is with the sons of men, for I love them and will honor them more. If I am the Judge of all the earth, they will judge the earth. If I am the King of kings, they will rule with Me. If I am coming in My glory on the cloud, they will come on the cloud with Me, they will be with Me at all times, where I am, they will be there also" (cf. John 14.3).

God honors all of these people by loving them, by living with them, by defending them, by giving them the keys of heaven and earth, by announcing their honor to other people, so that they can honor them also. He honors them by the favor He gives them in conversing with respect to His judgments.

This is a concise explanation of the favor which the righteous find with God, and the honor He gives them. On the other hand, we find that sin is contrary to this. Sin is deprivation of God, the angels, and the council of saints.

Sin is deprivation from God. The sinful person deprives himself of God by separating himself and his heart from Him. So sin, before all things, is lack of love for God. The Lord's saying is clear: "If anyone loves Me, he will keep My word" (John 14.23). The saying of the apostle is also clear: "If anyone loves the world, the love of the Father is not in him" (1 John 2.15).

Whoever loves God clings to Him and to whatever makes him closer to Him. As for whoever leans toward sin, he removes himself from the love of God, for he cannot love God and sin at the same time.

Sin is also disobedience to God, a revolution against God, and defiance of Him. It is a lack of fear of God that stops the person from taking God's commandments seriously. He breaks them in front of God, who sees the person committing the sin with such ease. This is a lack of shame before God. The righteous, however, are not like this. The righteous Joseph for example, when he was offered sin, said with strength and fear: "How then can I do this great wickedness, and sin against God?" (Genesis 39.9). Sin was offered to him, but his eyes were fixed on God. He regarded sin to be against God Himself, and not just against the woman and her husband. Similarly,

David the Prophet prays: "Against You have I sinned and done this evil in Your sight" (Psalm 50.4).

As long as sin is directed toward God and committed before God, then it is defiance of God. It is a revolution against His kingdom, His holiness and righteousness, and an attempt to remove Him from the heart, so that another may rule in His place. As God is unlimited, so the sin directed toward Him is unlimited, and its punishment as well. If an atonement is to be offered for it, it has to be an unlimited atonement. The forgiveness of sin, then, cannot occur without the sacrifice of Christ, in which He takes this sin on His shoulders and carries it from us, with all of its impurity and shame.

Sin is opposition to the Holy Spirit. The Spirit of God within you wants you to live in the holiness that is appropriate to the sons of God. He works in you for good and righteousness. If you walk in sin, then you are opposing the Spirit. "And do not grieve the Holy Spirit of God, by whom you were sealed" (Ephesians 4.30).

Therefore, everyone who commits a sin grieves the Spirit of God. The Bible also says: "Do not quench the Spirit" (1 Thessalonians 5.19). When the Spirit of God works in the heart of a person, He inflames him with love, with enthusiasm toward doing good, and with holy zeal for spreading the kingdom of God, for our God is a consuming fire (Hebrews 12.29). Everyone who keeps God inside him keeps a flaming fire. As it is written, God is the one "who makes His angels spirits and His ministers a flame of fire" (Psalm 103.4). The apostle commanded us to be "fervent in spirit" (Romans 12.11). For everyone in whom the Spirit of God works must be inflamed by spiritual fervor. Did not the Spirit of God, when descending on the pure disciples, descend on them with tongues "as of fire" (Acts 2.3)?

Therefore, whoever commits sin quenches the Spirit, according to the saying of the Bible. The quenching of this fervor leads a person to laxity. If he remains in laxity, he will reach spiritual coolness, and the spiritual means that inflame other people will have no influence on him. Despite all this, the Spirit of God still remains in him, even though He is grieved and the fervor for Him is quenched. The departure of the Spirit of God is the greatest fear we hold for the sinner—just as when He left King Saul and a distressing spirit from the Lord troubled him (1 Kingdoms 16.14). It is this grievous state that made David cry out in his prayers: "Do not cast me away from Your presence, and do not take Your Holy Spirit from me" (Psalm 50.11).

This dangerous state is what is called "blasphemy against the Holy Spirit." Blasphemy against the Holy Spirit is the complete, continual refusal of the work of the Holy Spirit in the heart. From the intensity of evil, the person reaches a stage of harshness of heart which refuses every work of the Spirit until death. Therefore he cannot repent, because repentance comes to him only as a result of the work of the Holy Spirit in him, for the Spirit convicts a person of sin (John 16.8). If he does not repent, he cannot gain forgiveness, for as the saints have said, "there is no sin without forgiveness, except that which is without repentance."[5] There is no forgiveness for the sin of blasphemy against the Holy Spirit (Mark 3.29; Luke 12.10).

We have not yet reached the stage of despair. The Spirit of God still works in us toward repentance, and we should submit to the work of the Spirit without refusal or stubbornness. If we have previously grieved the Spirit of God, let us not continue to grieve Him. If we have quenched His fervor in us, let us not continue to quench it. It is not right for us to continue in our stubbornness, for the Spirit may leave us like those who have fallen into the pit. I wish that we would hate sin, which resists the work of the Spirit of God in us. Sin is very dangerous, for it is the corruption of human nature.

Sin is the corruption of human nature. It is said that sinners "all turned aside and were altogether corrupted" (Psalm 13.3). A person is in God's image and likeness, except when he is in the state of sin. In that state, he is corrupted and has lost God's image. I do not agree with the one who falls and then defends his fall by saying, "This is human nature. I should be excused, this is my nature!" No, this is not the human nature which the good Lord created, who after creating everything saw that it was very good (Genesis 1.31).

Your human nature in its original state, my brother, is very good, but you complain about your present nature after it has been corrupted by sin. This is the corruption the apostle complained about: "But I am carnal, sold under sin.... O wretched man that I am! Who will deliver me from this

---

[5]Isaac the Syrian *Ascetical Homilies*, Homily II.

body of death?" (Romans 7.14, 24). Sin ruins our nature and degrades its heavenly quality.

Sin is degradation. Imagine a person in his position as a son to God, degrading himself to the level in which he becomes a son to Satan. By this degradation, the light which is in him becomes darkness. He forgets his high position and acts as one of the children of the world. The sinner is degraded before his own eyes, and his rank is lowered or destroyed. Can a son of a king sit on a heap of rubbish? Certainly not. How much more, then, can a son of God?

The sinner is degraded not only in his own eyes, but also in the way he views other people. An example of this is a youth who looks at a young woman lustfully. No doubt, if he were heavenly in his thoughts, he would have said to himself, "This young woman is a temple for the Holy Spirit, how can I touch or defile Him? I cannot at all destroy the temple of God." For "if anyone defiles the temple of God, God will destroy him. For the temple of God is holy" (1 Corinthians 3.17). Instead, the youth looks at the young woman with lust because her dignity has been degraded in his sight. This is the sin which corrupts human nature and changes it from being a temple for God to a tool for corruption.

Sin corrupts not only human nature, but all the earth. Therefore it was said in the book of Revelation about the great harlot that she "corrupted the earth with her fornication" (Revelation 19.2).

Sin is impurity, fornication, and disgrace. Sin is impurity, which is why the angels who fell were given the title of "unclean spirits" (Mark 6.7). The diseases that symbolized sin, such as leprosy, were considered an impurity. The same goes for the impure animals.

In the Holy Bible we see examples of the impurity of sin. Divine inspiration says through Ezekiel the Prophet: "The house of Israel dwelt upon their own land, but they defiled it by their conduct. Their conduct was like the uncleanness of a woman in her customary impurity" (Ezekiel 36.17). On breaking the Sabbath, He says: "They greatly defiled My Sabbaths" (Ezekiel 20.13). About the sins of the priests, He says in the book of Nehemiah: "They have defiled the priesthood" (Nehemiah 13.29). With respect to murder, the Bible says: "For your hands are defiled with blood, and your fingers with sins" (Isaiah 59.3). About fornication, it says: "And you have polluted the land with your harlotries . . . therefore the showers have been withheld" (Jeremiah 3.2).

The description of sin as impurity applies not only to the sins of fornication and murder, but also to the sins of the mouth and the tongue. Regarding sins of the tongue, the Lord Jesus Himself says: "Not what goes into the mouth defiles a man; but what comes out of the mouth, this defiles a man" (Matthew 15.11). The Lord used the word defilement to represent sin generally. Concerning the righteous, He says: "You have a few names . . . who have not defiled their garments; and they shall walk with Me in white, for they are worthy" (Revelation 3.4). About the sinners, He says: "But you entered and defiled My land, and made My heritage an abomination" (Jeremiah 2.7).

If you know, my brother, that sin is defilement, then no doubt you will flee from it. In the state of sin, you will feel that you are a "defiled person"! You will feel that every sinful word that proceeds from your mouth defiles you. For whatever comes out of the mouth is what defiles a man.

Because fornication was the strongest symbol of defilement, any sin was regarded as fornication. The Bible says about the sins of the sons of Israel that "Judah has fornicated," and "Israel has fornicated" (Ezekiel 16). All who are in these two kingdoms have sinned.

Sin is disgrace: "Sin is a reproach to any people" (Proverbs 14.35). It is also a sickness. Isaiah the Prophet says: "They forsook the Lord; they have provoked to anger the Holy One of Israel. . . . The whole head is in pain, and the whole heart in sadness. From the feet all the way to the head, there is no soundness in them, only wounds and bruises and festering sores. They have not been closed or bandaged, or soothed with ointment" (Isaiah 1.4–6).

Sin is also ignorance—ignorance of God, faith, goodness, and of whatever should be. The Lord said: "The ox knows its owner and the donkey its master's crib; but Israel does not know Me, and the people do not understand Me" (Isaiah 1.3).

What else is sin? Sin is also deficiency, defect, delusion, blindness, darkness, and forgetting of God. It is darkness, because it has departed from the light that is God. It is right, what was said about sinners, that they "loved darkness rather than light" (John 3.19), and "the senseless man walks in darkness" (Ecclesiastes 2.14). Two things will make us flee from sin: the disgusting nature of sin and the frightful results of sin. So what are the results of sin?

CHAPTER 3

If You Know the Results of Sin,
You Will Flee From Sin

I f you know the results of sin, you will flee from sin, for the results of sin are fear and unrest. Sin makes you lose your inner peace and fills the heart with fear and anxiety. The saint does not fear. David the Prophet says: "Though an army should array itself against me, my heart shall not be afraid; though war should rise up against me, in this I shall hope" (Psalm 26.3). As for the sinner, he is continuously fearful, losing his peace. "'There is no rejoicing,' says the Lord, 'for the ungodly'" (Isaiah 48.22). He also says that "the wicked are like the troubled sea" (Isaiah 57.20).

Fear started with the first sin, the sin of Adam and Eve. Adam did not fear God before sin. On the contrary, when God would come down to Paradise, Adam and Eve greeted Him with joy and rejoiced to talk with Him. After their sin, we read that Adam hid in the midst of the trees of the Paradise because he feared the face of God. When the Lord called him, Adam cried with fear: "I heard Your voice . . . in the garden, and I was afraid because I was naked; so I hid myself" (Genesis 3.10).

Imagine that the beloved God, whom everyone desires to see, becomes a fearful sight to the sinner, who flees from His vision! God, who is "fairer than the sons of men," "His mouth is most sweet, yes, he is altogether lovely," becomes fearful to the sinner! When the sinner sees Him, he fears Him, flees from Him, and hides in order not to see Him. The soul which loves God says with the bride of the Song of Songs: "I will rise now and go about the city, in the marketplaces and in the streets, I will seek him whom my soul loves." If she finds Him, she says: "I held him and would not let him go" (Song of Songs 3.2, 4). As for the sinful soul, it sees nothing other than the verse that says: "It is a fearful thing to fall into the hands of the living God" (Hebrews 10.31).

So God is fearful to the wicked. The righteous, however, are the friends of God who rejoice with Him. When Saint Antony the Great said to his disciples, "My sons, I do not fear God," they were amazed at this statement and answered, "Our father, these are difficult words." He then said to them, "This is because I love Him, and there is no fear in love, for 'love casts out fear'" (1 John 4.18).[1]

Imagine with me, my brothers, that God has now come into our midst. How many of us do you think will rejoice at His coming and embrace Him? And how many will be afraid, and try to escape? Sinners fear meeting God, and therefore they are afraid of death and tremble before it. They fear the great hour of judgment, when they will be exposed before everyone: in front of their enemies, who become malicious toward them, and in front of their friends, who thought that they were pure and righteous. When this hour comes, they shall "say to the mountains, 'Fall on us!' and to the hills, 'Cover us!'" (Luke 23.30; Hosea 10.8). These people will seek death and will not find it; they will desire to die, and death will flee from them (Revelation 9.6).

Truly, when Adam sinned, he began to fear. A new, frightful thing crept into him, which had not been present before: fear, alarm, and loss of peace. This fear—when Adam feared God—was the beginning of the psychological diseases inflicted on humanity as a result of sin, for it is with this fear that the soul began to be sick. The righteous person keeps his peace in quietness and joy. The sinner however, loses his inner and outer peace.

From the inside his conscience revolts against him, and the Holy Spirit rebukes him. Outwardly, he is afraid that his sin will be revealed, just as he fears its results and punishments. We have never seen a sinful person living continuously in peace of mind, no matter how insensible his conscience may be. There is no doubt that this conscience will awaken after a while, revolt against him, and trouble him.

Sin torments the conscience. An example of torment of the conscience is a story told about Pontius Pilate. Pilate knew that Jesus was innocent, and therefore said: "And indeed, having examined Him in your presence, I have found no fault in this Man concerning those things of which you accuse Him" (Luke 23.14). While he was sitting on the judgment seat, his wife sent to him, saying: "Have nothing to do with that just Man, for I have

[1]Antony 23, *Sayings of the Desert Fathers.*

suffered many things today in a dream because of Him" (Matthew 27.19). In spite of this, he passed the sentence of death against his own conscience. But to satisfy his conscience falsely, he took water and washed his hands before the multitude, saying: "I am innocent of the blood of this just Person" (Matthew 27.24).

The story goes that when Pilate was alone in his house, he found his hands stained with blood, so he washed them a second time, but the blood did not leave them. So he washed them a third time, saying: "I am innocent of the blood of this just Person." He still, however, found the blood staining his hands. He continued to wash his hands repeatedly, crying with fear: "I am innocent of the blood of this just Person." It is a story that demonstrates to us the degree of fear and loss of peace inflicted on the sinner as a result of his sin.

Sin is tiresome. A person does not feel sin's danger until he falls into it, or perhaps some time afterwards, when his conscience wakes up, either by itself or from an outside influence. The story of Judas Iscariot is an example of torment due to the late awakening of the conscience. Judas did not feel the enormity of his betrayal at first. He was busy with consultations, meetings, and agreements. He was occupied with money and the method of receiving it, and with the time and place of handing over his Master. He did not feel the Lord's warning to him.

Finally, when the Lord Jesus was judged and sentenced to be crucified, Judas' conscience awakened. It kept tormenting him, and he found himself faced with a repugnant and fearful sin. He then began to remember the words of the Lord to the disciples: "You are clean, but not all of you;" "one of you will betray Me;" "the son of Man goes as it has been determined, but woe to that man by whom He is betrayed" (Luke 22.22). Judas also remembered the saying of the Lord to him ("What you do, do quickly") and the last words of Jesus to him: "Friend, why have you come?" (Matthew 26.50). "Are you betraying the Son of Man with a kiss?" (Luke 22.48).

Judas could not bear all of this, for his conscience troubled him greatly. So he got up and went to the chief priests and gave back the thirty pieces of silver, saying: "I have sinned by betraying innocent blood." They replied: "'What is that to us? You see to it!' Then he threw down the pieces of silver in the temple and departed" (Matthew 27.4, 5). Through all of this, Judas' conscience continued to trouble him without ceasing. The vision of his sin was nailed before his eyes in all its ugliness, and finally he "went and hanged himself" (Matthew 27.5).

My brethren, how repugnant sin is! How great is its frightfulness, when the conscience awakens! A person may not feel its bitterness if he is still in a whirlpool of sins or preoccupations. However, as soon as he becomes aware or returns to himself, he becomes troubled and tortured by the vision of his sin.

That is why some criminals turn themselves in to justice, confessing their crimes. They do this because they cannot bear the rebuke of their conscience, the inner unrest which troubles them, nor the loss of peace which results from their feelings of sin. The Bible is correct in saying: " 'There is no rejoicing,' says the Lord, 'for the ungodly' " (Isaiah 48.22). There is a psychological theory about why criminals hover around the crime scene during the first few days after the criminal act. It is because the criminal is uneasy and afraid the crime will be discovered. He wonders if he has left any traces, or if the police have found him out. Therefore, when detectives and police discover a crime, they survey the crime scene secretly in order to discover anyone who might be lurking around the area.

What happened to Cain after his sin is an example of fear, unrest, and loss of peace. He lived as a lost man and a fugitive on earth, afraid that someone might kill him just as he killed his brother. He felt that God had banished him from the face of the earth and from before His face (Genesis 4.13–14). With this unrest, Cain spent his life in fear. He did not gain anything from his sin. He was continuously reminded of his transgression, and of the voice of his brother crying from the ground. This is how psychological diseases are inflicted on the sinner as a result of unrest, fear, confusion, disturbance, and the continual expectancy of evil.

In contrast to this, the righteous live in joy and peace. They are continuously joyful, neither disturbed, nor uneasy, nor confused from within. The Holy Bible says: "But the fruit of the Spirit is love, joy, peace . . ." (Galatians 5.22). Therefore, the person who does not live in peace does not have the fruits of the Holy Spirit in him. It was said of Saint Antony, in the story written about him by Saint Athanasius the Apostolic: "Anybody with a disturbed soul or a confused heart, after seeing the face of Saint Antony, was filled with peace."[2] The mere sight of the face of Saint Antony, in his quietness and joy, filled the heart with peace.

Sinners are not like this. Instead, they live in grief and torment, especially when their conscience awakens and inflames them with its whips. In addition to the torments of wicked men such as Judas and Cain, there are examples of the torment of the consciences of the saints. The best example is the story of David the Prophet. During sin, David the Prophet was elated by fleshly pleasure. He thus did not sense the danger of his actions, to the extent that he followed the sin of fornication with the sin of murder. He did all this with an unmoved conscience. But when Nathan confronted him with his sin, David started to feel the gravity of what he had done. His conscience woke up and began to trouble him, even though the prophet had said to him: "The Lord also has put away your sin. You shall not die" (2 Kingdoms 12.13).

When his conscience was awakened, David drenched his couch with his tears (Psalm 6.7). His tears became his food, day and night, and his soul clung to the dust. He lived in humiliation and cried out to the Lord: "For my bones are troubled; and my soul is greatly troubled" (Psalm 6.3–4). He accepted humiliation for the sake of the salvation of his soul, saying: "It is good for me that You humbled me, that I might learn Your statutes" (Psalm 118.71). Truly, when a person's sins are revealed to him, his tormented soul makes him feel as if he is in hell.

Do you think that there will be "weeping and gnashing of teeth" only in the lake of fire, burning with brimstone? No, there will also be "weeping and gnashing of teeth" on earth, when man is tormented in his heart from the horror of his sin. This happens at the times of repentance, when the penitent feels the extent of the ugliness of his sin and weeps for it with tears and a burning heart. He blames himself, wondering, "Where were my mind and thoughts when I did this?" His conscience reprimands him; his teeth shudder from pain, regret, shame, disgrace, and self-contempt. It is actually good for the sinner to suffer "weeping and gnashing of teeth" here on earth, rather than to suffer it in eternity without hope.

---

[2] Athanasius of Alexandria, *Life of Antony.*

We have now seen some of the results of sin: fear, loss of peace, bitterness, and torment of the conscience. There are also other results of sin, for sin changes a person completely. Some of these results include:

Loss of the divine image. Man was created in God's image and likeness. In the state of sin, man does not preserve this divine image, but rather loses it. He loses it from within and on the outside also, for sin leaves its impression on his face and features, on his voice, gestures, appearance, and attire. Even his words, his manner, and his language express the sin which is concealed in him, just as it was said: "Your speech shows it" (Mark 14.70). Therefore, our teacher Saint John the Beloved says: "In this the children of God and the children of the devil are manifest" (1 John 3.10). So you, O brother, whose sin has changed your appearance and manners, and you, O sister, whose sin has changed your face, attire, and voice, return to God with repentance. Repentance will change you, returning to you the divine image which you lost.

Loss of honor. Before sin, man was a holy breath which proceeded from the mouth of God. He was in God's image and likeness. After sin, however, the Lord says to him: "You are dust and to dust you will return" (Genesis 3.19). He returned to dust just as he was, unworthy of being called the image of God. He desired to have the divine glory, and instead he lost even the human glory that was given to him.

He desired to eat, therefore the Lord gave him herbs to eat (Genesis 1.18), which previously had been the food of animals (Genesis 1.30). The animals lost their awe of him, and he became afraid of them. They were given the capability of eating him, him who once was the master of them all (Genesis 1.26). Even the serpent had the ability to bruise his heel (Genesis 3.15). The earth rebelled against him and brought forth for him thorns and thistles (Genesis 3.18). The harshest statement of the earth's rebellion against man came when God said: "When you till the ground, it shall no longer yield its strength to you" (Genesis 4.12).

The sinful person has lost his honor and respect. He is a toy in the hands of the demons and of the wicked. He has no dignity. He has lost self-respect. Look at the how prodigal son desired the pods which the swine ate, and how he wished to be like one of the hired servants in his father's house! Look at Nebuchadnezzar the King: they stripped him of his majesty, and he became like an animal (Daniel 5.2–21). Look at Samson the Great, and how by sin he lost his power and honor, so that the people of Palestine despised and ridiculed him (Judges 16.19–25).

Do not let the devil deceive you, my brother, for he portrays sin to you as the enjoyment of desires, promising you honors and enticements. But when you taste sin, you find that it is bitter, leading you to humiliation and causing you to lose everything. You inherit depression and are led to despair; you hide your face in shame.

Loss of simplicity and purity. The righteous person is a pure person. He knows nothing but good. When he begins to sin, he comes to know evil also and loses his simplicity. He looks at things without his original perspective. His knowledge of new things degrades his condition, and he wishes this knowledge would disappear from his thoughts. Adam and Eve were naked in the garden before sin and were not embarrassed. They were living in simplicity, not knowing uncleanliness. However, with sin they lost their simplicity and had to make clothing for themselves.

You also, O brother, what has sin done to you? Has it caused you to lose your simplicity of thought and your purity of heart? Has it made you change your perspective toward people, your view of yourself, and your view toward things? This change is horrifying, and I hope you will not continue therein, so that you do not lose what remains of your simplicity and purity. I hope that you will return to God with repentance, so that your original purity will return to you, and so that the Lord will grant you a new white robe.

CHAPTER 4

If You Know the Punishment for Sin, You Will Be Afraid of Sin

In the previous chapter, we learned the results of sin: how it can shatter mankind's inner soul and make us lose the divine image, our honor, simplicity, and purity. Sin will make the soul inherit fear, unrest, torment, shame, and carelessness. It remains, then, for us to gain some idea of the punishment for sin.

If you knew the punishment for sin, you would be afraid of sin. We must be certain that just as God is merciful—and there is no limit to His mercy—He is also just, and there is no limit to His justice. Just as He is compassionate and forgives, He is also holy and hates sin.

There are some who, unfortunately, exploit God's mercy with a malicious intent. This leads them into carelessness and sin, with a false reliance on God's mercy. This type of person sins as he likes, and if you rebuke him, he will say to you, "God is merciful, compassionate, and kind. He will not deal with us according to our sins, and will not punish us according to our offences. He who forgave the adulteress will forgive me also. He who forgave Zacchaeus the tax collector and Augustine will forgive and pardon me. He who accepted Mary of Egypt and Moses the Black will accept me also with them."

He says this while at the same time overlooking the amazingly deep repentance these saints went through, by which God accepted them. This repentance was a turning point in their lives. They never again returned to sin. Every day, they increased in grace and progressed in the love of God. God's mercy to them was an opportunity neither for carelessness nor continuing in sin, God forbid.

We need to approach God's justice and mercy with a correct understanding, which leads us to repentance. This is a good opportunity to mention what Saint Paul said about the "goodness and severity of God" (Romans 11.22). The great apostle taught us, saying: "Therefore consider the goodness and severity of God: on those who fell, severity; but toward you, goodness, if you continue in His goodness. Otherwise you also will be cut off" (Romans 11.22). It is not right, then, to rely on God's goodness and forget His severity. Nor is it right to rely upon God's mercy while forgetting His justice.

God's mercy is just. God's attributes are never separated from each other, so that one stands out, apart from the others. Sometimes we mention them separately for the sake of details, and so that people will understand them, but they are divinely united. God is just in His mercy, and merciful in His justice. His justice is merciful and His mercy is just. His justice is filled with mercy and His mercy is filled with justice. We cannot separate His mercy from His justice.

This unity between mercy and justice is the foundation of the act of redemption. If God's mercy stood by itself, without justice, then His mercy would have been enough to say to man, "Your sins are forgiven." The matter would have been finished, without the crucifixion. However, with mercy He forgave sin, and with justice He paid the price of sin.

Since God is just, He was incarnate and died for us to pay the price of our sin. Justice must be fulfilled, even if the matter reaches the stage where God takes on flesh and becomes a man, taking the appearance of a slave, and is insulted, crucified, tortured, and killed. If God's justice is like this, how can we escape it?

It is possible to liken God's treatment of us to looking at a mirror. When you look into the mirror, at times you see a smiling, happy face. When you look into it at other times, you see a sad, angry face, although it is the same mirror. God shows you your condition, just like a mirror does. When you look at the face of God, you see your inner condition. If you have repented, you will see God in His goodness. But if you are reckless, you will see God in His severity.

God's goodness and severity are both represented in the angel who appeared to the two Marys at the tomb of Jesus. This angel caused both fear and joy. He frightened the guards, who "shook for fear of him, and became like dead men" (Matthew 28.4). This same angel was the cause of joy to the two women and the announcer of good news. In this way, God is fearful to some and joyful to others.

God's goodness and severity appear, generally, in the work of the angels. We all know about the angels of mercy. We must not forget that there are also angels of punishment and annihilation. We know how an angel awakened Elijah the Prophet when he was hungry and gave him food to eat. Elijah walked "with the strength of that food forty days and forty nights" (3 Kingdoms 19.8). When Hagar's son was on the verge of dying from thirst, God sent her an angel. He opened her eyes to see a well of water. Her son drank and lived (Genesis 21.15–19). An angel went down to the den and shut the lions' mouths, so that they could not hurt Daniel (Daniel 6.22). An angel went to the prison and released Peter after breaking the chains from his hands (Acts 12.7–10).

Angels surround believers and rescue them from evil. There are angels who bring good news, and angels who are "ministering spirits sent forth to minister for those who will inherit salvation" (Hebrews 1.14). Nevertheless, the angels' merciful nature does not preclude them from striking, carrying out punishment and destruction.

One example is the angel of destruction who struck every firstborn of the Egyptians. They all died in one night, "from the firstborn of Pharaoh who sat on his throne to the firstborn of the captive woman in the dungeon. . . . And there was a great cry in all the land of Egypt, for there was not a house where there was not one dead" (Exodus 12.29–30). Likewise, the angel raised his sword toward Jerusalem and counted the people when David the Prophet sinned. On that day, 70,000 men died (1 Chronicles 21.14). Other examples are the seven angels carrying trumpets, whose fearful blows are mentioned in the book of Revelation (8.9).

It is noteworthy that the first mention of angels in the Holy Bible is frightening. When God evicted man from the garden of Eden, He sent the cherubim with flaming swords to guard the way to the tree of life, so that man would not eat of it (Genesis 3.24). Goodness and severity manifested themselves simultaneously in the two angels who were sent to Lot. They rescued him and at the same time struck the people with blindness (Genesis 19.10–11). They were manifested concurrently in the story of Elisha the Prophet with Naaman the Syrian. When Naaman was healed from his leprosy, Elisha made the leprosy of Naaman cling to Gehazi, "and thus he went out from his presence leprous, like snow" (4 Kingdoms 5.27). This is how God is in His goodness and severity, and how His angels and prophets are. We should then beware of God's severity because of our sins.

God's fearful punishments. God's unlimited mercy did not prevent the passing of fearful punishments on humanity by divine justice, because of man's sin. By sin, man defied God's holiness, resisted His righteousness, and broke His commandments. Man deserved to be punished. Some examples are the great flood in which God destroyed man from the face of the earth (Genesis 6.7) and the burning of Sodom and Gomorrah.

The Lord rained fire and brimstone on Sodom and Gomorrah. "So He overthrew those cities, all the plains, all the inhabitants of the cities and what grew on the ground. But his wife looked back behind him, and she became a pillar of salt" (Genesis 19.25–26). When we contemplate both incidents—the flood and the burning of Sodom and Gomorrah—we ask ourselves, "Are our sins less than Sodom's? Are they less sinful than the sins of the people at the time of the flood? Are they less sinful than the sins of Lot's wife, who became a pillar of salt?"

Has God, who levied these punishments of old, changed in the New Testament? Is He not "the same yesterday, today and forever" (Hebrews 18.8), "with whom there is no variation or shadow of turning"? (James 1.17). Indeed, He is the One who made Ananias and Sapphira of the New Testament fall dead, because they lied in their conversation with Peter the Apostle. How many people lie in their conversation with priests, bishops, or even the patriarchs?

He is the One who permitted Paul, His servant, to say about the sinner of Corinth: "I have already judged . . . Deliver such a one to Satan for the destruction of the flesh, that his spirit may be saved in the day of the Lord Jesus" (1 Corinthians 5.3, 5). Some of the most terrifying things mentioned in the Holy Bible about God's punishment to sinners include the curses which God pours on whoever defies His commandments. A list of these curses is mentioned in the book of Deuteronomy, in which the Lord says:

> If you do not obey the voice of the Lord your God to keep and do all
> His commandments . . . all these curses will come upon you and overtake

you: Cursed shall you be in the city, and cursed shall you be in the country. Cursed shall be your storehouses and your reserves. Cursed shall be
the fruit of your womb and the produce of your land, and the herds of
your oxen and the flocks of your sheep. Cursed shall you be when you
go out, and cursed shall you be when you come in. The Lord will send
on you poverty, hunger, and consumption in all you set your hand to do,
until He destroys you and lays you waste quickly, because of your evil
habits in which you forsook Me. . . . The heaven over your head shall be
brass, and the earth under you shall be iron. . . . May the Lord give you
over to slaughter before your enemies; you shall go out one way against
them, and flee seven ways before them; and you shall be in dispersion
among all the kingdoms of the earth. . . . You shall not prosper in your
ways; you shall be only oppressed and plundered all your days, and no
one shall help you. . . . Also every sickness and every plague not written
in this book of this law will the Lord bring upon you, until He destroys
you. . . . Your life shall hang in doubt before your eyes; and you shall fear
day and night, and you will not believe in your life. In the morning you
shall say, 'Oh, that it were evening!' And at evening you shall say, 'Oh,
that it were morning!' because of the fear which terrifies your heart, and
because of the sight your eyes see. (Deuteronomy 28.15–68)

Truly fearful and terrifying are these curses! Because of the terrifying hardships which they contain, I refrain from recording all of them. They give
us an idea of God's holiness, which tolerates no sin whatsoever. We also
learn from them about God's justice, which punishes sin according to its
repugnance. I hope that we can read all of this and learn and repent, leaving
behind the sin that caused these curses.

Truly, the curse entered the world as a result of sin. When Adam sinned,
God said to him: "Cursed is the ground for your sake" (Genesis 3.17). As
matters proceeded, the curse advanced to man himself, and the Lord said to
Cain: "So now you are cursed from the earth, which has opened its mouth
to receive your brother's blood from your hand" (Genesis 4.11). "You are
cursed" is exactly what God said to the serpent beforehand: "You are cursed"
(Genesis 3.14). In this way the sinful person resembles the devil, "the old
serpent," and it is right to call sinners "the children of the devil" (1 John

3.10), or to say that they are a "brood of vipers" (Matthew 3.7). The curse of the flood was the curse of destruction (Genesis 8.21). So was the curse of the bondage which first fell on Canaan, when He said to him: "Cursed be Canaan; a servant of servants shall he be to his brothers" (Genesis 9.25).

The curses of the law (Deuteronomy 28) included many punishments: death, disease, plague, poverty, failure, injustice, unrest, and defeat. In the New Testament, the Lord Jesus cursed the leafy fig tree that did not produce fruits (Mark 11.21), which refers to hypocrisy without piety. It was a symbol to everyone who walked in this path. Who can read all of this without fear? Who can bear God's curse? Who can bear to lose the blessing which he originally received from the Lord?

We should repent, my brothers, because all of these matters are an example for us. They were written for us, on whom the end of the ages has come (1 Corinthians 10.11), to warn us. We need to wash our sins with the tears of repentance before the fearful day of judgment catches up with us, when weeping and repentance will no longer be of any use.

The terrifying torture of eternity. Just thinking about the day of death and the day of judgment sends a shiver to the sinful heart, leading it to humility and repentance. It is a terrifying, fearful day. Isaiah the Prophet describes it, saying: "Behold, the day of the Lord is coming . . . a day of anger and wrath, to make all the inhabited world a desert, and to destroy the sinners from it" (Isaiah 13.9). "In that day, a man will cast away his idols . . . so as to enter into the . . . clefts of the the rugged rocks, from fear of the Lord and the glory of His might when He arises to strike the earth" (Isaiah 2.20–21).

About this day, Malachi the Prophet says: "'For behold, the day is coming, burning like an oven . . . and all the proud, yes, all who do wickedly will be stubble; and the day that is coming shall burn them up,' says the Lord Almighty, 'that it will leave them neither root nor branch'" (Malachi 3.19).

Truly, the day of the Lord's coming is terrifying. The psalmist says about it: "Clouds and darkness surround Him; righteousness and judgment are the right ordering of His throne. Fire shall go out before Him and burn up His enemies on every side. His lightning gave light to the world; the earth saw and was shaken. The mountains melted like wax at the presence of the Lord, at the presence of the Lord of all the earth" (Psalm 96:2–5). Saint John the Apostle explains:

I looked when He opened the sixth seal, and behold, there was a great earthquake; and the sun became black as sackcloth of hair, and the moon became like blood. And the stars of heaven fell to the earth, as a fig tree drops its late figs when it is shaken by a mighty wind. Then the sky receded as a scroll when it is rolled up, and every mountain and island was moved out of its place. And the kings of the earth, the great men, the rich men, the commanders, the mighty men, every slave and every free man, hid themselves in the caves and in the rocks of the mountains, and said to the mountains and rocks, "Fall on us and hide us from the face of Him who sits on the throne and from the wrath of the Lamb! For the great day of His wrath has come, and who is able to stand?" (Revelation 6.12–17)

This is the condition of the sinners and the wicked on this day. As for the righteous, they will ascend to the Lord upon the clouds, and they will be with the Lord at all times in His glory. The righteous are in "joy inexpressible and full of glory" (1 Peter 1.8), the hymns of the saints are raised with the harps of God (Revelation 15.2–3), and these people enjoy the friendship of God and His saints in the heavenly Jerusalem. While these people are in paradise, the wicked are in unbearable torment, never knowing the taste of tranquility.

The Lord says about the wicked: "And these will go away into everlasting punishment, but the righteous into eternal life" (Matthew 25.46). He also says: "The Son of Man will send out His angels, and they will gather out of His kingdom all things that offend, and those who practice lawlessness, and will cast them into the furnace of fire. There will be wailing and gnashing of teeth. Then the righteous will shine forth as the sun in the kingdom of their Father" (Matthew 13.41–43).

How harsh this eternal torment is, with its wailing and gnashing of teeth in the outer darkness and the flaming fire! The pain is augmented when comparison is made between the condition of the wicked and the condition of the righteous. Saint Paul describes their condition, saying: "These shall be punished with everlasting destruction from the presence of the Lord and from the glory of His power, when He comes in that Day, to be glorified in His saints and to be admired among all those who believe" (2 Thessalonians 1.9–10). He also says: "Indignation and wrath, tribulation and anguish, on every soul of man who does evil, of the Jew first and also of the Greek; but glory, honor, and peace to everyone who works what is good" (Romans 2.8–10).

There is no doubt that we fear and tremble when we hear this apostle and saint saying: "For if we sin willfully after we have received the knowledge of the truth, there no longer remains a sacrifice for sins, but a certain fearful expectation of judgment, and fiery indignation which will devour the adversaries" (Hebrews 10.26–27). The apostle justifies this, saying:

> Anyone who has rejected Moses' law dies without mercy on the testimony of two or three witnesses. Of how much worse punishment, do you suppose, will he be thought worthy who has trampled the Son of God underfoot, counted the blood of the covenant by which he was sanctified a common thing, and insulted the Spirit of grace? For we know Him who said, "Vengeance is Mine; I will repay," says the Lord. And again, "The Lord will judge His people." It is a fearful thing to fall into the hands of the living God. (Hebrews 10.28–31)

Saint John the Beloved, famous for his detailed conversation about God's love, talks in his revelation about "the lake which burns with fire and brimstone" (Revelation 21.8). He describes the punishment of the sinner: "He himself shall also drink of the wine of the wrath of God, which is poured out full strength into the cup of His indignation. He shall be tormented with fire and brimstone in the presence of the holy angels and in the presence of the Lamb. And the smoke of their torment ascends forever and ever; and they have no rest day or night" (Revelation 14.10–11). "And they will be tormented day and night forever and ever" (Revelation 20.10).

He explains, as an example of this torment, the punishment of Babylon the fornicator, saying: "In the measure that she glorified herself and lived luxuriously, in the same measure give her torment and sorrow. . . . The kings of the earth who committed fornication and lived luxuriously with her will weep and lament for her, when they see the smoke of her burning, standing at a distance for fear of her torment, saying, 'Alas, alas'" (Revelation 18.7, 9–10). How fearful is this judgment! For this reason, the holy Church has set down to be read in the prayer of *al-settar* (the Prayer of the Veil[1]): "O Lord,

---

[1] *Editor's note:* The prayer quoted here is taken from the petition after the Gospel for the Prayer of the Veil, a prayer in the *Agpeya*.

how fearful Your judgment is, the people assemble, the angels stand. The scrolls are opened, the deeds are revealed, and the thoughts are examined. What type of judgment will my judgment be, I who am subdued in sin? Who will extinguish the flaming fire for me, unless You have mercy upon me, O lover of mankind?" God will not have mercy on the sinner unless he repents.

Truly, it will be absolutely shameful when every deed and thought is revealed before all people and the angels. Who will be able to bear this disclosure at that hour? It is also terrifying and shameful for the sinners to be separated from the righteous. Here on earth, all are assembled together, the most defiled fornicator with the most holy and righteous person. But there, this is not so. God begins separating the tares from the wheat, the goats from the sheep, the left from the right. He forever prohibits the sinners from the companionship of the saints and the angels, and from God. Imagine the righteous person when he passes away: the angels will carry him, just as they carried Lazarus (Luke 16.22). They will take him into the bosom of the saints, and introduce him to everyone.

This is Noah, this is Abel, this is Seth, and the rest of the fathers and patriarchs. These are Moses, Samuel, Jeremiah, Isaiah, Daniel, and the rest of the prophets. Here are Saint Antony, Saint Macarius, Saint Pachomius, and the rest of the fathers the monks. Come, let us show you Saint Paula, Saint Nofr, Saint Misael and the rest of the fathers who are spirit-borne. Look, here is Saint Athanasius, Saint Cyril, Saint Dioscorus, and the rest of the heroes of the faith. Here is Saint George, Saint Mina, Saint Demiana, and the rest of the martyrs. Here are the angels, the powers, dominions, principalities, cherubim, seraphim, and all the uncountable gatherings which are for the heavenly powers. It is an amazing festival of acquaintance, in which the righteous spirit becomes acquainted with the synod of angels and saints.

As for the sinners, they will be standing afar off, in the outer darkness, separated from the righteous by a great gulf. They are prohibited from the synod of the righteous, and from enjoying their company. There is no doubt that the words which explain the condition of the rich man in Hades are very moving. The Bible says: "And being in torments in Hades, he lifted up his eyes and saw Abraham afar off, and Lazarus in his bosom. Then he cried and said, 'Father Abraham, have mercy on me, and send Lazarus that he may dip the tip of his finger in water and cool my tongue; for I am tormented in this flame'" (Luke 16.23–24).

How amazing! Is this not the same poor Lazarus whose sores the dogs used to lick, and whom this rich man used to look at in disgust? Now, however, the situation has changed, and the great rich man desires Lazarus to come to him, but he is denied his desire. Sin is deprivation from the saints and, moreover, it is deprivation from God. Now, besides all the above-mentioned eternal punishment, there are other punishments for sin on earth.

Two punishments for sin: earthly and eternal. Besides all the aforementioned eternal punishments, there are other punishments for sin on earth. Man can escape eternal punishment by repentance. In contrast, man has to suffer the earthly punishment which God imposes on him even if he repents.

Our first parents are an example. When Adam and Eve sinned, their punishment was death. Jesus saved them from it by His death. But the matter does not stop there, for God placed on them another earthly punishment.

What was Adam and Eve's earthly punishment? Their eviction from the Garden was a joint punishment to both of them. What else? The Lord said to Adam: "Cursed is the ground for your sake; in toil you shall eat of it, all the days of your life . . . In the sweat of your face you shall eat bread" (Genesis 3.17–19). The punishment of toil and the sweat of the face remains clinging to every son of Adam to this day, despite the great work of redemption on the cross. The Lord said to Eve, "I will greatly multiply your sorrow and your conception; in pain you shall bring forth children" (Genesis 3:16). The Lord Jesus came and forgave the woman her sin. Despite this, she still conceives and gives birth in toil and pain. This earthly punishment, which fell on Adam and Eve, is a clear example of what man suffers on earth as a result of his sin, even if God forgives him for it in heaven.

The example of the adulteress. It is known that the Lord Jesus forgave many harlots. For example, He forgave the adulteress who washed His feet with her tears and wiped them with the hair of her head. Another example is the woman who was caught in this act. The Lord rescued her from being stoned, saying to the people complaining about her: "He who is without sin among you, let him throw a stone at her first" (John 8.7).

With this forgiveness, the Lord punished the adulteress by divorcing her and depriving her of a second marriage (Matthew 5.32, Matthew 19.9, Luke 16.18). Many people wonder why an adulteress should not be permitted to remarry, since the Lord has forgiven her. The answer is simple. It is possible for the Lord to forgive the adulteress if she repents, and in this way she does not lose her eternity. But she has to suffer earthly punishment as well. Because of her disloyalty to her husband, the Lord cannot trust her with another marriage. She becomes a lesson for others.

There are different types of earthly punishments. These can be a natural result of sin, a plague from God, or a punishment from society, civil law, or the Church.

Earthly punishment as a natural result of sin. There are many sins that carry their punishment in themselves. The adulterer, for example, can be afflicted with weakness, anemia, or venereal diseases. Whoever takes drugs is afflicted by losing his personality and his temper. Whoever smokes is afflicted with cancer, lung disease, high blood pressure, or other diseases. The student who neglects his studies has a punishment on earth, which is failure. Whoever gambles is afflicted with poverty and need. The mother who does not raise her son properly will suffer doubly on earth as a result of the bad behavior of this son.

All of these punishments on earth are different from the eternal punishment. The eternal punishment is eliminated by repentance, but the earthly punishment remains intact. So the mother who does not bring up her son properly repents and her sins are forgiven, but her son remains as a bitterness of heart to her on earth. The student who does not study and fails can repent and the Lord will forgive him for his negligence, but this does not bring back a year of his life lost on earth in vain. The person for whom sin causes disease can be forgiven his sin by repentance, but the disease remains with him as an earthly punishment as a natural result of sin.

Earthly punishment as a plague from God. One example is the plague of leprosy which afflicted Gehazi, Elisha's servant. This was his punishment for his love of money and his lying to his teacher (4 Kingdoms 5.27). The plague of leprosy, which afflicted Miriam the sister of Aaron and Moses, was her punishment for what she said against Moses (Numbers 12.10). The plague of boils that afflicted Egypt was a punishment for the hardness of

Pharaoh's heart (Exodus 9.10). The plague which afflicted the sons of Israel was a punishment for King David's sin. In one day, 70,000 died (2 Kingdoms 24.15).

Of this plague, the Lord says in His condemnation of the sinner:

> The Lord will make death cling to you, until He consumes you from the land to which you are going as an inheritance. The Lord will strike you with perplexity, fever, shivering, irritation, murder, blight, and mildew; these things shall pursue you until you perish. . . . The Lord will strike you with the boils of Egypt, with tumors, with the scab, and with the itch, from which you cannot be healed. (Deuteronomy 28.21–22, 27)

There are other plagues from God besides disease. Failure, for example, can be a natural result of man's carelessness and shortcomings, or a plague from God to remove the blessings (Deuteronomy 28). Other examples of these plagues are defeat, bondage, and even death. Sin is death and the punishment of sin is death. An example of this is what happened to Eli the priest when he did not instruct his children (1 Kingdoms 4.18).

Meditate on your life, my brother. Look to all that you have done or failed to do, in case there is a sin which is the cause of the plagues which afflict you.

Punishments for sin from society, civil law, and the Church. There are punishments for sin which afflict man on earth that are not imposed by God directly, but rather by society, the state, or the Church. The sinful person receives from society disgrace, shame, and dishonor. This can develop into contempt or rejection, isolating the person from society. There are earthly punishments which proceed from civil law, such as imprisonment, hard labor, execution, or exile, which are passed by judges on criminals. Punishment includes dismissal from work, monetary penalties, etc., and may be single or multiple.

There are also many punishments imposed by the Church; these are listed in the books of Church canons. Examples are the prohibition from Holy Communion for a certain period, the prohibition from entering the Church, suspension from priesthood or deposition, and other punishments that we will not mention in detail now. I say, however, that when the Church was severe and strict in its punishments, the congregation of believers was more holy, watchful, strict, and fearful of God.

Ask yourself, my brother: Have you committed a sin that placed you under a church judgment which has not yet been imposed on you? Maybe you have fled from such a judgment and are not worthy to enter the church, according to the canons. The earthly punishment is an order which God permitted to be placed even on His beloved saints, who struggled for His sake and performed miracles in His name.

Punishments for God's beloved saints include:

The example of David the Prophet. David the Prophet committed adultery and murder. He then confessed his sins to Nathan, saying: "I have sinned against the Lord." And he heard the divine pardon through Nathan's words to him: "The Lord has put away your sin. You shall not die" (2 Kingdoms 12.13). In this way the Lord removed from David the eternal punishment. The earthly punishment however, remained. How did this occur?

David repented with an amazingly deep repentance; his tears became his bread night and day, until he said: "All night I make my bed swim; I drench my couch with my tears" (Psalm 6.7). He prostrated himself in the dust and humbled himself before God. Nevertheless, the judgment of the Lord kept pursuing him.

> Now therefore, the sword shall never depart from your house forever, because you have despised Me, and have taken the wife of Uriah the Hittite to be your wife. Thus says the Lord: 'Behold, I will raise up adversity against you from your own house; and I will take your wives before your eyes and give them to your neighbor, and he shall lie with your wives in the sight of this sun" (2 Kingdoms 12.10–11).

All this came true. Fornication did not leave his house, being exemplified by the sins of his sons Amnon and Absalom. The sword did not leave his house, because Absalom stood against him. David left Jerusalem barefoot, crying, disturbed, and fearful of his son. He spent periods of humiliation and toil on earth as a result of his sin. Even when David wanted to build a house for the Lord, and had prepared everything—stones and steel, "and bronze in abundance beyond measure, and cedar trees in abundance"(1 Chronicles 22.3)—the Lord did not forget the blood that David shed. The word of the

Lord came to him, saying: "You have shed much blood. . . . You shall not build a house for My name, for in My sight you have shed much blood on the earth" (1 Chronicles 22.8).

Therefore the Lord prohibited him from building the temple, and this earthly punishment remained in spite of the forgiveness in heaven. The matter was repeated later when David sinned and counted the people, and the Lord was angered against him. David regretted it; his heart stirred him, and he realized his sin and repented of it, confessing it while crying out to the Lord: "I have sinned greatly in what I have done. But now, I pray, O Lord, take away the iniquity of Your servant, for I have done very foolishly" (2 Kingdoms 24.10).

Did the Lord accept this repentance from him, this confession and prayer? Yes, He accepted his repentance, forgave him his sin, and deleted the eternal punishment. However, the earthly punishment remained. Therefore, the Lord proceeded to punish His servant by offering him three harsh plagues which carry annihilation and destruction: famine, epidemic, and the sword of the enemy. David said submissively: "I am in great distress. Please let us fall into the hand of the Lord, for His mercies are great. Do not let me fall into the hand of man" (2 Kingdoms 24.14). The Lord, however, in spite of this humility, did not pardon him. He sent an angel of destruction to raise his sword on Jerusalem and kill 70,000 men, until David cried out to the Lord with unbearable pain: "I am the shepherd and I have sinned; but these sheep—what have they done? Let Your hand, I pray, be against me and against my father's house" (2 Kingdoms 24.17).

What is this, O Lord, that you have done with your servant David? Is he not the one of whom you said: "I have found David the son of Jesse, a man after My own heart" (Acts 13.22)? Why do you not have pity and forgive? He says, "Yes, I will forgive in heaven, but on earth he will receive his punishment." How frightening! Even with David, O Lord? Did not David love You and say to You: "O how I love your name, O Lord! It is my meditation all day" (Psalm 118)? Did he not awaken at midnight to thank You for Your righteous judgments, saying: "My eyes are awake through the night watches, that I may meditate on Your word" (Psalm 118)? And, "O God, my God, early will I seek you; My soul thirsts for You. . . . My soul follows close behind You" (Psalm 62:1, 9)?

David is a man of praise and prayer, a man of the flute, the lyre, and the ten strings. Why do You do this to David? If this is the case with David, the beloved prophet, then what can we say about ourselves? We do not share in the favor that he enjoys, nor his holiness, nor his repentance. We need, then, to be alert and awake to ourselves, because our Lord is just and will judge everyone according to his deeds, no matter what his spiritual position is with God Himself. This was not confined to David; it also applied to Moses.

The example of Moses the Prophet. Here is even a harsher example, in its significance, than David's. Who can describe the love between God and His servant Moses? Moses is the beloved of God and His spokesman. He is the man of wonders and miracles who split the Red Sea, who struck the rock and brought forth water. Through his prayers, the Lord changed the bitter waters to sweet waters, and the manna and quail descended. His raised hands were mightier than the army of Joshua. It was Moses whom the Lord Himself defended when Miriam and Aaron spoke against him, striking Miriam with leprosy and saying to Miriam and Aaron:

> Should a prophet of yours belong to the Lord, I would make Myself known to him in a vision; I would speak to him in a dream. Not so with My servant Moses; he is faithful in all My house. I speak with him face to face, even in visible form, and not in dark sayings; and he saw the Lord's glory. Why then were you not afraid to speak against My servant Moses? (Numbers 12.6–8)

Moses sinned when he struck the rock twice and said to the stubborn, rebellious people, "Hear now, you rebels! Must we bring water for you out of this rock?" The result was that God ordered him not to enter the promised land (Numbers 20.7–12).

What is this, Lord, that you do? Do you forget this long acquaintance for the sake of one sin, which happened during difficult circumstances? God insists, however, that Moses not enter the land. What is this that you say O Lord? As the saying goes, "the cook of the poison tastes it." You know how I labored for the sake of these people for tens of years, enduring their stubbornness with patience, and I led them in the wilderness while they were rebellious and unyielding. I am Moses Your servant, Your beloved friend, with whom you spoke face to face.

All of this was disregarded, for the Lord insisted on punishing him. Moses entreated the Lord, "I have sinned, O Lord; pardon, O Lord, forgive, O Lord forget this sin. I pray, let me cross over and see the good land." God is consistent in His principle: "I forgive in My kingdom." As for here on earth, punishment will be enforced even on Moses. When the begging of Moses the Prophet increased, God was angered and said to him: "Enough of that. Speak no more to Me of this matter" (Deuteronomy 3.26). Finally, after many requests and much beseeching and imploring, He permitted him to see the land from afar, from the mountain, but not to enter into it. God in His justice did not show partiality to His beloved Moses, in spite of his favor with God.

And you, my brother, what is your favor? Is your position with God higher than that of Moses? If this is the case, will you not sympathize with yourself and repent, in case you are subjected to God's justice as a result of your sin, for no previously holy life will plead for you? If Moses and David did not escape punishment, will you?

The example of Jacob, the father of fathers. God loved Jacob when he was in the womb, before he was born and before he did any good. The Lord said: "Jacob I have loved, but Esau I have hated" (Romans 9.13). He gave him leadership over his older brother while he was still in the womb, and said to Rebecca: "Two nations are in your womb, and two peoples shall be separated from your body. . . . And the older shall serve the younger" (Genesis 25.23). Jacob sinned and listened to the advice of his mother, who loved him more than Esau. He deceived his father and took the blessing.

God did not let him remain without punishment, in spite of appearing to him face to face (Genesis 32.30) and in spite of the promises, the blessing, and the revelation God bestowed upon him. God had appeared to him on the ladder which connected heaven and earth and said to him: "Your seed shall be as the dust of the earth . . . and in you and in your seed all the tribes of the earth shall be blessed. Behold, I am with you and will keep you wherever you go" (Genesis 28.14–15).

Despite all this, because Jacob deceived his father, the Lord permitted his children to deceive him also. They sold Joseph, dipped his tunic in the blood of a goat which they had killed, and informed their father that a wild beast had devoured Joseph. Jacob tore his clothes and mourned for his son many days (Genesis 37.31–34). His uncle Laban also deceived him, making him marry Leah instead of Rachel, whom he loved in his heart and labored many years for her sake. His uncle also deceived him in his wages and changed them many times.

Hardships continued to pursue Jacob. In his speech with Pharaoh, Jacob summarized his life concisely when he said: "The days of the years of my pilgrimage are ... few and evil" (Genesis 47.9). Truly his sin was forgiven, and God revealed His acceptance by the blessing, the revelation, and the promises. However, in spite of His love for him, He did not remove the earthly punishment.

Are you convinced, my blessed brother, of the danger of the punishment for sin? I would need more time if I were to give you other examples from the Holy Bible, but I will leave this matter for your personal meditations. I will now give you an example or two from the history of the fathers.

The example of Saint Moses the Black. Early in his life, he was a merciless murderer. He then repented, went to the monastery, and became a monk. He progressed in the life of grace until he became an example of meekness, kindness, and the love of his brethren. He would sometimes pass by the monks' cells and carry their jars secretly to the well, to fill them with water for them. God then gave him the gifts of visions and performing miracles. He advanced in holiness and became a spiritual advisor for many. He was ordained as a priest and became one of the pillars of the desert.

In light of his repentance, holiness, and spiritual gifts, did God forget his previous sins which deserved punishment? We hear that when the barbarians attacked the monastery, the monks fled, calling Saint Moses to flee with them. He said to them, "I know, my children, that the barbarians will kill me, because I killed many people in my youth." The Bible says: "All who take the sword will perish by the sword" (Matthew 26.52). This actually happened. The barbarians attacked Saint Moses and killed him, and so the prophecy was fulfilled. People wonder why such a great saint needed to die such a horrific death, even after he had repented of the sins he committed in ignorance when he was young. However, this is God's way.

The example of Saint Poemen. I read a story in one of the monastery's precious manuscripts about a saint called Poemen. He was very ascetic; he lived a life of poverty and want, and his cell lacked any coverings to protect him from the cold at night. This saint was visited by a youth who spent the night in a nearby cell. When he woke up in the morning, Saint Poemen asked him how he spent the night. The youth answered, "I was weary from the intensity of the cold because of the lack of coverings." The saint then said in embarrassment, "As for me, I slept in warmth." The youth then asked him how, and he answered, "A lion came at night and slept next to me, and warmed me with his body."

The youth was astonished at what had happened to the saint; how could a lion lie next to him and not devour him? The saint then said, "I know, my son, that the beasts must devour me one day. This is because a youth came to me one night, and I did not open to him. He was afraid, and according to what I was told the beasts devoured him." What Saint Poemen predicted actually happened.

These are examples of such earthly punishments. Many examples may be found by whoever reads the Bible and studies the stories from history which were written for our instruction.

Because of all this, it is not right for us to understand God's extensive mercy as separate from His justice, lest we hide behind God's mercy, compassion, and affection and thereby insult Him, neglect Him, and commit sin without realizing its danger. While we do believe in God's love for us, we must never forget to fear Him.

Some people are shameless about sin and think the matter very easy, for it only takes a few minutes with their spiritual father to confess and receive absolution. Then it is as if nothing has happened; God's commandments were never broken, and God's heart was never hurt. Truly, my brother, when the priest reads you the prayer of absolution, he adds your sin to the bitter cup which the Lord drank. You will be rescued from eternal punishment by the blood of Christ, if you have repented.

The earthly punishment, however, is another account you may have to pay. Be careful then, for the matter is not as easy as you think. However, for your comfort, and so that you do not fall into despair and fear, I say to you that God does not punish every sin with an earthly punishment. This is because the sins of man are innumerable: "For we all stumble in many things" (James 3.2). If God punished every sin with an earthly consequence, then punishments would continue without end until they matched the number of sins.

However, God vacates many punishments. In the midst of our hundreds of sins, He punishes us for one of them so that we will not become negligent, nor fall into carelessness. We will then become humble and benefit spiritually, just as in the case of David the Prophet. God in His mercy allows earthly punishments to call us to awaken and arise from our deep sleep. He also uses them to lead us to contrition.

We then feel that we have sinned and angered God, and consequently we repent and return to Him. Therefore, we are rescued from the eternal punishment. This is not because the earthly punishment has taken its place, God forbid, but because it has awakened us to repent, so that we may become worthy of forgiveness through the blood of Christ.

Our suffering here on earth is better than suffering in eternity, and better than its shame. The eternal judgments are fearful, but it is up to us to avoid them. At this present moment, it is in our hands to decide our destiny. Saint Paul the Apostle could say with courage: "Finally, there is laid up for me the crown of righteousness, which the Lord, the righteous Judge, will give to me on that Day" (2 Timothy 4.8). Will you be able to say the same words as Saint Paul? I wish that you could. Watch out, even when the crown of righteousness is given to you, and "hold fast what you have, that no one may take your crown" (Revelation 3.11). Live the life of repentance and awareness all your days.

Fear of the punishment due to sin motivates us to repent. Doubtless there are other motives, as will be explained in the next chapter.

CHAPTER 5

Other Motives for Repentance

So far, we have dealt with the motives for repentance which emanate from within a person, from the sentiments of his heart. Other motives for repentance are external; they come to a man without his even asking. Among these motives are the following:

The visitations of grace. God "desires all men to be saved and to come to the knowledge of the truth" (1 Timothy 2.4). Therefore, He strives for the salvation of all. His grace works in sinners so that they repent, "both to will and to do" (Philippians 2.13). The visitations of grace must come to every person.

The example of Saul of Tarsus. He witnessed about himself that he was formerly a blasphemer, an insolent man, and a persecutor of the Church (1 Timothy 1.13). Goads used to prick his conscience, urging him to leave off this harshness and severity. However, he would kick these goads and refuse to respond. Finally, the Lord appeared to him on the road to Damascus and rebuked him, saying: "Saul, Saul, why are you persecuting Me? . . . It is hard for you to kick against the goads" (Acts 26.4, 9.5). It is clear that Saul's inspiration to repent and to abandon his persecution of the Church did not start from within himself, but came from the outside, from the visitation of grace, through his encounter with the Lord. Jesus reconciled with him, restored him, and called him to His service.

The same situation occurred with Jonah the Prophet. He was escaping from the Lord, for He disagreed about the calling of Nineveh, lest God's mercy should spare it and Jonah's word not come to pass.[1] Indeed, when God accepted the repentance of Nineveh and this city was saved, Jonah sat on the east side of the city and "became angered even unto death," saying: "It is better for me to die than to live" (Jonah 4.1, 3). While he was in this state, the Lord's grace visited him to save him from his sinful grief. The Lord talked to him personally in order to be reconciled with him, to explain to

---

[1]See my book, *Meditation on the Book of Jonah the Prophet.*

him, change his heart, and lead him to repentance. In this way, grace through the voice of God was received by the prophet as it was by Saul.

Yet, grace does not require that God talk to man. God may send a person to rebuke the sinner, so that he may repent. For example, God sent Nathan to rebuke David to repentance. David did not feel that he was in sin, but rather progressed from one sin to another, from lust to fornication to murder. Grace visited him through Nathan telling him the danger of what he had done. Only then did he awaken to himself and say: "I have sinned against the Lord" (2 Kingdoms 12.13). He then began an act of deep repentance, wherein he drenched his couch with his tears (Psalm 6.7). Thus David's repentance did not start from his inner motives, for he was in a continual slumber of sin. Rather, his repentance started through an outside motive—a reprimand received externally. This initiated feelings of repentance within him, and the inner work began.

And you, O dear reader, are you aware that perhaps the person who rebukes you about your sin was sent to you by God's grace, to lead to you to repentance? If you refuse him and his reprimand, as harsh as it may be, then you are refusing God's grace, which works within you. As a result, you do not benefit from the visitation of grace. The visitation of grace is not restricted to superior methods, such as hearing the voice of God, the voice of a prophet, or dreams and revelations. The matter can be much simpler than this.

Grace may visit you through sickness; this would be God's voice to you. Saint Oghris had a disease that led him not only to repentance, but to monasticism also. The disease of Saint Timothy the Anchorite, and many other diseases mentioned in the Bible and in history, are all examples of visitations of God's grace. This type of disease may not afflict you, but may afflict one of your close loved ones instead. It drives you to your knees and makes you raise your hands upward. You cry from within yourself to the Lord. Such a disease crushes your heart and makes you look up to the Lord to be reconciled with Him for the sake of the person you love.

The visitation of grace can take the form of a tribulation or problem. This, too, may be God's voice to you, as He calls you to repent. The Lord may then have compassion upon you and remove you from this tribulation.[2] The Lord

---

[2]See my book, *The Spiritual Awakening*. It actually contains a section from *The Life of Repentance and Purity* and a chapter on the incentives for spiritual awakening, which is 28

may allow your enemies to overpower you; you return to God and ask Him to rescue you. There are many such examples in the book of Judges.

It is important, then, that your spiritual senses be trained to recognize God's voice calling you to return to Him. Therefore you must correlate whatever you go through—whether disease, troubles, or problems—with your relationship with God. Make all of them an occasion to strengthen your fellowship with Him, to deepen your prayers and increase your love for God.

The visitation of grace may come to you while you are reading a spiritual book, or listening to a spiritual sermon or touching hymn. A feeling within yourself will urge you to do something in regard to your relationship with God. You will find your heart in an unnatural state, moving within you, or perhaps the work of the Spirit moving within it. The Holy Spirit may rebuke you for a sin, and you will feel eager to live with God and reconcile with Him.

It is a visitation of grace; care for it and do not miss it. Grace visited Felix the Governor when Saint Paul the Apostle was talking about righteousness, self-control, and the judgment to come, and Felix became frightened (Acts 24.25). Unfortunately, he did not utilize this visitation of grace to his advantage. He said to Paul, "Go away for now; when I have a convenient time I will call for you."

As for you, if grace visits you, do not put your heart aside nor delay your repentance. Seek to benefit from every spiritual feeling which grace initiates within you, especially when you feel a revolt within you against the life of sin, or when you feel spontaneous love toward God—feelings that previously may not have been present within you. Grace visited Agrippa the King while Saint Paul was talking, and Agrippa said to Paul: "You almost persuade me to become a Christian" (Acts 26.28). Agrippa, however, was content with the conviction without taking another step.

But as for you, if grace visits you, do not be content merely with being convinced. For what benefit do you receive from being convinced that your way is sinful, unless you overcome and change this way in practice? Do not let the visitation of grace work in your mind alone, or in your heart only; it must work in your will also, so that you will arise and act accordingly.

pages long in the Arabic text. It should be added to our topic here, which we must leave for now.

The visitations of grace reveal to us a beautiful and comforting truth: even if you do not proceed toward the salvation of your soul, God, who loves you, proceeds with His grace to save you. He is the one who begins. God only asks you to respond to His voice within you. He wants you to work with Him when He starts to work in you. He wishes that you not harden your heart when you hear His voice. Hence the visitation of grace will lead you to repentance, as it has led many.

The visitations of grace give every sinner a burst of hope. He is assured that God loves him, that He will care for him and search for him, just as the Good Shepherd searched for His lost sheep. If there are no feelings in the sinner's heart to lead him to repentance, then God will plant these feelings in his heart by the work of His grace. He will prepare every means to make his heart move toward repentance.

PART THREE

THE MEANS OF REPENTANCE (HOW TO REPENT)

For every person there is a way that leads him to repentance, as grace finds suitable to him or his circumstances. Along the path to repentance, there are general principles which are suitable for everyone. The most important of these principles are given in the steps below. We will try to explain each of these points one by one, in order to meditate on their uses in the life of repentance.

Chapter 1: Sit with yourself, examine yourself, and come to a conclusion regarding your need for repentance.

Chapter 2: Give yourself neither excuses nor justifications.

Chapter 3: Do not delay repentance, but start now and seize the opportunity.

Chapter 4: Do not harden your heart when grace works within you.

Chapter 5: Avoid any initial step that leads to sin, flee from the little foxes that destroy the vines, and proceed with exactitude.

Chapter 6: Avoid stumbling blocks, and flee from the sources of sin.

Chapter 7: Do not be tolerant with sin.

Chapter 8: Reassess your behavior and stay away from sins.

Chapter 9: Flee from your beloved sins and treat your points of weakness.

Chapter 10: Be concerned with your eternity, and calculate the cost.

Chapter 11: Be mindful of the love of God.

Chapter 12: Wrestle with God and obtain power
from Him to help you repent.

Sit with yourself, examine yourself, and come to a conclusion regarding your need for repentance.

SIT WITH YOURSELF. It is your own will to repent, and it is also God's will that you repent. That is because He "desires all men to be saved and to come to the knowledge of the truth" (1 Timothy 2.4). The question then arises, to repent of what, and how? Therefore you need to sit with yourself, because you fall into one of the following categories:

1. You may not feel the wrong in which you find yourself. You do not know your exact condition, nor do you do realize your faults in their depth and ugliness. A whirlpool of preoccupations and concerns captivates you constantly, and you are drowning in them entirely. You have no time to think of yourself nor of your spiritual life, or perhaps this matter never crossed your mind. Therefore, you need to sit with yourself in order to assess your situation and recognize your faults.

2. You know your faults, at least the ones which stand out, but you have neither time nor opportunity to think about how to refrain from these faults and how to treat them. Before you think of treating a particular fault, you find yourself committing it again, or you have fallen into a different or maybe a worse fault. So it seems you are surrounded from every direction by your faults and sins, and there is no chance to get rid of them.

Again, you need to sit with yourself if you are to treat sin. You resemble a sick person who either does not feel his sickness, or else realizes it but still needs a strict examination and diagnosis, followed by the proper treatment.

A repentant person needs to sit down with the proper analytic tools if he is to know exactly what is happening within himself, as well as the type, extent, and danger of his sickness. He also needs to know the treatment and how to use it properly in order to be cured. He should pursue this treatment with a wise practitioner who is an expert in these sicknesses and their treatment. The sick person will gain nothing unless he removes himself from his preoccupations, no matter how important they may be, and assesses himself far away from other people. Here, the importance of being with oneself spiritually is manifested.

What is the program for this spiritual session, and how does one participate in it? Repentance and purification of spirit are the aim of this session. You must discover your sins and weaknesses, and blame yourself for them. You should identify the reasons for your falling: either they are external and were forced upon you, or there are internal reasons which caused you to sin. The latter may be habits, or other people's influences. Try to avoid all of these, refraining from them and treating them.

In this session you will reveal to God your weaknesses and sins. You reveal your weaknesses to obtain power from Him. You reveal with regret all your sins, and He will grant you absolution and forgiveness. Reveal them by praying with a contrite heart, as David did previously: "Purge me with hyssop, and I shall be clean; wash me and I shall be whiter than snow" (Psalm 50). You will come out of this session ready to confess these sins before the priest, so that he may read over you the prayer of absolution, advise you as to what is required, and allow you to partake of Holy Communion.

In your spiritual session with yourself, you must determine in your heart to abandon sin, with full acceptance and inner peace. Do not limit your session to searching the past, regretting, blaming, and rebuking yourself for your fall. Instead, in this session it is better that you set up a wise plan for the future based on your actual condition and experiences. Determine honestly to proceed in this plan with exactitude, with seriousness and obligation. In your determination to live a pure life in the future, do not get lost in many details, but give priority to your clear weak points and to the "mother virtues," such as the virtue of pursuing God's love, which contain within them the rest of the virtues and which will help you to realize the whole spiritual life.

Show your holy determination to God, so that He may bless it and strengthen you. I advise that this not be a vow that you dedicate, as some people do, nor a cause to call disasters down upon yourself, as some people do, saying, "May God punish me and do more if I ever do this again in the future." Such vows and woes contain within themselves a reliance on your human ability, as if you had the personal power with which to implement what you promised God, regardless of the obstacles and opposition you meet. Many have promised God, but they did not implement their promises. Then they return in grief, saying, "Often have I promised God with a broken promise, I wish that I had not made that promise out of fear of my weaknesses." The whole matter is nothing more than a holy desire through which you reveal your will and determination to God, so that He may grant you the power to implement it, for without Him you can do nothing (John 15.5). Thus, you convert your session with yourself into a prayer, in which you ask for the power to continue on the life of repentance and purity of heart.

There is no doubt that the devil, who does not want you to escape from his control, will resist your sessions with yourself with all his might, in the following ways. First, he fears that when you assess yourself, you will realize your bad spiritual condition and think seriously about repentance, and in this way slip from his hands. Second, he fears that if you assess yourself, you will be assisted by God and gain spiritual power from Him, whom the devil cannot resist, and you will conquer him with this divine power.

The devil knows that many who assessed themselves have repented, as in the example of the prodigal son (Luke 15.11–24). While this young man was busy with his friends, he remained in his delusion. He had neither the time nor desire to be with himself. And yet the story of his repentance was worthy to be recorded in the Bible, from the mouth of the Lord Himself. When he sat with himself, examining his condition, his life, and the position he had reached, he realized the bitter truth.

He realized in his session with himself the deplorable condition into which he had deteriorated. He asked himself: "How many of my father's hired servants have bread enough and to spare, and I perish with hunger?" (Luke 15.17). However, is it enough to realize one's bad condition? No, a solution must be found. He said: "I will arise and go to my father, and will say to him 'Father, I have sinned against heaven and before you, and I am no longer worthy to be called your son. Make me like one of your hired servants'" (Luke 15.19).

He realized his deplorable condition, found the solution, reached a decision, and implemented it straightway. The Bible states: "And he arose and came to his father" (Luke 15.20). He began a new life in which he was reconciled with the father. If he had not sat with himself in this session of destiny, he never would have reached a decision—nor repentance, contrition, return, reconciliation—nor release from the devil's grasp as he put on the best robe.

Another example is Saint Augustine. He was unable to repent while still in the whirlpool of his preoccupations, friends, sins, and pleasures, as well as the whirlpool of philosophy and thought. But when he sat with himself, in a deep session, he was able to reach the faith and repentance necessary to return to God, escaping forever from the grasp of the devil and becoming a blessing for many.

This is not just a normal session, then, but a momentous session. Believe me, the most important work of the fathers, of every advisor and preacher, is the invitation to the sinful person to assess himself in the presence of God, in the light of His commandments, as did Saint Augustine and the prodigal son, of whom it is rightly said: "He returned to himself" (Luke 15.17).

The devil therefore endeavors to prevent man from being with himself in two ways. First, he prevents you from being with yourself by presenting you with your many preoccupations and hundreds of thoughts. He reminds you of matters that you consider very important, and to which you should be devoted. All these strategies lead you back into your whirlpool. For example, on occasions such as a birthday or the New Year, the devil can create parties in order to preoccupy you with them, so that you will neither retreat nor think about yourself and the goals of your life.

If you wish to be with yourself at the start of the Coptic calendar year, the devil will prevent you by involving you with spiritual activities, meetings, and talks. It is very easy on the feast of *El Nawruz* (Coptic New Year) to talk about the martyrs—their suffering, their tolerance, their bravery, and their glories—to the point that we forget ourselves. We talk about history and forget the reality in which we live. We talk about our great forefathers, but we do not think about how to emulate them. The stories of the martyrs are undoubtedly enjoyable, but they should lead us to think about ourselves, for the martyrs left for us an example to follow. It is an attempt, even on a spiritual manner, to prevent man from sitting with himself.

However, if you insist on sitting with yourself and pursuing the other recommended activities as well, then the devil will resort to his second trick. In this second way, the devil will try to enter into your session with yourself and void its benefits. He never loses hope. As long as he cannot prevent you from sitting with yourself, he will deny you its spirituality. He does this by offering you thoughts and feelings. He prevents you from rebuking yourself and eases your feelings of regret. So how does this happen?

CHAPTER 2

Give yourself neither excuses
nor justifications.

IF YOU REMEMBER ANY SIN, the devil will present you with excuses and justifications, instead of allowing your heart to be contrite and letting you rebuke yourself for the sin with tears of repentance. You, however, know very well that your aim in this spiritual session is to purify yourself, not to justify sin. Purifying the self is attained by identifying sins and rebuking yourself for them, not by pampering the self or easing its responsibility and casting the blame on other people.

Therefore, in your session with yourself, be as honest as possible. Do not be kind to yourself and do not pamper yourself, for this will not benefit you spiritually, nor will it lead you to repentance. Instead, reveal all your errors and weaknesses with all of their defilement and repugnance. Do not try to present excuses and justifications, but instead offer repentance, regret, and contrition of heart. You know that the tax collector went out justified, rather than the Pharisee, because he was humble before God and asked for mercy, since he was a sinner (Luke 18.13). The Bible states: "You are inexcusable, O man" (Romans 2.1). It also says: "They have no excuse for their sin" (John 15.22).

You will not receive forgiveness by justifications. By repentance, however, you will be qualified for forgiveness. The tax collector is distinguished from the Pharisee by his self-judgment. In the same way you can distinguish the thief on the right hand from his companion, for he says: "And we indeed justly, for we receive the due reward of our deeds" (Luke 23.41). Happy is the man who reveals his sins when he sits with himself. Happier still is he who presents his sins to the Lord with contrition and tears.

Condemn yourself, as this will lead you to repentance and will increase your humility and contrition of heart, which enables you to confess and will bring you closer to the Lord. The Bible says: "The Lord is near those who are brokenhearted" (Psalm 33.19). Saint Antony rightly said in this matter: "If we judge ourselves, the Lord will be pleased with us."[1] So, when you sit with yourself and remember your sins, do not excuse yourself nor put the blame on someone else while forgetting what you have done, as Adam and Eve did.

Blaming others does not make you righteous, even if they deserve the blame. Therefore, you must concentrate on what you have done, because you alone are responsible for it. Doubtless it is a trick from the devil: instead of calling yourself to account, he makes you concerned with others' responsibility for your sins, so that you forget your own responsibility.

Even trickier is how he lessens sin's seriousness. The devil does not allow the sin to appear in its true repugnance, showing it rather as a simple matter, not worthy of your grief and regret. He would give sins other names, philosophizing about sin and hiding it behind good intentions. In this way he stretches your conscience in order to hide the sins for which you refuse to bear responsibility, or at least refuse to bear responsibility for the results. All this will doubtlessly lead you to negligence and carelessness; it will not help you repent, but perhaps push you to continue on the same path, casting away from you humility and contrition of heart. As for you, then, be strict with yourself and rebuke sin. If at times you cannot withstand others who talk to you frankly about your faults, then at least you can rebuke yourself on your own. Be frank with yourself when people avoid confronting you to spare you embarrassment, out of good manners and decency or because they are unwilling to hurt your feelings. As Saint Macarius the Great said: "Judge yourself, my brother, before they judge you."

If there is in your nature any hardness or severity, then use it against yourself. Do not use it against others. You are the one who requires this severity, so that you may be deterred from sin and not return to it. Discipline it with a rod of steel, and raise it in the fear and obedience of God. If you need to examine yourself regularly, then you also need to punish yourself instead of having God punishing you.

In your judgment of yourself, remember the saying of the great Saint Antony: "If we remember our sins, God will forget them, and if we forget

[1]Antony 4 *Sayings of the Desert Fathers*.

our sins, then God will remind us of them." When David the King did not feel his sin and did not remember it, God sent him Nathan the Prophet, who explained the repugnance of his sin, saying to him: "You are the man" (2 Kingdoms 12.7). When David judged himself, saying, "I have sinned against the Lord," immediately afterwards he was told: "The Lord also has put away your sin. You shall not die" (2 Kingdoms 12.13). As for you, do not wait for God to send another Nathan to expose you, but rather sit with yourself in order to judge your sin, to repent and be qualified for forgiveness.

Some people are accustomed to sitting with themselves at the beginning of a new year, during fasts, or on other important occasions in their lives. Sit every day with yourself, and reckon with sin. Examine your life and be reassured continuously of its purity. Be vigilant toward its safe orientation, pursue the life of repentance you started previously, and beware that you do not lose the fervor which started you on the path of God.

Avoid justifications and excuses. If you wish to live in the life of repentance, then try to find neither excuses nor justifications for every sin into which you fall. Excuses will never accord with the life of repentance and humility. Justifications mean that the person who sins does not want to take responsibility for his fault. He sins and presents the matter as if it were something completely natural, giving reasons for its cause as if there were no fault in the matter. How can the type of person who finds justifications for his sin repent of it?

Justifications are an attempt to cover up sin, not to repent of it. By finding justification for sin, does it not become easier for the sinner to continue in it, since he has an excuse? One person covers sin with an excuse, whilst another covers it with a lie. With his justification, he wants to come out of a sin unhurt, faultless, blameless, and covered in a robe of false glory.

However, sin is sin, regardless of the reasons surrounding it, or the circumstances accompanying it. In the "Holy, Holy, Holy,"[2] we ask for absolution and forgiveness even for hidden sins, for those we committed without knowledge or involuntarily, and we do not regard any of those as justifications. Whoever said that the path of hell is furnished with excuses and justifications was correct.

---

[2] *Editor's note*: The prayer "Holy, Holy, Holy," is in the *Agpeya*.

The history of justification is old. The sin of justifying is as ancient as humanity, since the time of our parents Adam and Eve. Adam tried to justify his sin by saying the woman gave him the fruit to eat. Eve in turn said that the serpent deceived her. However, God did not accept any excuses from Adam or Eve. He did not even find their excuses worthy of a reply or deserving of discussion. On the contrary, He punished Adam for the excuse which he presented by saying: "Because you heeded the voice of your wife, and ate from the one tree. . . ." (Genesis 3.17). Unfortunately, we inherited the sin of justifying from Adam and Eve, down through the generations.

Even a great saint such as Abraham, the father of fathers, fell into this exact sin when he said that Sarah was his sister (Genesis 20.2–11). For this reason Abimelech, the king of Gerar, took her to his house. He would have come closer to her if the Lord had not prevented him in a dream, warning him of death as a result of this action. Abimelech reprimanded our father Abraham, saying to him: "How have I offended you, that you have brought on me and on my kingdom a great sin? You have done deeds to me that ought not be done" (Genesis 20.9). Our father Abraham answered with an attempt to justify his actions: "Because I thought, surely the worship of God is not in this place; and they will kill me on account of my wife" (Genesis 20.11).

It is very easy to respond to this justification, wherein Abraham placed responsibility on someone else. We can say, "Our father, why did you come to this place which does not have the fear of God? Did you enter this place with God's guidance, who said to you from the beginning of your calling 'Get out . . . to a land that I will show you' (Genesis 12.1)? Is it possible for you, father, to sacrifice your wife for the sake of your safety, to subject her to this danger of being wife to a strange man, and to subject this stranger to God's wrath? Why did you resort to these human methods for your protection without resorting to God's assistance?"

It appears that once our father Abraham found the justification, he continued and made it a firm policy. Therefore, he said to his wife with complete sincerity: "This righteousness shall you do for me in every place: in every place we enter, say of me, 'He is my brother'" (Genesis 20.13). In this way it was possible, in every place in which he dwelt, for the same problem to be repeated, because Abraham had found a justification for this (Genesis 20.12), and so he never said of Sarah, "She is my wife." It is unlikely that a person will say, "I have sinned," so long as the method of justification is available.

Though the sin is very clear, irrefutable even, one often presents justification and excuses. An example of this is the man who was given one talent. He took it and buried it in a hole in the ground, without trading with it or profiting from it as his friends did. When his master reckoned with him, he was not embarrassed to present justifications and excuses—and as the saying goes, "an excuse is fouler than an offence." So he said: "Lord, I knew you to be a hard man, reaping where you have not sown, and gathering where you have not scattered seed. And I was afraid, and went and hid your talent in the ground" (Matthew 25. 24–25). Of course, his master did not accept his excuse and ordered that he be thrown into the outer darkness.

Jonah the Prophet's disobedience of the Lord was clear, but also had a justification. Jonah fled from the Lord and refused to go to Nineveh, according to the Lord's command, and instead went to Tarshish in a ship. Later, when the people of Nineveh repented, "it displeased Jonah exceedingly and he became angry." In spite of this, he presented a justification for his attitude to prove that he was right, and said:

> O Lord, was not this what I said when I was still in my country? There-
> fore I fled previously to Tarshish; for I know that you are a gracious and
> merciful God, slow to anger and abundant in loving kindness, one who
> relents from doing harm. Therefore now, O Lord, please take my life
> from me, for it is better for me to die than to live (Jonah 4.1–3).

This is the excuse which the prophet presented to justify his disobedience to the Lord, and his grief at the salvation of 120,000 souls. Who can accept these words?

Another obvious sin was that of King Saul, who, although he was not a priest, offered a burnt offering to the Lord. Despite the obviousness of this sin, he justified it. For when Samuel the Prophet reprimanded him, he did not say, "I have sinned," nor did he regret and repent of it, but he instead presented excuses and justifications. He said to the prophet: "When I saw the people scatter from me, and you did not come within the appointed days, and the Philistines gathered at Michmash. . . . Therefore I forced myself, and I offered a burnt offering" (1 Kingdoms 13.11–12). Of course, the prophet did not accept these excuses. He made him listen to God's punishment: his kingdom would not continue, and the Lord would choose another commander for the people instead of him.

Elijah, the mighty prophet, also found an excuse when he was afraid of Jezebel! He received her threats (3 Kingdoms 19.2), became afraid, and fled. When God asked him about his flight, inquiring, "Elijah, what are you doing here?" he found a justification. He said twice: "They . . . killed Your prophets with the sword. I alone am left, and they seek to take my life" (3 Kingdoms 19.10,14). In this justification, he overlooked all of God's amazing works with him: how He strengthened him when meeting and rebuking Ahab the King (3 Kingdoms 18.18), and how he strengthened him in killing 450 prophets of Baal (3 Kingdoms 18.22, 40). Thus there was no need for him to fear and flee as long as God's hand was with him.

God, of course, did not accept this excuse from Elijah. He ordered him to carry out a number of important matters. One of them was to go and anoint Elisha the son of Shaphat as prophet in his place (3 Kingdoms 19.16). As for his statement, "I alone am left," the Lord answered him by saying that He had reserved 7,000 knees who had not bowed to Baal (3 Kingdoms 19.18). Truly, there are many justifications, but all of them are unacceptable, and therefore pointless.

With such justifications, man seeks to be blameless before other people, and perhaps before himself also, so as to ease his conscience if it protests against him. Even if the people accept these excuses, and even if man deceives himself and numbs his conscience to accept these justifications, God will not accept them.

God is all-knowing and has refused all of the above examples of justification. Before God, every mouth may be stopped (Romans 3.19). While justifications are never suitable with God, submission and confession of sin are in order. There are other justifications which appear as a type of pampering for the soul.

An example of this is the virgin in the Song of Solomon, when the Lord knocks on her door. He remains at her doorstep all night, until His head is covered with dew and His locks with the drops of the night, calling to her with very tender expressions. In spite of this, she excuses herself from opening to Him, saying: "I have taken off my tunic; how can I put it back on? I have washed my feet; how can I dirty them?" (Song of Songs 5.3). Did the Lord accept her excuses? No, He turned away and was gone, making her suffer the bitterness of abandonment: "I sought him, but did not find him; I called him, but He did not answer me" (Song of Songs 5.6).

Excuses for not serving the Lord are another example of justifications that are unacceptable. Moses excused himself from serving by saying to the Lord: "I am not capable, neither before nor since . . . but I am weak in speech and slow of tongue" (Exodus 4.10). God did not accept this excuse, but treated the matter of the slow tongue for him. Jeremiah also excused himself from serving by saying: "I cannot speak, for I am a youth" (Jeremiah 1.6). The Lord did not accept this excuse but rebuked him, saying: "Do not say 'I am a youth,' for you shall go to all to whom I send you, and whatever I command you, you shall speak. Do not be afraid . . . for I am with you to deliver you" (Jeremiah 1.7–8). In the same way the Lord did not accept the excuses of the one who said to Him: "Let me first go and bury my father," but rather said to him, "Follow Me, and let the dead bury their own dead" (Matthew 8.21–22).

By contrast, how amazing is the young shepherd whose flock is attacked by a lion? He does not consider his weakness before the fierceness of the lion a good excuse. Young David acted similarly in 1 Kingdoms 17.

Futile justifications and excuses also are challenged by the examples of the saints, who rejected the method of justification. When will the sinner get rid of the justification for his deeds? David the Prophet, after he had taken a census of the people, did not try to offer a justification for this. His heart condemned him, and he said to the Lord: "I sinned greatly in what I have did. But now, I pray, O Lord, take away the iniquity of Your servant, for I have done very foolishly" (2 Kingdoms 24.10). This is the way a humble penitent, who confesses his sins, speaks before God.

As for the unrepentant and immodest man, he tries to find a justification when committing a sin, after the sin has been committed, and also when he speaks about it generally. I would say with sorrow that the continuous excuses and justifications by such a person will shake his principles and values. As long as every sin has its justification, then there are no principles to be followed or pieties in which to persist.

We will mention here four general excuses that people use when they do not proceed correctly in their lives. Some may say, "Everybody is like this. Shall we deviate from society?" They say this as if they believe the individual should not be blamed if the fault is commonplace. It implies that the shortcomings of society are no longer shortcomings; a common fault becomes an excuse for an individual fault. This is certainly not the case. An error is an error, whether it is common or individual. This is the reason why social workers try to reform the corruption of society along with the pastors, priests, and other upholders of principles who attack these excuses. When we look at the Holy Bible, we see the extent of judgment for this excuse.

Noah, the father of fathers, lived in righteousness in an age full of corruption. In those days the corruption of the people reached such a stage that God drowned the earth with the flood. He "saw man's wickedness ... was great in the earth, and every intent of the thoughts within his heart was only evil continually" (Genesis 6.5). "So He blotted out all living things which were on the face of the earth" (Genesis 7.23).

Was general corruption an excuse for Noah and his family to proceed like the rest of their society, saying, "Everyone is like this, shall we deviate from society?" No, instead Noah proceeded with perfection before both God and the people. It was inevitable that he deviate from that corrupt society. If the phrase "deviate from society" troubles you, we will use a better one: "stand out from society." The Bible advises us, "Do not be conformed to this world" (Romans 12.2)—that is, do not be like it.

The same words can be said also about Lot in Sodom. The whole city was corrupted, and for this reason the Lord burnt it with fire (Genesis 19). There were not even ten righteous people in it to prevent God from burning the city for their sake (Genesis 18.32). Did Lot use this as an excuse to proceed like them, rather than deviating from society? And through this, would he have followed the proverb which says: "If you were in a distant country where there are calves, throw them freshly cut grass"?[3] No, the righteous keep their high principles, no matter how common the error may be. On the contrary, we can say that if an error is widespread, it requires more caution. Only three were saved from Sodom: Lot and his two daughters. The rest perished.

---

[3] *Editor's note:* This is a traditional Egyptian saying, which stresses pragmatic conformity when faced wit insurmountable adversity; similar to the English proverb, "When in Rome, do as the Romans do."

Another example is the righteous Joseph in the land of Egypt. He was the only one in the land of Egypt who worshipped God, whereas everyone else worshipped the ancient Egyptian gods: Raa, Amon, Isis, Osiris, Ptah, Hathor, etc. Joseph did not permit himself to follow society.

Daniel and the three young men also were like this in the land of captivity. They were distinguished from others even in their food, although they were prisoners of war, enslaved and abiding under laws. The Bible beautifully tells us that each "purposed in his heart that he would not defile himself with the king's food, nor with the wine he drank" (Daniel 1.8). You, also, are to live by your sound spiritual practices, even if you live by them all by yourself.

If you cannot influence society with your spirituality, then at least neither assimilate nor submit to it. Do not let common errors influence you. God's children should obey their consciences and not be swept away by the current, using the excuse that the world's general atmosphere is like this. It is a weak heart that hides behind excuses. It is the same for the lovers of sin, and for those who falter between two opinions (3 Kingdoms 18.21). However, the heart that loves God is strong, and no matter how many difficulties it meets along the path to repentance, it tries to overcome them.

Why, then, do you take a weak stand before those who insult your devoutness? Those who ridicule your spiritual methods try, by weakening your morale, to draw you into their ways and make you lose the fruits of your repentance. So, if you have truly repented, do not let such people be the cause of your relapse. Unless you become very strong and speak convincingly to prove to them the exaltedness of the spiritual life, you are better off keeping silent and remaining firm in your spiritual path, without hesitation.

Some people use obstacles as excuses. You may say that only the powerful can overcome obstacles. We will take the thief on the right hand of Christ as a magnificent example of someone who refused to use obstacles as a justification. There were many obstacles standing in front of the faith of this thief; even if he did not believe, like his companion, he could have found more than one excuse. In whom did he believe? He did not see the Lord in His power, His transfiguration, or His miracles. Indeed, those who had seen many of Jesus' magnificent miracles weakened at the time, and one of his most prominent disciples denied Him. Furthermore, the voice of the crowd echoed in the thief's ears: "Crucify Him, crucify Him." How was the thief to believe in a person crucified before him, in weakness, bleeding, surrounded by ridicule, reproach, and defiance from every direction, while He remained silent? The priests and chief priests were against Him. The elders of the people, the leaders and the teachers of the law, were against Him. The rulers were against Him. Even the other thief who was crucified next to Him ridiculed Him also.

Those who carried the paralytic offer another example of how to overcome obstacles (Mark 2.1–11). It would have been very easy for these people to make excuses to the paralytic, telling him that they could neither help him nor take him to Jesus. The house where Jesus was staying was full of people and very crowded. All the paths were blocked, there was no outlet nor entrance, and no way to get to the Lord. But they did not shrink from these obstacles, because their love of doing good was stronger than the obstacles. They carried the paralytic on a stretcher, uncovered the roof of the house and let down the sick person in front of the Lord to cure him. How great is this charitable intention, how powerful this will! Truly, as the saying goes, where there is a will, there is a way.

The strong heart finds a hundred ways for the thing it wishes to do. The fathers said, "Virtue asks you to desire only it, and nothing else." It is enough for you to desire. You will find that grace will open every door which closed before you. The Holy Spirit of God will strengthen you, and the spirits of the angels and the saints will surround you. Therefore do not let obstacles be an excuse, but think correctly about how to overcome them.

Zacchaeus the tax collector likewise found obstacles before him in coming to the Lord. Even just seeing the Lord was impossible for him. Jesus was surrounded by the crowd, and Zacchaeus was short in stature. He was also a chief tax collector—that is, a person hated by everyone, far from any spiritual piety—and they ridiculed him when he asked to meet the Lord. So he thought of climbing up a sycamore tree to see Him. Another obstacle standing in front of him was his great position. However, he overcame all of this. Therefore, he was made worthy of hearing the Lord say to him: "For today I must stay at your house" (Luke 19.5). Truly, if the inner drive in the heart of Zacchaeus had been weak, he would have found justification in the obstacles before him and would not have reached the Lord.

How strong is your inner drive? Would you allow obstacles to become your excuse? Here is an example from the age of martyrdom, involving a youth with whom no method of torture worked. They wanted to make him fall by enticing him with respect to his chastity, but they failed. They tied him to a bed so that a woman could come and sin with him. When the youth saw that there was no way out, he bit his tongue until it bled and spat blood in her face. She was terrified and left him, and the youth preserved his chastity. If he had been weak from within, he would have found a justification for falling. However, his inner strength made him victorious, and he gave no weight to obstacles or justifications.

Some make excuses on the basis of the severity of outside pressures, or outside enticements. The heart that is firm within does not submit to outside pressures, nor does it fall on their account, nor use them as justification for its fall. A person who justifies his position by outer pressures is one whose love for God and His commandments is not firm. In his heart is a betrayal from within, and he is truly faithful neither to God nor to the commandments.

Take the righteous Joseph as a magnificent example of victory over outside pressure. There is no doubt that outside pressure was very harsh on him. He was a servant enslaved to a woman. It was the woman who asked him to sin. She persisted in this, and he refused. She continued to persist. He was under her authority: she could ruin his reputation and throw him into prison, as she finally did. If he had been weak from within, he would have found something to justify his fall. However, he said: "How then can I do this great wickedness and sin against God?" (Genesis 39.9), and he endured for the sake of his righteousness.

The pure heart that is firm in its righteousness does not recognize justifications, nor submit to outside enticements. An example of this can be found in the story of David and King Saul. Saul tried many times to kill David, who was without offence, pursuing him from one desert to another. Finally, he fell into David's hands. David saw him sleeping in a cave, and his men said to him: "This is the day of which the Lord said to you, 'Behold, I will deliver your enemy into your hand, that you may do to him as it seems good to you'" (1 Kingdoms 24.4). The enticement was great; David could get rid of the enemy by whom he was threatened, and become king. However, David refused all this, saying: "The Lord forbid me, that I should do this to my lord, for he is the the anointed of the Lord." So David rebuked his men (1 Kingdoms 24.6–7).

There were many possible justifications. Who said that Saul was the Lord's anointed? The Lord had announced His rejection of Saul (1 Kingdoms 16.1). "The Spirit of the Lord departed from Saul, and an evil spirit from the Lord tormented him" (1 Kingdoms 16.14). David knew this, for he was the one who played the harp to refresh Saul so that the distressing spirit would depart from him (1 Kingdoms 16.23). Saul was a rejected and sinful person. If David got rid of him, he would have saved the people from Saul's evil. No, said David, for he is the Lord's anointed one.

You, O David, were the true anointed one of the Lord. Samuel the Prophet anointed you as king, and the Spirit of God came upon you (1 Kingdoms 16.12–13). So you became the official replacement for this wicked man. If you had captured the king, you would not have defied him, for this was your right, and all the people would have been happy with you. It was the Lord who drove him into your hands. It would only reflect the nature of the war between the two of you if you had killed Saul.

However, David did not accept any of these justifications. He said, "How can I stretch out my hand against the Lord's anointed? He is a sinner and an evildoer, he is rejected, he is my enemy, he is what he is, but still he is the Lord's anointed, and I will not stretch out my hand against him." This is an ideal picture of the pure heart which rejects justifications and enticements.

Some make excuses, saying, "I am weak, and the commandments are difficult." You say that you are weak, but only if you do not consider God's assistance. You are not alone. You might be weak, but you can still say, "I can do all things through Christ who strengthens me" (Philippians 4.13). As long as your prayers exist, then you are not weak, because the power of God works in you. It gives you victory over every sin, and lifts you up from every fall.

If David had looked upon himself as weak, he would not have fought against Goliath. This feeling of weakness was a justification for every man in the army to remain in his place, rather than stand and fight Goliath. David, however, did not permit such justifications to protect him from God's commandments, nor from the work of the Spirit. There were justifications available to David which would have exempted him from fighting Goliath, but he did not use them. First, he was not one of the soldiers in the army, but merely came to bring food for his brothers. He could have shortened his mission and departed, wishing them all the best.

Second, Goliath was a man to be feared, with his magnificent body and powerful weapons. No one would blame a young boy like David for refusing to fight with him.

Third, no one asked him to carry out this matter, nor even to consider it.

Fourth, all the army leaders were afraid of the man. Not even King Saul came forth to fight him. So, then, it would have been easy for David to rely on these justifications and depart, saying, "What have I to do with this matter, and why should I intervene in someone else's responsibilities?" However, David's zeal drove him to go forth to meet Goliath and save the people from him. The excuses were present, but he refused to use them or hide behind them. Everyone witnessed the difficulty of the deed, but with faith he was victorious.

The Lord punished those who weakened the Israelites' morale by talking about difficulties. They saw the land flowing with milk and honey, and yet they said: "The people who dwell in the land are strong; the cities are fortified. . . . We are unable to go up against them, because they are stronger than we. . . . There we saw the giants, the descendants of Anak, and we seemed like grasshoppers to them, but so we actually were" (Numbers 13.28, 31, 33). With this conversation that shattered morale, "all the congregation lifted up their voices and cried, and the people wept that night" (Numbers 14.1). The Lord rejected these people who made the matter difficult and impossible.

Therefore, do not say that the Lord's commandments are difficult. For if they were difficult, the Lord would not command us to do them. How can He command us to do something which cannot be carried out? God cannot command us to do the impossible. He gives the commandment, no matter how difficult it seems, and at the same time He gives the capability for its execution. He gives the commandment, and with it He gives grace. The Holy Spirit works within the heart in order to qualify it for work, and participates with it in the work. Otherwise, no one would have been capable of overcoming Satan, who is like a roaring lion, seeking whom he may devour (1 Peter 5.8).

Abraham, the father of fathers, did not refrain from performing a commandment that seemed very difficult. The Lord said to him: "Take now your son, your only son Isaac, whom you love . . . and offer him there as a whole burnt offering" (Genesis 22.2). Our father did not use as an excuse the difficulty of this commandment, which was above the standard of nature. This was the son of promises, the son of his old age; what would he say to the boy's mother? However, he woke up early and proceeded to execute God's commandment. God, who gave Abraham the power to carry this out, can also give you power. He made young Jeremiah a fortified city and walls of brass on all the earth (Jeremiah 1.8). Along the path of repentance, do not be afraid of any sin nor any habit or particular characteristic, nor of the devil, but say, "I can do all things through Christ who strengthens me." Do not let fear be a justification for you to abandon spiritual labor. Abraham did not withhold his son from God, nor did he try to find a justification to restrain himself. What about you? What is the difficult thing the Lord asks of you, that you cannot do? Does He ask you to sacrifice your only son? Is what is asked of you perhaps very simple?

Blessed are those giants who were victorious over their hearts from within, and who did not find an excuse in the difficulty of the commandment, as we do when justifying ourselves. Truly, the kingdom of heaven needs hearts like a rock, never softening in the face of obstacles, nor weakening in the face of difficulties, hearts to carry out the Bible's commandment: "Be strong, therefore, and prove yourself a man" (3 Kingdoms 2.2). Here, true manhood appears in the life of purity.

Those who do not want to struggle adopt justifications. With some people, as long as they have an excuse to present, then the path of sin and shortcomings becomes easy. Those who turn away from His love, without honesty toward the commandment nor any obligation to it, fail to take into consideration the Lord's feelings. When a person excuses himself, he deceives himself; his conscience becomes shaken, not firm.

Through the wide gate of excuse both truthfulness and lying may enter. Excuses may be untrue, or the obstacle easy to overcome. There is no true obstacle with the power to defeat the will. Excuses become a chance for carelessness, or for the love of sin. They become a veil for pride, which refuses to recognize errors. So they become secondary rather than true reasons. In general, justifications and excuses show the lack of repentance.

The amazing thing is that the unrepentant person, despite his errors, sees his beautiful self as it appears in his own eyes. Everything he does, in his view, has its reasons and wisdom. Every sin has its justification. Every shortcoming in carrying out the virtues also has its justification. He does not find error in anything he does. He talks as if he were infallible, never sinning. He defends and justifies. It is difficult for the words, "I have sinned," to proceed from his mouth. If you increase the pressure on him, the most he will say is, "What? Maybe some people understand this deed in a different way than what was meant by it. But I meant, ... " So another series of justifications takes place.

As if he were a god ... not sinning! "I said, 'You are gods" (Psalm 81.6). These "gods," who do not sin, cannot repent. Of what will they repent? Truly, those who are well have no need of a physician. These people are not in need of Christ, the Forgiver and Savior. What sin can you see Him forgiving or saving them from? Even those who have shortcomings in every spiritual duty, such as prayer, fasting, attending church and Holy Communion, also find justifications for their shortcomings, and it is as if they had not sinned.

You may ask one of them, "Why don't you pray? Why don't you attend church?" He will certainly not say to you, "I am a sinner," but justifies his shortcomings by saying that he has no time on his hands. If you discuss this with him, he will place before you a long list of preoccupations. You ask him, "Why isn't God among your preoccupations? Why don't you include Him in the organization of your time?" He then enters into another justification to try to philosophize the error, and says, "What is in the heart is most important. So, as long as my heart is pure, then there is no need for prayer! For God is the God of hearts." Of course the reply is clear. The pure heart cannot dispense with prayer, but helps in prayer. The pure heart contains the love of God. Whoever loves God speaks with Him and prays. The spiritual person unites the two matters, the purity of heart and prayer. As the Bible says: "Do this and do not leave that."

Purity of heart is necessary for prayer, for the prayer that proceeds from a pure heart is what is accepted before God. Therefore, the person who answers with the above words does not understand the meaning of the phrase "purity of heart." For if his heart is pure, then it is impossible for him to say that he has no need for prayer. Thus, he who has no need for prayer lacks purity of heart. You may ask another person, "Why don't you fast?" He replies, "Are all the people who fast saints? So-and-so fasts, and does this . . . so-and-so fasts, and does that." If you say to him, "What have you to do with them? God will not ask you about them, but will ask you about yourself," he will then return to the same justification, philosophize the matter, and say, "Life with God does not rely on eating and drinking certain foods. What is important is purity of heart," as if fasting does not assist in purity of heart.

In vain does one talk to such a person about the spirituality of fasting, saying that whoever proceeds in it in a spiritual way will grow in the life of the spirit. God commanded us to fast because of its benefits, and even the prophets used to fast in the purity of their hearts. The Lord Jesus Himself also fasted. So we do not find logic here, only mere justifications to escape responsibility.

Another person makes the excuse that he lacks spiritual advisors and good examples. It seems that his excuse, too, is exaggerated. Whoever is in need of advice undoubtedly will find it. If he does not find advisors, there are books which fill the world and contain everything. If in prayer he asks the Lord, He will advise him. He has his conscience, and also the Holy Bible. Saint Antony lived alone in the desert and did not have any predecessor to advise him, yet he did not make excuses based on a lack of advisors, but opened the way alone—and, with the grace of God, he made it and in turn advised others.

As for good examples, there are many. Do not look for every ideal quality in one person, but take each person as a model for a certain point. There are also examples in the stories of the saints and the righteous who passed away. There is a saying that whoever wants to arrive at God will find the means. So, the only question remaining is: Do you want this? It was kind of the Lord to ask some of those sick men who came to Him for healing that deep and immortal question: "Do you want to be made well?" (John 5.6).[4]

Yes, if you want, God is willing to work with You and strengthen you. He is the One who washes you, and you become whiter than snow. He is the One who purifies you from every sin, every defilement of the body and spirit. However, most importantly, you must want. But if you do not want, then there is no need for justifications. Be honest with yourself.

[4]Read my book *The Return to God*, for it is from this series on the life of repentance and purity. It will complete the understanding of repentance for you, and the means toward it.

CHAPTER 3

Do not delay repentance, but start now and seize the opportunity.

D<small>O NOT DELAY REPENTANCE</small> and lose your opportunity. Some have lost their opportunity for repentance. In God's mercy toward sinners, He offers every sinner many chances for grace to visit him and work in his heart, to help him repent. As a result of God's work within him, he finds his heart ignited with a holy desire toward repentance and a return to God. He might have been influenced by a sermon, a book, a spiritual meeting, a good example, or an occurrence of death. Disease may have shaken him from within, or perhaps circumstances led him to repent.

The wise person is the one who utilizes these influences, and does not let the chance slip away from him. It is like what happened with the prodigal son who, when grace visited him and influenced his heart and thoughts, said, "I will arise." And he arose and went to his father, and repented. The ignorant person, however, lets his chance pass by without benefiting from it. He looks for it later, but in vain. Hence, this dangerous phrase was said about Esau: "He found no place for repentance, though he sought it diligently with tears" (Hebrews 12.17). He was late in coming to his father after the blessing was transferred to Jacob, who became the chosen one, through whose descendants all of the nations of the earth would be blessed. Esau wept and "he cried with an exceedingly great and bitter cry" (Genesis 27.34). After the passage of time, however, and after the crying was over, he did not gain anything.

Look at the virgin in the Song of Songs and what happened to her, and learn a lesson. She was asleep, like any sinner, but her heart was awake to the Lord's call. She heard His voice calling to her, "Open for me," but she was slow and made excuses. She finally arose to open, but only after the chance had passed, after her beloved had turned away and gone. She then cried and said: "My soul went after him because of his word. And I sought him, but did not find him; I called him, but he did not answer me" (Song of Songs 5.6). The poor virgin was exposed then to many sufferings. Later the Lord, for the sake of her love, gave her another chance.

But you may lose the chance for good! This happened to Felix the Governor, and to King Agrippa. Each had the chance when Saint Paul the Apostle stood before him, defending himself. Regarding Felix, the Bible says: "Now as he [Paul] reasoned about righteousness, self-control, and the judgment to come, Felix was afraid" (Acts 24.25). Grace worked within his heart and moved him toward faith and repentance. However, he did not utilize the chance, but delayed it to another time, and answered Saint Paul: "Go away for now; when I have a convenient time I will call for you" (Acts 24.25).

With great regret, the book of Acts makes clear that Felix never found the time to call Paul. In this way, he lost the chance of a lifetime. The great Saint Paul spoke in front of King Agrippa in the same way also, in his deep and convincing style, with every work of the Spirit that was within him. Agrippa was greatly influenced. Grace worked within his heart, and he said to Paul: "You almost persuade me to become a Christian" (Acts 26.28). The poor king, however, did not grab the chance. He stood up from the judgment platform and left. He left behind repentance and faith, and the chance was lost. The Bible does not say anything after that about Agrippa. Just this one little incident stood between him and God.

I wish that he had done something like the Ethiopian eunuch, who grabbed the chance and gained salvation. The grace of God arranged for Philip to meet this eunuch along the road. Philip explained to the eunuch what he had read in the book of Isaiah. The man was influenced, and God worked within his heart. He believed. He did not let the chance slip away, but said to Philip: "See, here is water. What hinders me from being baptized?" (Acts 8.36). So straight away he went down into the water and was baptized, "and he went on his way rejoicing" (Acts 8:39). This is a brilliant example of capturing the chance. How about you, my brother? How many like Philip did God send you along the way, by whom you were influenced, yet you let the chance slip from your hand and did not benefit?

Therefore, do not delay repentance. For many who delayed never repented, and their lives were lost. Look at how many times the Jews rejected the Lord and followed other gods, and how the Lord sent prophets and apostles to them to attract them. But they lost all of these chances. The Lord then placed them into the hands of their enemies, rejecting their prayers and sacrifices. He said to them, "When you spread out your hands, I will hide My eyes from you; even though you make many prayers, I will not hear" (Isaiah 1.15). He also said to Jeremiah the Prophet: "Therefore, do not pray for this people, nor consider them worthy to be shown mercy. Do not pray nor come to Me about them. I will not hear you" (Jeremiah 7.15). Do you want through your continual delay to reach a similar condition?

The continual delay of repentance means the rejection of repentance. This is what happened to Pharaoh, until he perished. How many times did Pharaoh say to Moses and Aaron, "I have sinned. Entreat the Lord for my sake. . . ."? In spite of this, he did not repent. Look at his saying after the plague of hail and thunder: "I have sinned this time. The Lord is righteous, and my people and I are wicked. Entreat the Lord, that there may be no more mighty thundering and hail, for it is enough. I will let you go" (Exodus 9.27–28). In spite of this, Pharaoh neither repented nor kept his promise, but resorted to delay. After the plague of the locusts, he said to Moses and Aaron: "I have sinned against the Lord your God and against you. Now therefore, pardon my sin yet this time, and entreat the Lord your God that He may take away from me this death" (Exodus 10.16–17). The Lord removed this plague from him, as He had removed the others, but Pharaoh did not repent.

The expressions of repentance were in his mouth, but repentance was not in his heart. He screamed out of fear, without being convinced. He promised he would repent, but did not fulfill his promise. He kept delaying his promises to the Lord day after day, plague after plague, until divine anger caught up with him. He drowned in the Red Sea and perished. The delaying of repentance, in his case, was a practical rejection of repentance. There were chances presented to him by the Lord through the ten plagues. He was influenced by them, and would decide to repent definitely. He did not, however, utilize these chances for the salvation of his soul. The love of the world was in his heart more than the love of repentance, and so he perished.

Another example of those who lost the chance of repentance are the vinedressers (Matthew 21). To these the landowner sent his servants many times. They did not listen, nor turn from their evil. Finally, he sent his son. It was another chance for repentance, but they did not repent. What happened then? He said to them: "The kingdom of God will be taken from you and given to a nation bearing the fruits of it" (Matthew 21.43).

Let us take the mighty Samson as a further example of delaying repentance. He started well, and hence the Spirit of God descended upon him. His sin began when he knew Delilah, gave her his leadership, and submitted to her advice. This woman deceived him more than once. She handed him over to his enemies. Even though he knew this, he did not repent (Judges 16), but continued in what he was doing. Finally, he broke his vow. His enemies took him and plucked out his eyes. They bound him with bronze fetters and he became a grinder in the prison (Judges 16.21). This is what sin and delaying repentance did to him. God gave him another chance on the day of his death, as one of the men of faith (Hebrews 11.22–23).

Slowness in repentance makes a person perish, just like what happened to Achan the son of Carmi. He took of the accursed things and hid them. As a result of his sin, the people were defeated before the small town of Ai. Nevertheless, his conscience was unmoved, and he did not confess his error. The Lord said: "There is an accursed thing in your midst, O Israel" (Joshua 7:13). Joshua announced this truth, but still Achan did not move. Joshua then began to cast lots in order to find out who was responsible for God's anger. Even then, Achan did not come forth to confess. The lot fell on his tribe of Judah, and on his family of the Zarhites. In spite of all of this, Achan still did not come forth until God pointed toward him by name. So he confessed what he had done, but only after the chance for repentance had passed. He confessed as one who was revealed by the Lord, and not as one who reveals himself. They stoned him (Joshua 7.25).

Lot was lucky that the two angels did not permit him to slow down. This happened when God wanted to burn Sodom. The Bible says: "The angels urged Lot to hurry." When he lingered, they took hold of his hand, his wife's hand, and the hands of his two daughters, and they brought him out and set him outside the city. They then said to him: "Flee for your life" (Genesis 19.15–17). Lot had to flee quickly from that place of evil in order not to perish. There are many dangerous matters which require haste, and one of them is repentance. Sluggishness and delay are not appropriate.

The foolish virgins came late, after the door was closed, and that is why they lost the kingdom of heaven. They stood in front of the closed door, saying with grief and despair: "Lord, Lord, open to us." But they could hear only the fearful reply: "Assuredly, I say to you, I do not know you" (Matthew 25.12). They had come after the chance had passed, after the door was closed. Truly, how dangerous is what the Lord said of sinful Jezebel in the book of Revelation: "And I gave her time to repent of her sexual immorality, and she did not repent" (Revelation 2.21).

The heart stands in awe before the statement, "I gave her time," and keeps quiet. As this sinful woman did not repent within the time that the Lord gave her, He explained the plagues that would be placed on her. He also said that He "will give to each one according to his works" (Revelation 2.23). God, in His prolonged patience, gave this sinful woman time in which to repent.

Man should not then delay his repentance, despising God's prolonged patience. The apostle rebukes us about this, saying: "Or do you despise the riches of His goodness, forbearance, and longsuffering, not knowing that the goodness of God leads you to repentance?" (Romans 2.4). The apostle sees that such a person demonstrates that his heart is hard; he is unrepentant and treasuring up for himself wrath on the day of wrath (Romans 2.5).

There are also examples of those who did not delay. I like David the Prophet's haste in repentance. He was human like us, capable of sinning. However, his heart was gentle and sensitive, responding quickly to the voice of God. His repentance was true and without delay. This was revealed when Abigail rebuked him gently because he wanted to avenge himself on Nabal the Carmelite. He did not argue with her, nor justify his position, but said to her: "Blessed is your conduct and blessed are you, because you have kept me this day from coming to bloodshed and from avenging myself" (1 Kingdoms 25.33). When he took a census of the people, his repentance was quick. His heart was stricken, and he said: "I have done wickedly" (2 Kingdoms 24.17).

When Nathan alerted him to his sin toward the wife of Uriah the Hittite, he did not argue, but said: "I have sinned against the Lord" (2 Kingdoms 12.13). His psalms are filled with phrases of true repentance and contrition, and he drenched his couch with his tears (Psalm 50, Psalm 6).

The repentance of the people of Nineveh and of Saint Baeesa[1] was very similar. Jonah the Prophet gave Nineveh time to repent. He called out: "Yet three days and Nineveh shall be overthrown" (Jonah 3.4). This great city did not delay its repentance until the end of this period drew near, but repented immediately with sackcloth and ashes. It was a deep repentance which included everyone. The Lord, then, removed His anger from them.

Saint Baeesa's soul was taken by the Lord on the very day of her repentance, on the same evening that Saint John the Dwarf visited her. If she had delayed her repentance, what do you think her destiny would have been?

Happy, then, is the person who utilizes the chance God sends him for his repentance, and does not harden his heart. Who knows, maybe this chance will not recur. The Philippian jailer was guarding the prison when the Lord sent an earthquake at midnight. The doors of the prison were opened, and the chains were loosened for the release of Paul and Silas. This jailer did not delay, but said to Paul and Silas: "Sirs, what must I do to be saved?" (Acts 16.30). He believed. He took Paul and Silas to his house "the same hour of the night." This was done without delay: "And immediately he and all his family were baptized" (Acts 16.33).

Is there not a lesson for us in the story of the Philippian jailer, when we read the word "immediately" and the phrase "the same hour of the night?" This occurred at midnight (Acts 16. 25). Why, then, should we delay our repentance?

We read about a similar situation that occurred in the repentance of Zacchaeus. The Lord said to him, "Make haste and come down." Zacchaeus did this immediately and took the Lord to his house. The Bible tells us "he made haste and came down, and received Him joyfully" (Luke 19.6). So the Lord then declared: "Today salvation has come to this house."

Procrastination does not align with repentance. The phrases which suit this occasion are "I will," as in the story of the prodigal son (Luke 15); "immediately," "the same hour," as in the story of the Philippian jailer (Acts 16); and "make haste," "today," as in the story of Zacchaeus (Luke 19).

All of the stories of repentance in the lives of the saints also show clearly a lack of postponement. Mary of Egypt, when she was not able to enter into

---

[1]*Editor's note:* The life of "Baeesa" (Thais) is in Benedicta Ward, *Harlots of the Desert* (Kalamazoo, MI: Cistercian Publications, 1987).

the Church of the Resurrection to take a blessing from the icon, immediately carried out what she had decided upon for her repentance. Consequently, she became a saintly anchorite. When Pelagia[2] was influenced by Saint Nonius' sermon, she did not leave him until he gave her the grace of baptism. You can find more details about these examples in the history books.

There are examples of people who met the Lord and did not benefit. The first man in the world to lose the chance of repentance perished. It was Cain. The Lord Himself spoke to him, and warned him regarding his sin, before he became entangled in it. He said to him: "Sin lies at the door . . . but you should rule over it" (Genesis 4.7). He advised him to repent: "If you do well, will you not be accepted?" However, Cain missed the chance and did not listen to the advice. He let his thoughts and feelings control him. So he fell, and his fall was great.

It is amazing that there were many who met with the Lord and lost this chance. The rich young man had a chance to meet the Lord and hear advice for his salvation. Regretfully, however, he went away sorrowful (Matthew 19.22). The Lord said: "And come, follow Me." He did not do it. In this way he lost the chance. Neither did the Pharisee who invited the Lord to his house (Luke 7.36) benefit from this chance. It was the same also for many others who lived at the time of Christ and met with Him.

As for you, if the Spirit of God speaks in your heart, do not lose the chance. Millions of people who are in hell wish for a few moments of life, which you have—just a few moments in which to repent—but cannot find them. They have lost the chance, and the door has been closed. How about you, my brother? You have all of this life, why do you not think about repentance, and grab the chance? As the apostle said: "Walk circumspectly . . . redeeming the time, because the days are evil" (Ephesians 5.16).

Know that the postponement of repentance is one of the works of the devil, who does not want repentance. He knows that keeping you from repentance in a direct way is something your conscience will not accept. Therefore, he will never say to you, "Do not repent," and yet every time your heart moves toward God, he will say to you, "That's okay, but not now. We have many chances before us." He then keeps leading you in a series of never-ending postponements until your life ends.

[2]Ibid.

The outcome of such postponement is never for your own good. If you are influenced spiritually and have decided to repent, then do not delay, for you cannot guarantee yourself. You cannot guarantee that these spiritual feelings will remain with you. You might search for this desire to repent, and not find it. You cannot guarantee the circumstances which surround you. You cannot guarantee the next morning, or what might come with it. So, utilize your present condition. You cannot guess what kind of obstacles the enemy will put in your way, for he has known of your decision to repent, and how grace has visited you. If you remain in sin, awaiting another chance, your condition might become worse. As sin increases, it is transformed from just a fall or a practice to a habit. It then completely controls you, binding you with chains which are not easy to loosen. You then enter into a series of falls of which you will not know the end.

The devil postpones your repentance until he dominates you completely. You end up in a state in which you do not know how to repent, or in which you do not want to repent, for he has inserted sin in the depth of your heart, and at the same time he has paralyzed your will. At this time, he makes you fall into despair.

Here we will discuss another point: What does postponement demonstrate? It demonstrates your lack of love for God, for in breaking His laws you reject life and reconciliation with Him. It also demonstrates that the love of sin still remains in the heart. It demonstrates the lack of seriousness in the desire to repent, for serious desire leads to implementation. It also demonstrates that your mistaken concern with yourself is more profound than your concern for God's feelings and His relationship with you. I call it your mistaken concern with yourself because whoever is concerned with himself is concerned with his eternal salvation, and hence with his repentance. Therefore, do not by any means postpone your repentance, but as the apostle says: "If you will hear His voice, do not harden your hearts" (Hebrews 3.7,15).

CHAPTER 4

Do not harden your heart when grace works within you.

D O NOT HARDEN YOUR HEART.[1] God calls everyone to repentance, but hearts differ in their degree of compliance. Because of His excessive love for mankind, God "desires all men to be saved" (1 Timothy 2.4). He Himself strives for our salvation. For the sake of our salvation, He sent the prophets and the apostles, and He sent His divine inspiration to call us through His Holy Book to return to Him and repent, as "these times of ignorance God overlooked" (Acts 17.30). He placed in us a conscience to reproach us. He sent us His Holy Spirit to work within us. He gave us pastors, priests, preachers, and teachers, so that we can hear God's voice through their teachings. What is most important, however, is whether we listen. Who accepts His word? What is the extent of our compliance with the voice of God?

Here, hearts differ in type in the same way that the flexible branch differs from the dry branch. The flexible branch complies with you. You straighten it, and it becomes straightened; you stand it upright, and it remains upright; you change its position, and it changes. It is obedient in your hands. The dry branch, however, does not respond to you; if you want to straighten it, it resists. As the poet says, "The branches will be straightened if you straighten them, but if you try to straighten wood, it will not comply." Hard hearts of this kind the Lord works with, but they do not respond.

Such hearts are exactly the same as the sick person who does not respond to treatment. The doctor gives him the medicines appropriate to his disease, medicines to which others have responded. His body, however, does not respond to them. These treatments do not affect him. So, the disease continues, in spite of the treatment, or the condition becomes worse than before.

---

[1] This section was taken from three lectures about the hardening of the heart, which were delivered on November 28, 1969, July 29, 1977, and August 5, 1977.

So, with a hard heart, the means of grace do not result in any change. One's characteristics continue as they are, along with one's sins.

Certainly, the hardened heart does not wish to be made whole. Or perhaps, because of the hardness of his heart, he does not want to confess that he is sick and in need of healing. He remains in his disease, just as he is, like the hard-hearted Pharisees who lived at the time of Christ. They saw His miracles, but did not benefit, and afterwards said that He was a sinner. They heard His teachings and did not respond.

Instead, they said He was a deceiver and a violator of the law. Solomon the Wise said: "Though you grind a fool in a mortar ... yet his foolishness will not depart from him" (Proverbs 27.22). This is because the hardness of heart does not permit the sinner, who is attached to his ways, to change or to leave his sin behind. He rejects God, no matter how God strives toward him to save him.

It is amazing how the compassionate Lord strives toward man, and yet man rejects God! The great God strives toward the dust and ashes, and dust and ashes closes his heart in front of God. God speaks and calls, and this poor creature closes his ears and his heart, refusing to open to the Lord. God knocks on the door until His head is covered with dew, and His locks with the drops of the night (Song of Songs 5.2). However, man closes his door, and pays no attention to this great heart which has come to him, "leaping on the mountains and skipping over the hills" (Song of Songs 2.8). It is hardness of heart.

Sometimes we see a person being harsh toward his fellow man, and we feel uncomfortable. Many people, however, become harsh toward God Himself. It is amazing how man can be harsh in his dealings with God—the compassionate and kind God, in whose hand is found the spirit of this person, and who deals with everyone with complete gentleness. However, not every heart is like this. There are kind hearts that cannot stand to leave God at the doorstep, but get up and open to Him without delay, dreaming of hearing His divine voice.

Here are some examples of kind hearts. The gentle and kind-hearted Saint Augustine spent a long period away from God because the divine voice was not clear to him. When he realized it, he complied on that very night with all his heart and feelings, and became a saint. Mary of Egypt remained far from God for a long time, and far from His voice. But when she felt the voice of God calling her at the holy icon, she was completely changed. She yielded to the Lord and spent the rest of her life in His love. In the same way Pelagia was influenced by the mere sight of the saints, and by a single sermon she heard. She had a gentle heart that was easily influenced. In spite of her fornication and wealth, she repented quickly. Her yielding to God was amazing.

What is amazing in these stories of repentance is how fornicators yield to the Lord quickly. In fact this is not amazing, because most of these fornicators did not have hard hearts. They had, instead, emotional hearts, which yielded to love quickly. However, these hearts went astray when they directed their feelings toward the body. The body defeated them. When they found true love from God, or from His saints, they returned quickly. Compassion and love were already there, but lacked guidance and direction. This is contrary to the owners of the hard hearts who did not respond quickly, and might never respond at all. Therefore, the Lord rightly said to some of the elders of the Jews who were hard-hearted: "Assuredly, I say to you that tax collectors and harlots enter the kingdom of God before you" (Matthew 21.31).

How wonderful it is that many fornicators were transformed from sinners into saints! When the burning compassion they had was directed to God, their hearts were inflamed with His love. They were capable of reaching the life of holiness quickly. Besides Augustine, Mary of Egypt, and Pelagia, we may talk about other sinners who responded to the Lord quickly, and were transformed into saints: for example, Baeesa, Saint Thais, Saint Martha, Saint Mary the niece of Saint Abraham the solitary, Saint Evdokia, and many others.[2] Male examples include Saint Jacob the Struggler, Saint Timothy the Anchorite, and Saint Oghris at the start of his life. None of them required much effort from God in their return to Him.

God did not have to beseech them, nor call them with persistence. Just one session with Jesus changed the Samaritan woman's entire life. She was transformed from a sinful woman ("for you have had five husbands, and the one whom you now have is not your husband") to the saint of Samaria. She had a gentle heart that could respond quickly to the Lord, more than the

[2]See my book *The Spiritual Awakening*, to gain an idea about these saints.

severe Pharisees who spoke about high principles, but did not carry them out. David the Prophet, after his sin and fornication, could not withstand the one sentence from Nathan: "You are the man." So, he cried out that night, "I have sinned against the Lord." He repented with an amazing repentance, in which every night he made his bed swim and drenched his couch with his tears (Psalm 6.7).

The gentle heart may need only a word to change its lifestyle. Thais heard one phrase from Saint Besarion, which made her fall to the ground and break out in tears. Then she departed with him from the place of sin to live as a saint. Baeesa heard one phrase from Saint John the Dwarf, which influenced her together with his tears for her. Repenting, she departed with him for the desert. That night the angels lifted her spirit, pure as a beam of light.

The stories are many, all rotating about one orbit, which is the gentle heart that responds quickly. This occurs not only with fornicators, but with many others as well.

Saul of Tarsus was changed by one declaration from the Lord. Saul was very harsh in carrying out the law. He was persecuting the Church. But his heart was not hard. It had zeal, which he counted as holy, and he did what he did in ignorance (1 Timothy 1.13). When the Lord Jesus appeared to him and said but one statement, he accepted the word with joy. He was changed into the opposite of what he had been, and believed and suffered for the sake of the Lord.

Peter the Apostle cried bitterly at the mere sound of the cock's crow. He did not require much rebuke. It is enough that he heard the cock crow. Then a revolution broke out within him. It wrung his heart and eyes. A little is enough to make a kind heart repent.

Jesus looked up to Zacchaeus the tax collector and spoke to him. Zacchaeus could not resist, but proclaimed his repentance in front of everyone (Luke 19.5). Jesus spoke to many scribes, Pharisees, and priests, but they did not benefit. Zacchaeus' heart was not too hard to repent, like theirs, despite what we known about the injustice of tax collectors. Matthew the tax collector also needed only one call from the Lord to change his life: "Follow me" (Matthew 9.9). He then left everything, arose, and followed Him. Peter and Andrew the fishermen acted similarly when the Lord called them: "Follow

Me, and I will make you become fishers of men" (Mark 1.17). The sensitive heart not only obeys the voice of God but responds to any sign from Him, even from afar, since it is opened to God regularly.

The matter then depends on whether the heart is hard or soft. Both types appear together in the story of David and Nabal the Carmelite. David requested some sheep from Nabal the Carmelite, because he and his men were in need of food. Nabal did not respond, because of the hardness of his heart. David warned him, but he did not take notice, again because of the hardness of his heart. Neither request nor threat worked with Nabal. When Abigail his wife learned of the incident, her heart was moved quickly and she responded. She met David and presented to him the food that his men needed. David's heart was moved by her, and she was able to rebuke him in a decent manner for trying to avenge himself. In this story David, although he is firm but strong, presents an example of the kind heart that accepts reproach quickly and turns from its errors. He said to her: "Blessed is your conduct and blessed are you, because today you kept me from coming to bloodshed and from avenging myself" (1 Kingdoms 25.33).

The kind heart accepts reproach, but the hard heart revolts. David accepted reproach from a woman. In the same way Saint Antony accepted reproach from the woman who said to him, "If you were a monk, you would have lived in the mountain." He did not merely accept the word and carry it out, but even considered it to be God's voice to him. In contrast to this was Saul the King, who was known for the hardness of his heart. When his son Jonathan talked to him on behalf of David, asking, "Why should he be killed? What did he do?" (1 Kingdoms 20.32), Saul's anger increased against Jonathan, and he cast a spear at him to kill him. He swore at him with abusive language and disgraced him (1 Kingdoms 20.30–34). The hard heart accepts neither guidance nor advice. It does not change its thoughts, but its pride convinces it to stay firm. Therefore the Bible rightly says: "God resists the proud" (James 4.6). The Lord never stood against the poor tax collector, but He stood against the harsh and proud Pharisee, and against the harsh scribes and Pharisees, who in their harshness laid heavy burdens on men which were hard to bear (Matthew 23). These harsh people lose themselves, lose the people, and lose God.

Hardness of heart delays repentance. Pharaoh may well be the most prominent example of such hardness. None of the plagues was able to soften his heart. If he at times said, "I have sinned against the Lord" (Exodus 10.16), he would return after that with his heart hard as ever.

Every time he made a promise, he would go back on his promise after God had removed His anger. As the Bible says: "But Pharaoh's heart was hardened, and he did not heed them [Moses and Aaron]" (Exodus 8.15). Pharaoh remained in his hardness of heart until he perished. God wanted to attract him to Himself through these plagues. But he refused to listen to the Lord despite all of God's wonders, which he himself had experienced.

Another example is the rebellious people in the wilderness. All of God's wonders were with them in the land of Egypt, as well as in the wilderness; all of His great charity was for them. None of this softened their hearts. The ten plagues, the splitting of the Red Sea, the manna and quail for food, the water God burst open to them from the rock, the pillar of fire that gave them light at night, and the cloud, which sheltered and led them during the day—none of these made them repent.

The Lord described them many times as "stiff-necked people" (Exodus 32.9; 33.3, 5; 34.9 Deuteronomy 9.6). "They are impudent and stubborn children" (Ezekiel 2.4), "argumentative and hardhearted" (Ezekiel 3.7). Because of their hard-heartedness, they did not respond to the Lord, nor did they obey Him. Instead, they continually complained to Him. They did not repent at all, no matter how good He was to them. He even said about them: "All day long I have stretched out my hands to a disobedient and contrary people" (Romans 10.21).

Imagine God stretching out His hand to reconcile with the people, and the people rejecting God's continuously outstretched hand all day. They did not stretch their hand out, either for pardon or for reconciliation. What benefit did they gain, then, from their hard-heartedness? They lost the Lord, did not enter the promised land, and all of their complaining generation perished in the wilderness. God was angry with them and ready to destroy them, had it not been for Moses' intercession on their behalf (Numbers 32).

The hardness of their hearts clouded their minds. They could not remember any of God's good deeds. They did not soften and return to Him. None of the sayings and warnings of the prophets brought about any change.

It was as if for them God's seeds had fallen on a rock. Neither water, nor fertilizer, nor a working hand, nor agricultural experience can be of any benefit to seeds on a rock. By the same token, a hard heart does not feel the sting of the conscience, nor does it respond to the voice of the Spirit within. Such a man may listen to or read the word of God, but he does not benefit. He may go to church, but he remains unchanged; even partaking of the sacraments of confession and Holy Communion, counting God's blessings, and learning of God's warnings do not make a difference. He is a rock, a hard heart which is not influenced. The saying of our father Abraham, the father of fathers, applies to him: "Neither will they be persuaded though one rise from the dead" (Luke 16.31).

For this reason the Bible alerts us, saying: "If you will hear His voice, do not harden your hearts" (Hebrews 3.7). God's voice comes to us from many sources. God talks to us through His Bible, sermons, and spiritual advice. We may hear it through incidents in which God's hand is very clear, or through the quiet session with the self. The most important thing in all of this is for us to accept the voice of God with attentive ears and an open heart, a soft and non-resisting heart.

In this way, even if we hardened our heart once, we will not continue to do so. The virgin in the Song of Songs did not open the door to the Lord the first time, because her heart was hardened toward Him. But the second time her heart softened. She said: "My beloved put his hand by the opening of the door, and my heart was stirred by him" (Song of Songs 5.4). She got up to search for this beloved everywhere, saying: "I implore you, O daughters of Jerusalem. . . . If you find my beloved . . . tell him that I am wounded with love" (Song of Songs 5.8).

I wish we would fight the hard heart within us. If our heart is kind, every spiritual means will influence us, leading us to repentance and to the love of God.

The sensitive, kind person will be influenced by every spiritual matter. If he hears the liturgy, some hymn, or a sermon, or reads a spiritual book, he is influenced. He is also influenced in remembering his loved ones who have departed. If he sins, he reminds himself, "What if the spirit of so-and-so were to see me now?" In this way, he turns from his sin instantly. Looking at a picture of Jesus crucified affects his feelings and he weeps, joining Saint Mary the Virgin at the cross: "But my heart burns when I gaze at you hanging on the cross, which you endured for the sake of all; O my son and my God."[3]

I compare the eyes of a sensitive person to a sponge filled with water. The slightest touch or pressure makes it hard for it to hold the water. In the same way, a kind-hearted person finds it hard to hold back his tears. If he sins, he returns quickly and does not continue in the error. This was evident with David the Prophet and with Peter the Apostle after his denial. Reject, then, my brother, all hardness of heart, so that your heart becomes kind and sensitive, responding to every spiritual influence without delay.

Know that hardness of heart has dangerous hazards. It leads to spiritual laxity, falling into sin, and non-productivity. If hardness of heart continues as a way of life, it will make your life dry out completely, to be burned in the end (Hebrews 6).

Do not say, "What can I do? This is my nature." No, your nature originally was in God's image and likeness (Genesis 1.26). Every error that follows is an artifact you can get rid of by repentance, and by accepting the work of the Holy Spirit within you. Many hard people were transformed into meek people. For example, Saint Moses the Black was transformed from a murderer into a meek monk with a very kind heart. He became an advisor to many, and his heart was completely free of any hardness toward God and people.

We will explore, then, the reasons for hardness of heart, and then we will investigate how to treat it. Some common reasons for hardness of heart are listed below.

I. The practice of sin: Sin hardens the heart. Continuing in the practice of sin hardens the heart even more, for as long as a person lives in sin, he forgets about God and His commandments, His death, and His redemption. Forgetfulness hardens his heart. Sin becomes an easy and simple practice in which he neither hears the voice of his conscience, nor that of the Spirit. Repentance from sin removes this hardness. Meditating on the repugnance

---

[3] *Editor's note:* Taken from the petition of the Ninth Hour in the *Agpeya.*

of sin removes hardness from the heart. We discussed this in detail in chapter one of this book.

II. The pleasure of sin: If a person enjoys sin, he easily forgets God's love and the commandments. His heart becomes hardened. The pleasure of sin casts a shadow over the mind and heart. When Eve saw that the tree was appetizing to eat, her heart was hardened. She forgot God's commandment and the judgment of death. She overlooked the life of purity and the love of God. The desire for the tree was overwhelming.

In the same way, Samson forgot his vow when the pleasure of sin anesthetized him. When he was with Delilah, he was not with God. His sinful desire made him forget everything. The Spirit of God still called to him, but it no longer influenced him. He forgot that Delilah was unfaithful to him and had handed him over to his enemies more than once. His heart was hardened through desire from hearing even the voice of the mind. He became stubborn. Nothing affected him. Samson gave up his honor and his vow (Judges 16).

For the same reason, the rich young man rejected the Lord's commandment. He was searching for the commandments and learned them from a young age. However, the love of money was in his heart. The pleasure of having money hardened the heart of that youth. When he heard the Lord's commandment he went away sorrowful, for he had great possessions (Matthew 19.22).

The pleasure of sin hardened the heart of Pharaoh. In front of him were hundreds of thousands of people, whom he utilized in his works. How can he let these people leave, and lose this free labor? The pleasure of the sin of exploitation and lordship hardened his heart. He did not benefit from all of the plagues which fell upon him and on all of Egypt. Every time his heart responded, the joy of sin would retract him.

Ahab acted in the same way when he desired the vineyard of Naboth the Jezreelite. The act of possession gave him great pleasure. He broke God's commandment and submitted to Jezebel's advice. He killed Naboth unjustly, after he had devised an accusation around him, and he called upon false witnesses. The pleasure of having that vineyard blinded his conscience completely. His heart was hardened and could accept injustice and murder.

The pleasure of sin makes the voice of conscience lose its influence, and hardens the heart. Man either forgets God's commandments, or else delays their execution in order to harbor a desired sin for a longer period. During this time, he blocks his ears to any inner voice that rebukes him, and to any external voice that advises him. His heart becomes stubborn, resisting change. The mind calls him to stay away; his conscience—and every spiritual influence—calls him, too. However, the heart that has been hardened by sin says, "Yes, I will stay away, but not now." He delays repentance. Delaying hardens the heart and makes it less responsive to the spiritual call. Hardness of heart makes man delay repentance. The delaying of repentance hardens the heart even more. Every time man delays his repentance and continues to feel that he is enjoying sin, his condition increasingly worsens. His practice of sin makes him realize its joy and benefits. The pleasure of sin invites him to increase his practice. In all of this the heart is hardened and is not influenced by spirituality.

There is no solution but for him to stop enjoying sin. Either he is convinced that he is in a state of loss, that sin harms him here and deprives him of his eternity, or some outcomes of sin shake him greatly. God may strike him with a plague, and he collapses. Or, he is bored with sin and becomes tired. Now he thinks differently. There is still another important treatment, which is to increase in one's nourishment of the spirit, until sin loses its pleasure. Man's view of sin must change. This may be what the apostle meant by saying: "Be transformed by the renewing of your mind" (Romans 12.2). With the renewing of the mind, man no longer enjoys sin.

III. External harmful influences also cause hardening of the heart: Associations, friendships, and surroundings have a great influence on the condition of the heart. If you associate with people whose hearts are sensitive to God's commandments, then their attitude will be reflected upon you, and you will learn precision in spiritual conduct. If you associate with people who are careless, they will teach you hardness of heart. If it were not for his association with Jezebel, King Ahab's heart might not have been hardened to kill Naboth the Jezreelite (3 Kingdoms 21). Jezebel was the one who presented to him the sinful thought. She helped him to execute it. She planned everything for him, simplifying the punishments. She hardened his heart, and he responded.

Similarly, the advice of the young men succeeded in hardening Rehoboam's heart. They advised him to say to the people: "Being from the loins of my father, my meanness will be more burdensome.... Whereas my father chastised you with whips, I will chastise you with scorpions" (3 Kingdoms 12.9–10). They explained honor in a way that ruined him. His heart was then hardened, and he carried out their advice.

There are those who simplify sin to others and assist them in doing it. There are things the heart naturally rejects. However, some encouragement or an offer of guidance usually overcomes this natural obstacle. The person then submits, and falls into sin. A simple example is the person who is encouraged to smoke for the first time, or the hippies who used to do horrific things such as nudity in front of other people, practicing sex in front of friends, or other kinds of immoral behavior, including murder and drinking blood. Their followers were disgusted with this at first, but they were finally led to practice these things, as mentioned in their memoirs. Their hearts were hardened. The saying "tell me who your friends are, and I will tell you who you are" is quite correct.

The worst thing is an insensitive conscience which justifies every error, finds an excuse for every sin, and puts the mind at the service of every selfish wish. If you come across this type of person, stay away from him. He may implant in your heart thoughts and desires that were not originally yours. He may harden your heart by justifying sin, by regarding it as a natural thing, or even mocking your precision in the spiritual life, regarding this as an extravagance or a difficulty. Your heart hardens.

Evil company may include books, media, and publications, or sound recordings, films, and illustrations. These may influence your thoughts in a certain direction and lead you where God does not wish you to be. They may teach you things that could be harmful to you and implant thoughts that may change your spiritual outlook. Your heart will then be hardened. They present to you new concepts of freedom, power, personality, and happiness, which may confuse your principles and beliefs. Be cautious, then, and be careful in choosing what to read and view. Examine what you hear, even inside your home.

Examine every new thought that occurs to you. Practice discerning the spirits. Do not accept every piece of advice, nor every thought and opinion, but be strong from within, and you will acquire the virtue of differentiating and testing the spirits (1 John 4.1). Do not lose your spiritual principles. Be very careful in choosing your friends. Seek much guidance in every new thing you meet. Examine everything in the light of the Bible's teachings, the lives of the saints, and firm spiritual principles.

IV. Submitting to obstacles assists in hardening the heart. We should overcome obstacles, not submit to them. Nothing is easier for the devil to do than to place obstacles in front of you at every juncture of your spiritual life. Fearing for one's health stands as an obstacle in the way of fasting; lack of time may stand in the way of prayer, spiritual reading, meetings, and service. Monetary needs might stand as an obstacle to your giving tithes to God. Preoccupation stands as an obstacle to sanctifying the Lord's day. What is called wisdom appears to cover every wrong action. Worldly wisdom becomes an obstacle in the way of your spiritual progression. With such wisdom you learn to lie and to practice adulation, favoritism, and fear.

Your submission to obstacles teaches you carelessness and hardens your heart. The strong-hearted person does not acknowledge that there is an obstacle which can stand before him. Nor does he permit these obstacles to harden his heart, but he lives a life of continual victory. In the victory over every obstacle he finds a spiritual joy. When confronting obstacles placed by the devil, he remembers the saying of the apostle: "Resist him, steadfast in the faith" (1 Peter 5.9).

V. Disregard of God's kindness usually leads to hardness of heart: A person sometimes sins and, because he does not encounter divine, deterring punishment, despises God's commandments and loses his fear of Him. His heart is hardened. Yet we see this person being precise in his professional behavior, for which he can be blamed, questioned, or punished. This reminds us of the apostle's saying: "Or do you despise the riches of His goodness, forbearance, and longsuffering, not knowing that the goodness of God leads you to repentance? But in accordance with your hardness and your impenitent heart you are treasuring up for yourself wrath in the day of wrath" (Romans 2.4–5).

Talking about the fear of God sometimes benefits a hard heart, while the one who is moved by love can benefit from words about God's love. In contrast, the contemptuous might benefit when reminded of God's fear. The apostle says: "Do not be haughty, but fear" (Romans 11.20). He also asks for "perfecting holiness in the fear of God" (2 Corinthians 7.1). This might remind us that pride is one of the reasons for hardness of heart.

VI. Pride: Pride hardens the heart. The proud person thinks only about himself and his honor. He places neither God nor people before himself. For the sake of executing his will, he can do anything and could not care less. In this way, he attains a hard heart. The humble person, on the contrary, has a contrite heart before God. He obeys and is not hard. If man could evaluate himself as dust, he would be led to repentance. Then his hardness of heart would leave him, and grace would join him instead.

VII. The loss of reverence for spiritual means leads to a hardened heart: Whoever practices the sacraments without spirit loses his reverence for them. Hence, they no longer influence him. Since he does not benefit from them, his heart is hardened. Formerly, when he entered the church, his heart was humbled and fearful. He felt that he stood in front of God in His house. Now, he enters the church continuing in his sin; he roams in it, talking and discussing, and the Church has no influence on him. It is the same with the altar. He becomes accustomed to partaking of Holy Communion and confession recklessly. Similarly, his prayer and reading are without spirit. His fasting is a bodily act. Because his heart has been hardened by continuation in sin, these spiritual means no longer change him.

When a sick person becomes addicted to certain medicines, they lose their effect on him. For example, too many painkillers very soon lose their effect on the pain. An employee who meets his boss and associates with him on a regular basis no longer fears or reveres him as much as the other employees do. A person who has lived in holy places and visits them regularly is no longer influenced by them in the same way as a person who visits them for the first time. Therefore, whoever practices these spiritual means needs to practice them with spirit, depth, understanding, and humility, if he would regain his reverence, benefit from them, and turn his heart to God.

Avoid any first step that leads to sin, flee from the little foxes that destroy the vines, and proceed with exactitude.

A VOID THE FIRST STEP, and beware of the little foxes.[1] If you want to repent, then beware the first step leading to sin. In most cases sin does not attack you all at once, with all of its strength, but creeps toward you over a long period of time and reaches you after many progressions. So, then, detect where sin begins and observe its stages.

Sin usually starts with contact, then with stimulation, and then with kindling. Sin contacts you first through stumbling blocks, recklessness, or wicked acquaintances. If you give it a chance, it will influence your thoughts or emotions. So, if you underestimate this inner stimulation, it will then increase and be transformed into kindling. At both of these stages the influence of sin is internal. This is more dangerous, and the matter may become worse.

The matter then develops into an inner struggle, which may end in submission and falling into sin. It is a struggle between the conscience and sin, or between spirit and matter. Struggle indicates that a person is rejecting and resisting sin. It is a tiresome stage, but it is better than submitting and falling. A person puts himself into such a situation by neglecting the initial stages.

You cannot guarantee victory in the struggle between you and sin. You might be successful in it after toil, or you might fail and give up your weapon, that is, submit to the enemy and fall. It is the nature of sin that it should be accomplished. Once you fall into sin, the enemy will not leave you alone.

---

[1] The topic of the first step was delivered in Saint Mark's Hall at Anba Rewais on Friday October 6, 1966. It was also discussed at the Church of the Angel at Damanhour as part of a series of lectures about the life of repentance. As for the topic of the little foxes, it was presented in the Great Cathedral on Monday, June 7, 1980, as part of a group of lectures on the Song of Songs.

Instead, he will continue his warfare until the sin is repeated and becomes a habit or a characteristic behavior. As such, you will no longer resist it; you will submit to every suggestion the devil makes to you as his slave, and thus sin dominates you. The captivity of Babylon is a symbol. The psalmist says: "By the rivers of Babylon, there we sat down and wept when we remembered Zion" (Psalm 136.1). He also says: "How shall we sing the Lord's song in a foreign land?" The devil is never satisfied by making his prey a slave to sin, but continues to make him slide into an even more disgusting state.

This stage develops further into the humiliation of bondage wherein man desires sin but does not find it, even after asking and pleading for it with all his strength. He becomes the person who seeks money and possessions, or the desires of the flesh, but cannot obtain them; one who asks for majesty (or pride or revenge or spite) and proceeds with all his desire, hoping to find it. He pleads with and begs the devil to grant him sin. The devil continues to humiliate him until he despises this person. At which of these stages do you find yourself?

I wish that you would cut your struggle short by avoiding the first step. This is easier and guaranteed. It also demonstrates your purity, your rejection of sin. You neither negotiate nor deal with the enemy. To this effect, Saint Dorotheos compares the seedling to the big tree. He says that it is very easy to uproot a seedling from the soil: you grab it with your hand and remove it with ease. However, if you wait until it becomes a big tree, it will be very difficult for you to uproot. Even if you succeed at this, there is still another danger.

You might overcome an evil thought from within you after a bitter struggle. However, during the struggle you might have defiled your mind, and perhaps your heart. Even if you cast this thought out of your conscious mind, it remains in your memory and your subconscious. It might return to you after a while, or appear to you in your dreams or your suppositions. What need is there for all of this toil? It is better to eradicate the thought at the beginning, before it sets in with increasing chances of ruining your spirituality. Try to overcome sin at the beginning, that is, at the stage of contact.

As much as you can, try to avoid contact with sin. The first psalm says: "Blessed is the man who walks not in the counsel of the ungodly, nor stands in the way of sinners, nor sits in the seat of the troublesome" (Psalm 1.1).

One of the saints noted a kind of development in the psalm: walking, then standing, then sitting. The first stage (walking or proceeding) is less dangerous than standing, which is less dangerous than sitting, or settling. The last stage, that of the scornful, is more horrific than the stage of sinners, because the former are reckless sinners. Therefore, do not allow sin to develop with you, nor to induce you to develop with it. Deviate from it at the first step, if you wish to repent and keep your heart pure.

On the whole, at whatever stage you find yourself, do not allow it to develop to a worse one. Hold on, while you are relatively strong, at the beginning of this deadly stage of contact. If you are affected, then your will has begun to respond to sin, and in the kindling you have weakened. In struggle, you enter into a stage of life or death. When you fall, it means your will has given up quickly in this war. When you become a slave to sin, that is the end of your will. You then become a person deprived of his will. Watch yourself then, and beware the first step.

Know well that every time man takes a step forward along the path of sin, his will becomes weaker. He is inclined toward sin, making room for the devil within himself. Every time he takes another step toward sin, the love of God decreases in his heart, and his fall becomes certain. Therefore, the psalm says: "O wretched daughter of Babylon, blessed is he who . . . shall dash your infants against the rock" (Psalm 136.8). The daughter of Babylon (the land of captivity) is sin. Her children are the desires or thoughts of sin at the first step, before the sin can grow. Happy is he who takes them and dashes them—that is, gets rid of them—against the rock. The Bible says: "And that Rock was Christ" (1 Corinthians 10.4). That means, happy is he who resists sin in the mind, at its very beginning, and seeks help through the power of the Lord Himself to annihilate it. We will try to give examples from the Bible about the development of the stages of sin.

How did the situation develop with the fall of our mother Eve? Let us take a lesson for our lives from this first sin. Did Eve fall when she took from the tree and ate, or when she gave to her husband and he ate with her? For this was the last stage in the problem, a very natural development following everything that preceded it.

The problem actually started when she sat with the serpent, who made her listen to some amazing words: "You shall not die by death. . . . In the day you eat from it your eyes will be opened, and you will be like gods, knowing good and evil" (Genesis 3.4–5). Here, doubt entered the heart of Eve, and she started to lose faith in the truth of God's words: "In the day that you eat of it you shall surely die." At last her faith began to be shaken, and she doubted God's promise. Doubt handed her over to the desire for divinity and knowledge, and not merely the desire for the fruit. Here, her inner stimulation reached its peak. Eve lost her simplicity and her inner purity. She looked at the tree and saw "the tree was good for food, was pleasant to the eyes, and a tree desirable to make one wise" (Genesis 3.6). Eve passed by the tree every day, since it was in the middle of the garden, but she had not looked at it like this. So, where did this look come from?

A strange thought entered into her heart, which was transformed into a desire. The desire dominated the heart, and the will submitted to it. At that stage neither Eve nor Adam was capable of abstaining from eating. The condition of their hearts had completely changed. Their original state of purity and simplicity was lost. Doubt, then, took the place of faith. The desire increased greatly, and the will was greatly weakened. Eve then fell, and Adam followed.

Eve should have kept away from the first step. In other words, she should not have sat with the serpent, which "was more cunning than all the wild animals" (Genesis 3.1). She could have spared herself from listening to words which were against God's commandment. As she listened, she should have rejected and not believed them. She should not have let the sinful thought enter her heart and be transformed into a desire. If such a desire tempted her, she should have resisted it. But she let the matter develop in her heart and lead her from one sin to another, until she reached the extremity of falling. She could have avoided all of this, if she had kept away from the first step.

Do you wish, then, not to fall? Keep away from the serpent. Keep away from "evil company [which] corrupts good habits" (1 Corinthians 15.33). Beware of evil external influences. Protect your eyes from viewing sin. Keep away from the first step that may lead you gradually to a total loss. Samson fell as a result of another serpent. Samson was a great judge who had honor and reverence, one whom the Spirit of God used to move (Judges 13.25) and upon whom the Spirit of the Lord came (Judges 14.6). This Samson revealed his secret, broke his vow, and his enemies despised him. They put out his eyes and made him labor at the mill-stone in prison (Judges 16.21).

Did Samson's distress come suddenly, or was it the outcome of a few developing stages? It had developments, for one step led to another. First, he went to Gaza and sinned there (Judges 16.1). Then he became acquainted with a woman called Delilah, and his relationship with her developed into love, devotion, and then living with her. In all of these, his conscience did not bother him. His enemies felt this and used it against him. She tried to learn the secret of his power in order to hand him over to his enemies. She asked him more than once. She betrayed him to his enemies, and he knew it. Nevertheless, he kept up his relationship with her. He lost his personality with her. He let the matter develop until he told her his secret, and then she sold him to his enemies for silver. He agreed to give her his head, to shave his hair. So, he lost his power and they captured him. He could have avoided all of this if only he had avoided the first step, or if he had awakened to himself at any of the stages through which he passed, before they culminated in tragedy.

Lot's tragedy also passed through various stages and developments. Along with Sodom perished all of Lot's riches. He lost everything, all of his relatives and his wife also. He would have perished with the city were it not for the two angels who took him away with his two daughters (Genesis 19). When I analyze Lot's problem, however, I turn back the hands of the clock to the years when he lived in friendship with the man of God, Abram, next to righteousness and the altar. It was then that the problem began.

Lot loved riches and abundance. He desired the fertile land. The matter reached the point that he separated from Abram, the man of God. This was his first loss. So, while searching for the fertile land, he saw Sodom. The land was watered "like the garden of God, like the land of Egypt" (Genesis 13.10). "Then Lot chose . . . for himself." This was a spiritual error, for "the men of Sodom were exceedingly wicked and sinful before God" (Genesis 13.13). In spite of this, Lot did not consider the spirituality of the place, only its greenery. So he left Abram and the altar to go into the abundant land in the company of the wicked. He went to a place which had material wealth, not the place where he could worship God. His spirituality thus became of secondary importance to him. "For that righteous man, dwelling among them, tormented his righteous soul from day to day by seeing and hearing their lawless deeds" (2 Peter 2.8).

Things became even worse. He mixed with the people of the land. His daughters were married to them. He lost his spiritual reverence living among them, so that later, when he warned them of God's destruction, "to his sons-in-law he seemed to be joking" (Genesis 19.14). The Sodomites even attacked his house when the two angels entered it, and the matter ended with the destruction of the city and the loss of everything he had.

It would have been more appropriate for him to stay alert from the beginning, and never to have left Abram. He should have fought in his heart against the first step, which was the love of the abundant land, the love of wealth and spaciousness. He could have avoided that great loss.

Let us now contemplate David's sin and identify its first step. David committed fornication, which led him to murder to cover his sin. He pursued a method of lying and perverseness in order to deceive Uriah the Hittite (2 Kingdoms 11.8–13). Was fornication then, the first step? No, for he previously had seen the woman bathing and desired her. Yet even this was not the first step, for it was preceded by David leaving his bed, walking on the roof of the king's house, and looking into peoples' homes and the privacy of their personal lives. However, this step was preceded by still another fundamental step.

The first step in the fall of David was his life of luxury. This luxury enticed him to stay in his palace while the people were occupied with the war in the desert. He did not go out to battle with them, nor even contribute his sentiments. Uriah was nobler than he in this point, for when David invited him to go home and to rest, Uriah answered: "The servants of my lord are encamped in the open fields. Shall I go to my house to eat and drink and lie with my wife? ... As your soul lives, I will not do this" (2 Kingdoms 11.11).

Previously, David's life was different. He was pursued by Saul, escaping from one desert to the other. He lived in caves, fought by himself, and slept on the ground; he did not sin at that time. Later, however, he lived in luxury, in palaces with servants, attendants and slaves. He sent the army to fight, while he stayed in his house on his bed. He stood on the roof and looked at the people. He lacked the desire to be with his fighting army.

Luxury led him to desire sin, instead, and to attempt to cover it. Because of his many sins, he later drenched his couch every night with his tears (Psalm 6). When God wanted to correct him for his first step, He permitted Absalom to rise against him. David went out from his palace barefoot (2 Kingdoms 15.30). Shimei the son of Gera cursed him along the way, and God returned David to his original rank.

Let us contemplate, then, how Solomon was able to burn incense to the idols. Solomon was the wisest person of his generation on earth. Twice God appeared and spoke to him (3 Kingdoms 11.9). He granted him wisdom, majesty, and a big heart. How, then, was he able to fall into such amazing ignorance? There is no doubt that it did not come upon him suddenly, but developed gradually.

The first step was that he married foreign women (3 Kingdoms 9.16–24). The Bible says: "But King Solomon loved many foreign women, as well as the daughter of Pharaoh. The women of the Moabites, Ammonites, Edomites, Sidonians, and Hittites" (3 Kingdoms 11.1). This was against God's commandment, which disallowed marriages with foreigners.

Next he built high places on the mountains for the gods of these foreign women, "burning incense and sacrificing to their idols" (3 Kingdoms 11.6). Solomon's situation ended in tragedy through the development of his sin; the Bible says: "For it was so, when Solomon was old, that his wives turned his heart after other gods . . . For Solomon went after Ashtoreth the goddess of the Sidonians, and after Milcom the abomination of the Ammonites. Solomon did evil in the sight of the Lord" (3 Kingdoms 11.4–6). All of this developed after the first step: his marriages to foreigners.

More time would be required if we were to discuss the development of sin among these great people, and how the first step in sin led them to more horrific steps. My advice is: Remember that you are not stronger than the prophets, the wise, and the great people who fell. Be aware, then, of the first step toward sin and run for your life. You are not stronger than Adam, who was in Paradise, in a superior natural state, nor stronger than David, on whom the Spirit of God descended and who was the Lord's anointed. You are not stronger than Samson, the Lord's consecrated one, whom the Spirit of God moved, nor stronger than Solomon, whom the Lord spoke to twice, and who was the wisest person of his generation. You are not stronger than

Abraham, the father of fathers and beloved of God who, in order to rescue himself, lied and called Sarah his sister and subjected her to be lost (Genesis 20.11–13). The Bible is correct in saying that sin "has cast down many wounded, and all who were slain by her were strong men" (Proverbs 7.26).

Let us, then, be aware of sin in all its power—not only when it intensifies against us and attacks like "a roaring lion, seeking whom he may devour" (1 Peter 5.8), but from the first step. We take her little ones and dash them against the rock. We should act accordingly with the obvious, horrific sins and with every sin, no matter how simple or small it may seem, in order to fulfill the divinely inspired saying: "Catch us the foxes, the little ones that spoil the vineyard" (Song of Songs 2.15). The vine in general is the Church, while in particular it is the heart of every believer. The foxes are the cunning sins that appear small and unlike ferocious beasts.

Their danger lies in their small size, since no one gives them any importance. As a result, they allow sin to progress and grow until it reaches a destructive stage which is difficult to resist. This commandment calls us to exercise precision and attention, to search our lives for these little foxes and resist them. We also learn an important lesson, that we must not neglect any sin, no matter how small it appears. A single hole in a ship, if neglected, can lead to a drowning disaster. The river Nile, with its great channel, started with drops of rain that fell on the mountains of Ethiopia. It progressed until it came to Egypt as a river. The great hill of rubbish which was placed on the Holy Cross started with one basket of rubbish. The longest journey in sin started with one step.

We should be alert and take great care in every step that leads to sin. We must cast out the little foxes, which may be laziness, carelessness, laxity, unnecessary talk, or unruly conduct. Know that whoever gives importance to the little ones will also give importance to the great ones. As the English saying goes, "Take care of the penny, and the pound will look after itself." Thus do not neglect the small things, but give importance to resisting them.

There are little foxes which entered even into the lives of the saints. We will take Abraham as an example. Our father Abraham sacrificed his wife Sarah twice, saying that she was his sister. When taken before the king of the country, she was desirable in his eyes, for she was a woman of beautiful countenance. This happened once in Egypt (Genesis 12.10–20), and another time in the land of Gerar (Genesis 20.1–14). If it had not been for the Lord's intervention, Sarah would have been lost, and she would have become the wife of someone other than Abraham while he was alive. How did our father Abraham fall into this situation?

The first step might have been fear for his life. He feared and thus said to Sarah: "Therefore it will happen, when the Egyptians see you, so they will say, 'This is his wife' and they will kill me, but they will let you live" (Genesis 12.12). Would you sacrifice your wife? This is too much. Abraham's fear of death was preceded by the fear of famine. The Bible says: "Now there was a famine in the land, and Abram went down to Egypt to dwell there" (Genesis 12.10). Egypt, with its wealth, symbolizes the reliance on human assistance.

However, a little fox got Abram. This unseen little fox was the weakness of faith in the heart of Abram with respect to God's support during the time of famine. This weakness in faith led him to rely on human assistance instead, and so he went down to Egypt. The devil knew these points of weakness and led him to fear for his life there, as he had feared for his life because of hunger. Fear led him to sacrifice his wife, to lie and say that she was his sister. The little fox that entered into him was able to destroy the vine from all of these directions.

Another little fox—self-righteousness—entered into Job. Job's problem was that he was a blameless, upright man, and he knew himself to be blameless and upright. For this reason he fell into self-righteousness. He was, as the Bible says, "righteous in his own eyes" (Job 32.1). God kept purifying him through temptation until he said: "I have uttered what I did not understand, things too wonderful for me, which I did not know" (Job 42.3). It is very easy for a small weak point to drag us to many problems.

A little fox attacked the righteous Joseph, who boasted about himself. He told his brothers about his dreams, and about those who bowed down to him in the dream. This aroused their jealousy, which was transformed into hatred. "So they hated him even more for his dreams and for his words" (Genesis 37.8). The situation developed until they finally sold him as a slave. Therefore, it was good that the Virgin Mary did not talk about all of the marvels which happened with her, but kept all these things in her heart (Luke 2.51).

The colored tunic was another little fox that caused problems. Jacob made a tunic of many colors for Joseph, the son of his old age. This aroused the jealousy of his brothers. "But when his brothers saw that their father loved him more than all his brothers, they hated him and could not speak civilly to him" (Genesis 37.4). Do you also do this, when submerged in your dealings with people, and show more love to one than the other?

Truly, who would have thought? Who would have thought that this first step in many sins would end in the selling of a brother, the deceit of a father by his children, and Pharaoh's bondage, that all these were a result of a colored tunic and the telling of a young boy's dreams? However, these are the little foxes which destroy the vines. The Bible therefore says: "See then that you walk circumspectly, not as fools but as wise" (Ephesians 5.15). Be very strict, for a sin you thought to be simple may drag you into many problems, whereas strictness will definitely benefit you and teach you vigilance. We will give you an example of this.

Whoever gives importance to decency within his own room will no doubt act decently outside. He who, in his own private room, is too embarrassed to act indecently on account of the spirits of the angels and the saints, will no doubt proceed with decency in front of other people. Decency becomes one of his characteristics. On the other hand, whoever does not care to sit modestly in his private room will not mind sitting the same way in front of other people.

The devil is smart. He does not attack you with a horrific sin all at once. He does not ask you to open a wide door so that he may enter into your life. He only wants to gain your permission to enter through the eye of a needle. You may not notice, and thus permit him entrance. This is sufficient for him. He then keeps widening the opening until he destroys your life. Therefore circumspection is better.

Many are the sins which are able to enter through the eye of a needle. The devil, for example, does not ask you not to pray, only to delay it. If he finds that you are accustomed to prayer, then when you wake up he will say to you, "Wait until you have washed your face." Before you awaken, he has placed in your mind many thoughts to occupy you and make you forget, and many other things to delay you. As for you, do not give him a chance but continue in your prayers, even while you are going to wash your face. Be very careful, then, and avoid the first step that leads you into negligence and laxity, or causes you to sin.

The first step to sin may not be a sin in itself. A sinful relationship may begin as an innocent friendship without any errors. It might be a matter of wasting all your time at home on television and films, which started out with viewing an innocent educational film or soccer match, and ended with study time lost along with missing church meetings. Man, then, must be circumspect and aware.

The first step toward sin differs from one person to another. Luxury was the first step in David's sin, while jealousy was the first step in Cain's and Joseph's brothers' sins. The marriage to foreigners was the first step in Solomon's sin. The sinful external influence was the first step in Adam and Eve's sin and also in the sins at the time of the judges (Judges 3.5–6). The love of women was the first step in the fall of Samson. Fear was the first step in the sins of Peter and Abraham.

Search, then, for the first step in your sins. Be very aware of it. If you fall in the first step, do not continue into the second. Your first step might be that you have gone to Gaza, or to Sodom, or to Gerar. Perhaps a weakness in your personality might cause you to submit to the advice of the wicked. Perhaps the love of God is not in your heart. Perhaps your first step is conceit or excessive self-confidence, which fails to lead you to awareness. Perhaps the first step in your fall is one of the stumbling blocks. Whatever it is, we will try to search for it with you, in order to get rid of it. Let us benefit from the study of how the first step caused the fall of others, especially those who were mighty in the life of the spirit. "How the mighty have fallen, and the warriors of war perish!" (2 Kingdoms 1.27).

By being careful about the first step, you will learn the life of circumspection. Make sure you get rid of the little foxes that destroy the vines. As Saint Syncletica said: "A mouth denied water will not ask for wine. A stomach denied bread will not ask for meat."[2]

---

[2]Amma Syncletica 4, *Sayings of the Desert Fathers.*

CHAPTER 6

Avoid stumbling blocks, and
flee from the sources of sin.

Avoid stumbling blocks, and you will escape from the sources of sin.[1] Avoid all types of stumbling blocks, both those that others put in your way and those you put in other people's way.

Stumbling blocks are dangerous. Literally, stumbling means falling. Whoever makes another stumble is responsible for that person's fall. In this, he carries or shares the guilt of the stumbling person. The Lord Jesus said: "Woe to that man by whom the offence comes" (Matthew 18.7), for "it would be better for him if a millstone were hung around his neck, and he were drowned in the depth of the sea" (Matthew 18.6, Luke 17.2).

The phrase "woe to that man" demonstrates the grave danger of this sin. Saint Paul the Apostle recognized the danger of making others stumble, and wished that none would perish as a result of him. He famously said: "If food [the eating of meat] makes my brother stumble, I will never again eat meat, lest I make my brother stumble" (1 Corinthians 8.13).

Those who cause stumbling will precede other sinners for judgment. Jesus said: "So it will be at the end of this age. The Son of Man will send out His angels, and they will gather out of His kingdom all things that offend, and those who practice lawlessness, and will cast them into the furnace of fire" (Matthew 13.40–42). He will put those who offend before those who practice lawlessness, because they are the cause of many sins.

Causing others to stumble is a dangerous matter, but making the young and naïve to stumble is even more dangerous. This is what the Lord said in the woe which He poured on those "by whom the offence comes" in

[1]This is from a lecture on "Stumbling Blocks" given on Friday, January 23, 1970 in the Great Cathedral, and another lecture with the same name given at the university group meetings, and a third lecture titled, "Run for Your Life," which I gave on Friday, August 25, 1972 in the Great Cathedral.

Matthew 18.6 ("Whoever causes one of these little ones who believe in Me to sin"). "It would be better for him if a millstone were hung around his neck, and he were thrown into the sea, than that he should offend one of these little ones" (Luke 17.2).

This is because the little ones and the naïve fall easily. They believe everything quickly and without discussion. They do not doubt whoever is talking to them. They cannot differentiate between true or false matters. Therefore the guilt of whoever causes them to stumble and the guilt of the person who accepts their words cannot be compared.

This lack of equivalence was found in Eve's stumbling in sin. Eve was very simple, extremely pure. She had no experience with sin. She did not know evil. She did not doubt anyone's word, since she did not know that there were other creatures who lied. The serpent was "more cunning than any beast of the field." It knew how to lie, and how to shape the stumbling with cunning. Therefore, because of the lack of equivalence of the two sides, the serpent was able to make Eve stumble. Eve was, with respect to the serpent, "one of these little ones."

It is the same with the stumbling of children. They are at an age in which they believe everything, imitating every movement and feature. They repeat the expressions they hear without understanding. They are soft dough, which can be shaped with ease. Therefore it is very unlawful for anyone to corrupt them. The stumbling blocks presented to them by their parents, brothers and sisters, neighbors, teachers, relatives, and various types of advertisements are very dangerous. Dealing with children should be done with great care, as with sensitive equipment.

Therefore refrain from making others stumble, especially the naïve and the little ones. Be very cautious not to weary the thoughts of the simple and naïve. Imagine a person who has the simplicity of a child, whose heart has not been opened to sin. When this person comes in contact with a person who is relatively broader in mind and experience, who opens his eyes to stumbling, his thoughts become contaminated. The acquired stains of thought will deprive him of his simplicity, make him doubt, make him stumble and fall. Will the other not bear the judgment of the simple one who stumbled?

Whoever makes a little one stumble is like someone who opens fire against an unarmed person. The words "little ones" are taken then in their relative meaning and not their literal one. That is, whoever is smaller than you in knowledge, in will, in position, and whom you can make fall, is a little one. Truly, this is a very dangerous matter for two reasons: (a) The feeling of guilt over corrupting a righteous person and (b) what would happen if the person who made another fall were to repent, while the one who stumbled did not repent? How will the conscience of the former be at ease, when he can see the one whom he made to fall?

Therefore, take great care not to be a stumbling block for others. It is within your power to repent. You can repent if your heart returns to God. However, the repentance of the person whom you made to stumble is not in your hands. If he continues in the sin into which he fell because of you, and his soul perishes, will your soul be taken in place of his soul? Even if God forgives you through repentance and you are saved, does there not remain in your heart a severe pain, when you see him who perished through you? This is true if you were the cause of the other's stumbling.

If instead the stumbling came to you from others, then my advice to you is as follows: Keep away from stumbling stones and flee from every cause of sin. Remember the angel's saying to Lot: "Flee for your life. . . . Do not stay anywhere in the plain . . . lest you be destroyed" (Genesis 19.17). Remember also how the righteous Joseph fled from stumbling, which insistently urged him. His flight protected him from falling into that sin. In the same way, when the Lord chose our father Abram and wanted to make him a holy nation, He kept him away from stumbling by taking him out from his country and kindred (Genesis 12.1).

Your flight from sin and its stumbling demonstrates your rejection of sin. The flight from stumbling is a virtue, for it demonstrates that the heart does not desire sin from within. Therefore, do not make the mistake of thinking that escaping is weakness. It is not wise for man to be lax with his power, subjecting himself to temptations and entering into wars which may weary him. Therefore, do not call departure from stumbling a weakness, but consider it rather as preservation.

The fathers advised some people about the "substance of sin," saying that whoever is close to the substance of sin will encounter two wars, internal and external, but he who is far from it has one war. Not only do the fathers advise flight from stumbling, but so does the Holy Bible itself, which says: "Flee also youthful lusts" (2 Timothy 2.22), the reason being that "evil company corrupts good habits" (1 Corinthians 15.33). The first psalm is clear when it says: "Blessed is the man who walks not in the counsel of the ungodly, nor stands in the path of sinners, nor sits in the seat of the troublesome" (Psalm 1.1). Such friendship is all stumbling. The Lord Jesus Himself says in the Sermon on the Mount: "If your right hand causes you to sin, cut it off and cast it from you" (Matthew 5.29–30). He repeated these same words on another occasion, in Matthew 18.8–9. This repetition demonstrates the Lord's concern with this point in particular, that is, the avoidance of stumbling blocks. It is not necessary for us to take the Lord's words here in a literal way, but we can explain these verses according to their spiritual meaning.

If a stumbling block comes to you from the person dearest to you, the one as dear to you as your eyes,[2] or even if it comes from the person who helps you the most, who is like your right hand, stay away from him. If the stumbling comes from within you and not from the outside, be firm and keep away from it according to the Lord's commandment, even if the matter leads to your martyrdom.

From where does the stumbling originate? The stumbling could be internal, from within a person. "Out of the evil treasure of his heart he brings forth evil" (Luke 6.45). So from within him there initiate desires and thoughts that disturb him. The stumbling might be from his senses, which gather visions and conversations that weary him. It might be from his desires, pastimes, hobbies, thoughts, and feelings, or from what he has stored in his subconscious of pictures, news, and thoughts. He therefore makes himself stumble. If a desire does not come to him from the outside, he brings it about to himself from within, by his personal conduct. Truly, "a man's foes will be those of his own household" (Matthew 10.36). His household is his heart and thought. If this applies to you, then try to control yourself, as the apostle said, "bringing every thought into captivity to the obedience of Christ" (2 Corinthians 10.5).

[2]*Editor's note:* "As dear as your eyes" is a common Arabic idiom, similar in English to the idiom "the apple of your eye."

There are external stumbling blocks both from humans and from the demons. In the first sin of humanity, both types are found. Eve stumbled because of the devil, and Adam stumbled because of Eve. The devil makes people stumble in a direct way, through other humans and through his servants who "transform themselves into ministers of righteousness" (2 Corinthians 11.15).

There are stumbling blocks from the demons such as revelations and false dreams, for the devil, as the Bible says, can, "transform himself into an angel of light" (2 Corinthians 11.14). In *The Paradise of the Desert Fathers*, it is mentioned that the devil once appeared in the form of an angel to a holy monk, saying, "I am Gabriel the angel, God has sent me to you." The monk answered him very humbly, "Perhaps you were sent to another person and were lost along the way, but I am a sinful person and do not deserve that an angel appear to me." The devil then departed.

The devil can appear as a spirit of a person who has departed. He says, "I am the spirit of so-and-so" (one of your relatives or friends). He tells of things related to this person or his house or his family, to convince the person who sees him. He also appears in the form of one of the saints or anchorites, in order to deceive people.

The devil might appear in a dream. There are many dreams from the devil. Saint Antony knew of a certain incident because, he said, "The demons came and informed me."[3] Therefore my advice to you is, do not believe in dreams, nor be led by them. Some dreams are from God, for example, the dreams of Daniel, Joseph the Righteous, and Joseph the carpenter. But there are dreams from the devil through which he makes people stumble, and there are also revelations from the devil.

Also, do not follow the spirits, for they have deceived many. The Bible says: "Do not believe every spirit, but test the spirits, whether they are of God; because many false prophets have gone out into the world" (1 John 4.1). These are sent from the devil. The false Christs and the Antichrist in the end of the age were referred to by the apostle when he said: "The coming of the lawless one is according to the working of Satan, with all power, signs, and lying wonders, and with all unrighteous deception among those who perish" (2 Thessalonians 2.9).

[3] Antony 12, *Sayings of the Desert Fathers*.

Therefore we must distinguish the thoughts of the devil and his tricks. He fights through thoughts as well as revelations, dreams, and spirits. Do not believe him lest, as the apostle says, "Satan should take advantage of us; for we are not ignorant of his devices" (2 Corinthians 2.11). Therefore do not follow every thought which comes to you, thinking it is from the Spirit of God. Do not say with courage, "The Spirit said to me . . ." Be patient with thoughts, to find out whether they are from God or not, and seek advice. Saint Macarius the Great had a thought to visit the anchorite fathers in the inner desert, and it seemed to be a holy thought. However, Saint Macarius said, "I kept suppressing this thought for three years to see whether or not it was from God."[4] So, do not run after thoughts to carry them out. The devil presented to Jesus three thoughts. He rejected them all and answered him back. You, too, should reject every thought which comes to you from the devil. Remember what was said by your godmother at baptism: "I renounce you, O Satan, with all your evil thoughts . . . and all your soldiers . . . and all the rest of your hypocrisies." Reject every thought which neither advances you spiritually nor builds you up, whether it comes to you from the devil or from people.

Flee from the stumbling blocks of the devil in the same way as from the stumbling blocks of people. These stumbling blocks have a general type which covers all of society, and a specific type for you personally. The people with whom you associate, whether they are enemies or friends, can be stumbling stones for you and others.

The stumbling might come from your dearest relatives and loved ones. The majority of youth who become corrupt do so through the corruption of their very dear friends, who influence them. The stumbling came to Samson from Delilah, the person whom his heart loved most. The stumbling came to King Ahab from his wife Jezebel. We will not forget how the stumbling came to our father Adam from Eve. Stumbling comes to many children at home from their parents. If the home is not religious, then they may hear abusive language and quarrelsome words. They take from their parents all of the wrong characteristics and habits.

The stumbling came to Jacob, the father of fathers, from his mother Rebekah. She was the one who made him disguise himself in his brother

[4]Macarius the Great, *Bustān al-Ruhbān (Paradise of the Fathers*, Arabic).

Esau's clothes and deceive his father Isaac, in order to receive the blessing from him. She was the one who made the plan and prepared everything. When Jacob was worried that this deception might be discovered, he said: "I shall bring a curse on myself and not a blessing." His mother said to him: "Your curse be on me, my son; only obey my voice. . . ." (Genesis 27.12–13). It is very easy for stumbling to come to a daughter from her mother. A mother can destroy the life of her daughter after her marriage by intruding, and imposing her opinion on her and her husband.

The stumbling came to Lord Jesus from His disciple Peter, and so He rebuked him. This stumbling was in the form of wrong advice. When the Lord was explaining to His disciples that it was necessary for Him to go to Jerusalem "and suffer many things from the elders and chief priests and scribes, and be killed, and be raised again the third day," Peter did not like the idea of his great Teacher surrendering Himself. "Then Peter took Him aside" and said to Him with an erroneous love: "Far be it from You, Lord; this shall not happen to You!" But the Lord turned to him and said: "Get behind Me, Satan! You are an offence to Me" (Matthew 16.21–23). In this way the Lord rejected this stumbling from His disciple and friend.

You must reject the stumbling that comes to you from your loved ones, even if it is from your closest relative. The Lord Jesus said: "A man's enemies will be those of his own household. He who loves father or mother more than Me is not worthy of Me. And he who loves son or daughter more than Me is not worthy of Me" (Matthew 10.36–37). Love is offered first to God, and from His love proceeds all other love. Obedience is rendered first to God, and from this obedience proceeds all other obedience. The Bible said about the obedience of parents: "Children, obey your parents in the Lord, for this is right" (Ephesians 6.1). It is thus an essential obedience, but "in the Lord."

Jonathan did not obey his father Saul in his persecution of David but rather rebuked him, saying: "Why then do you sin against innocent blood, to put David to death without cause?" (1 Kingdoms 19.5). King Saul was a cause of stumbling to his son Jonathan, but Jonathan overcame this stumbling. In the same way King Solomon, even though he had great respect for his mother Bathsheba, did not obey her in her intercession for Adonijah, his brother (3 Kingdoms 2.19–23).

The limit of obedience precludes stumbling. From your association with people and your experiences in life, you can realize the sources of stumbling for you. Benefit, then, from this experience by surrounding yourself with a pure atmosphere as much as you can. Those whom you cannot avoid physically, avoid with respect to your thoughts and direction of life. As the Bible says: "Have no fellowship with the unfruitful works of darkness, but rather expose them" (Ephesians 5.11). If you cannot reprove it, then at least do not walk in its current, nor submit to the stumbling.

Take care that you yourself do not become a stumbling block for others. If you do, then you will be responsible before your conscience and before God, and perhaps before people, as the cause of someone else's fall.

Regarding the responsibility for being a stumbling block to others, a youth was tripped up by a young lady and fell into lust. What is her responsibility? If this beautiful young lady was well behaved, and her beauty alone was the cause of the stumbling of this youth, then she would not be blamed at all, and there is no responsibility on her part in this stumbling.

There are female saints whose beauty caused some people to stumble. Probably the most famous example of this is Saint Justina,[5] who was very beautiful. A man fell in love with her, and since he could not possess her, he used magic to try to reach her. The mere mention of her name drove out the demons utilized in the magic. Even Cyprian the magician believed because of this, and he became one of the saints of the Church. Can we say that Saint Justina bore a responsibility for the stumbling? Definitely not. The responsibility is completely upon whoever desired her, and the stumbling was caused by his desire.

In the same way we can talk about Saint Sarah, the wife of our father Abraham. She was very beautiful. Her beauty attracted the kings, and even Pharaoh took her to his palace once (Genesis 12.14–15). Abimelech the king of Gerar took her another time (Genesis 20.2). She bore no blame in either occasion. Naturally, she was not to blame for being beautiful, but rather the blame lies with whoever desires.

---

[5] *Editor's note:* See the Coptic *Synaxarion, Tut* 21; also see Theofried Baumeister, "Cyprian the Magician," *The Coptic Encyclopedia* 2, (1991 edition) http://ccdl.libraries.claremont.edu/cdm/singleitem/collection/cce/id/550/rec/1

When, then, is a woman responsible for the stumbling? When she means to allure the man and attract him to herself in a provocative way; or if the man falls because of her manners, speech, or allurements; or if, in her make-up or clothing, she was actually a cause of stumbling to the normal person. In this way the young lady would be responsible for making the youth's heart fill with desires that make him commit the sin, either through his own senses or physically. He stumbles when she occupies his thought. As a result, he neglects his responsibilities and loses his spirituality.

However, if all of the above is caused by the young lady's natural beauty, then she is not to blame. We say this so that pure young ladies do not doubt themselves and fall into delusions or the complex of blame because of their beauty. What has been said about the woman in this example can also be said about the man.

What, then, is the offence of these people? What was Joseph the Righteous' offence, in that Potiphar's wife desired him because he was handsome? Can we say that he made her stumble? Or that his conscience troubled him at her fall into desire because of him? Certainly not. With the same reasoning, what is the offence of the two angels whom the people of Sodom coveted? Angels do not have bodies and, in addition, they had the purity of angels. The stumbling here is in the corrupt heart that desired. A similar argument can be made about Zechariah the young monk, whose story was told in the *Paradise of the Fathers*. He was very handsome, and many people stumbled because of that. He was compelled to go down to the salt lake and disfigure his body and his looks, to avoid the stumbling caused by other people's errors.

You cannot escape the responsibility of your error by unjustly blaming it on someone else, saying that he made you stumble in spite of your righteousness. The words of the Lord Jesus about the simple eye are very beautiful. He said: "If therefore your eye is good, your whole body will be full of light. But if your eye is bad, your whole body will be full of darkness" (Matthew 6.22–23). Many stumble because their eyes are not simple. Sin is in their eyes, and therefore everything can arouse sin within them. I wish then that every person would train himself to have this simple eye.

Just as we talked about the scope of the young lady's responsibility in the stumbling of the youth, we can say there is also a responsibility for a youth who causes a young lady to stumble. She may stumble through his use of a lot of praise and sweet words, and the affection he shows her with abnormally increased kindness. He makes her stumble through his great persistence toward her, pursuing her intensely until she weakens, feels obligated, and responds to him. He also makes her stumble through the promises he makes to her and his repeated assurances. She believes him. In this way he keeps her in suspense and wearies her. However, if she stumbles just because of his personality, then he bears no blame.

As for you, then, keep away from both of these types of stumbling. First, avoid the stumbling that actually arouses, which contains a type of seduction or enticement, or which makes you responsible for making others fall. Try also, as much as you can, to keep your eye simple. Second, avoid even the natural, innocent opportunities that cause you to stumble because of your weakness. Say to yourself humbly, "I do not want to search for where to place the responsibility, on someone else or on me. Rather, I will keep away in order not to fall, even if it is because of my weakness, or even if someone else is completely innocent, as the wild beast was innocent of the blood of the son of Jacob, or as the son of Jacob was innocent of the sin of Potiphar's wife."

We can analyze the remaining types of stumbling blocks in similar fashion. By the other stumbling blocks, we mean those that are outside the sphere of sexual matters. A person misunderstands you, although your words are very clear and do not mean at all what he understood. Someone may say to you, "You are referring to me with these words," whereas you are completely innocent and do not mean him. It is his own thinking, doubting, and feeling that are wrong.

In all of this, we say that the stumbling does not come from the speaker, but is the responsibility of the one with wrong understanding. In spite of this, you are obliged for the sake of love to clarify your correct intention, and to explain what was obscure to another person's understanding. You should also be aware of times when your speech is not correctly understood. Keep away from stumbling also. Be very careful in speech and conduct, especially when there are suspicious people around who understand your words in their own personal way. There is a type of person who will say regularly, "I have been thrown into confusion by people's conduct. I have been thrown into confusion by their words." He means that he stumbled because of them and their words. This may be true or perhaps exaggerated. He may have inner complexities, or the complexity may actually reside in others' conduct. The Lord Jesus said: "Offences must come" (Matthew 18.8). This is because we do not live in an ideal world, but in a world which is full of stumbling blocks. It contains wheat and also tares. The tares will remain with the wheat until the day of harvest (Matthew 13.30). What is our position then?

We must not search for the person who is responsible for the stumbling, but instead search for salvation from it. Salvation is in escaping the stumbling blocks, not in examining who is responsible for them. This examination could very easily make us fall into other errors. However, it is not admissible to say that we are thrown into confusion by the stumbling blocks of other people.

It is not right for stumbling blocks to make us lose our inner purity, nor is it right for stumbling blocks to make us lose the peace in our hearts. We are not in heaven but on earth, and on earth there must be errors. What is important, then, is to flee from these errors. We will not be delivered from them by grumbling and complaining, and we will not be rescued from them if we are thrown into confusion by them. However, we will be rescued from stumbling blocks by purity of heart, and by not responding to them, and at the same time we will not cause others to stumble.

If we are strong from within, then stumbling blocks will not harm us in any way. We will be like the house which was built on the rock, upon which the rain descended and the winds blew, but did not harm it (Matthew 7.25). The responsibility is not completely, in every situation, on the person who causes the stumbling blocks.

There are temptations from the other person; if it were not for him, the fall would not have occurred. The alcohol (methylated spirits) might say, "The matchstick made me burn, and I burned." But I say, if the alcohol were not a flammable substance, then the matchstick could not make it burn. The same matchstick does not affect the cup of water, for if it comes close to the water, it goes out. Anyway, whether you are water or alcohol, escaping is safer. Escaping at least involves meekness, and meekness saves many people. Saint Antony saw the trap of the devil set up, and so he cried, "O Lord, who can escape from it?"[6] The voice came to him, saying: "The humble escape

[6] Antony 7, *Sayings of the Desert Fathers.*

from it." Stumbling is a first step; if you fall into it, then do not complete the rest of the steps.

The presence of stumbling blocks is not an excuse for you, nor is it a justification for your errors. For God placed in you His Holy Spirit and gave you power to resist. If you responded to the stumbling blocks, then you lost this divine power and did not use it. Victory is possible. Remember Joseph the Righteous, who was stronger than the stumbling blocks and was victorious in spite of the severity of the war to which he was subjected. The stumbling is a mere offer; if it does not meet with acceptance, it passes by.

There are different types of stumbling. Many concentrate on talking about stumbling in sexual matters. It is truly important and dangerous, but it is not everything. The stumbling in this field comes in many ways, from sexual stimulation by way of enticement, which some individuals use; by way of different amusement and pleasure aids, with offending pictures, foolish songs, and sexual jokes; or by way of futile stories which are heard or read, and also by films. The stumbling comes through association with bad company, and it also comes from within the soul.

As for you, avoid all stumbling blocks and control your senses. Know that "the senses are the door to thinking." As Saint Isaac said: "What you see and hear brings wrong thoughts to you, and becomes a stumbling to you."[7] Thought then gives birth to desire, and desire leads to a physical sin. But in case you ask, "What should I do? Should I close my eyes, when the stumbling is in every place? It is inevitable that I see and hear," I say to you that you are not responsible for the first look, as long as it comes accidentally.

However, you are responsible for the second look and its promptings. If the offending view which you see arouses or delights you, and you look at it again with your free will, then you have sinned here, whether it is a live picture or a printed one, because you look at it with your free will. If the first look is with your desire and will, then you are responsible for it also.

We can say the same things about hearing bad things. Flee from them. What if you cannot? If you are required to hear it, then do not give it your attention or thought. Let it be a sound that passes by. Do not let it enter into the depth of your heart, do not think about it, do not repeat it in your mind, and do not comment on it.

[7]Isaac of Nineveh, *Mystical Treatises* LXXIX.545.9.

As much as you can, flee from offending encounters. If you are compelled to have them, make them as short as possible. Do not stay alone with a person whom the devil uses to combat you, and you weaken from within in his presence. Try during such encounters to raise your heart to God in prayer. Do not remain in the encounter with all of your heart and affections.

This is a short word about sexual stumbling, for it is a long topic and books have been written about it. This is not the place for it. We would like to say here, however, that not all of the stumbling blocks are sexual.

There are stumbling blocks of thought, for example, and they are of different kinds. Among them are wrong philosophies. When you read them, they confuse your thoughts and bring doubts to you, if you are reading without the previous preparation of true, sound thought. You must be careful of what you read.

There are heretical books that attack religion. There are many heretics. There is a reply to everything they write, but they form a stumbling block with regards to those who have not studied or lack knowledge. This causes them to doubt, which is more dangerous to them than the sins of the flesh from which they can easily be delivered.

Those who mislead in religious thought are many and cause stumbling. Jeroboam the son of Nebat was a stumbling to Israel, and made him sin and digress from God's worship (3 Kingdoms 15.1). He was one who misled the people before the coming of Christ. Judas of Galilee rose up in the days of the census and drew away many people after him (Acts 5.36–37). Also in the time of Christ the scribes, Pharisees, Sadducees, and the like were misleading the people. They were great stumbling blocks. They held the keys of knowledge, but they did not enter and did not let anyone else enter who desired to do so. They made the people stumble through their teachings.

One of the mental stumbling blocks is inaccurate doctrinal thought. Such thoughts contain an innovation or heresy, or a theological idea which has not been handed to us by the holy fathers, or which does not agree with the settled doctrine of the Church. These thoughts make people stumble and arouse doubt within them. Do not then accept these thoughts, as the apostles said (Galatians 1.7–8; 3 John 10.11).

Flee from these stumbling blocks of thought, for you are in the age of repentance. You are a person who is searching for salvation. What do you have to do with these thoughts which confuse your intellect and bring you into fields of argument or perhaps into disputes, which do not agree with your endeavor of purity of heart through repentance? I would suggest leaving it to the specialists to reply. Be devoted to spiritual books, for the more you read of them the more your love of God will increase, and you will feel your heart come closer to Him.

Similarly, flee from every other stumbling of thought, such as the ones which make you offend people and judge them. There are individuals who, when troubled by thoughts or news of judgment, pour these completely into the ears of others; they do not care whether or not the news makes them stumble or enters into their hearts, making them doubt, judge, or belittle people, or love them less. As for you, flee all of this and try to keep your love for everyone. Keep away from those who distort people's image in your sight, in order to preserve your purity of thought.

There are stumbling blocks from those who disclose their secrets to people. They cannot keep a secret; they reveal even their private secrets and sins to people, so the listener stumbles by hearing them. He also stumbles on account of the names which are mentioned in these stories, and he might fall into sin because of this. Even though the Church is very careful in making confession secret, people still continue to tell others, and their stories become stumbling blocks.

Another stumbling of thought is wrong and harmful advice. An example of this is the counsel of Ahithophel. Ahithophel was the advisor of David. He left him and joined Absalom's conspiracy, so that he could offer him advice with which to destroy David, the Lord's anointed, and all who were with him. David went to pray, saying: "O Lord, my God, defeat the counsel of Ahithophel" (2 Kingdoms 15.31). Undoubtedly, Ahithophel's advice was a stumbling to Absalom and an encouragement to him in the revolt against his father David. The Lord, however, heard David's prayer and destroyed Ahithophel's counsel.

Another example similar to Ahithophel's offensive counsel is Balaam's counsel to Balak (Numbers 22). The Bible gave it the name "the error of Balaam" (Jude 11). The book of Revelation says of Balaam that he "taught Balak to put a stumbling block before the children of Israel, to eat things sacrificed to idols, and to commit sexual immorality" (Revelation 2.14). This was so that God's wrath would come upon them, and so that His enemy would overcome them. Undoubtedly it was an evil and offensive counsel.

Choose your counselors, then, and keep away from every offensive counsel. Whether it comes from those of whom you seek advice or from those who voluntarily advise you in your life, remember that, although they may seem to sympathize with you, their sympathy is not spiritual.

Bad examples cause stumbling to some. Do not let this matter offend you, no matter how high in stature the person whose conduct causes you to stumble. Do not let it change any of your principles, nor your love of God and the Church. Remember that it was said about Elijah the great prophet: "Elijah was a man with a nature like ours" (James 5.17). Let your firm example be found in the Lord Jesus and the lives of the saints. As for other people's errors, do not let them make you stumble, no matter how great those people are. Good is good, no matter how people may choose to avoid it. The Holy Bible mentions to us the sins of the prophets, so that we may know that man is man with his weaknesses, in any position whatsoever. As for the specific stumbling blocks in your life, examine them, know their causes, and keep away from them. For repentance does not agree with stumbling blocks.

Search for the reasons which make you stumble and lead you to sin. What are they? Are they close to you? How can you avoid them? Are they within you, or do they come to you from others? Keep away from these stumbling blocks as much as you can, so that they do not influence you. Flee from friends who drag you down and make you lose your spirituality. Repeat regularly what we say in the Lord's Prayer, "Lead us not into temptation, but deliver us from evil."

Do not be tolerant of sin.[8] Man falls many times into sin because of tolerance. How is this? It is known that sin starts with an external war that wants to enter and dominate. Through tolerance, the external war is transferred to the inside of the heart. How does this development occur? What is the role of tolerance in this? The sin from the outside might be a stimulating fantasy, a picture in a book, a word spoken by someone, or anything which could be desired or owned. Then man becomes tolerant of it with his senses,

[8]I delivered a lecture on this in the Great Cathedral on Friday, October 28, 1977.

with his hearing or viewing, although the thought comes to him weakened at first and can be easily cast out.

However, the tolerated thought goes down to the heart and is transformed into a feeling. If a man awakens to himself, he can get rid of this feeling, completely sure that this wrong feeling keeps him away from the love of God and leads him to sin. This wrong feeling in itself is a sin; it is a lack of inner purity and defiles the heart.

However, tolerance of feelings transforms them into stimulation or desire. Here, the person begins to submit to the thought and enter into an inner struggle between his desire and his conscience. The nature of desire is to dominate. You can get rid of it, if you cast it out firmly. But through tolerance the desire or stimulation begins to spread, to the extent that this inner war now covers man's thought, heart, and senses, and perhaps his body also.

If you tolerate desire, the desire tries to express itself practically; that is, it tries to satisfy itself in a practical way. If a man tolerates this, the action will be carried out. The sin then becomes complete. Furthermore, sin does not stop there, but wants to be repeated. So, man either repents after his fall, or his sin is repeated.

However, he sometimes tolerates sinning so that it is transformed into a habit or a characteristic. Thus, he submits to its domination and becomes enslaved to it. He does it sometimes against his will and cannot control himself. An example is a person who becomes angry spontaneously or talks without control of himself. Whoever commits fornication, accumulates money, or mocks others does that without examining himself and controlling what he does.

The righteous, instead, are firm. They are not tolerant with themselves. They closely observe every thought and feeling. They firmly observe their senses, their conduct, and every word that proceeds from their mouths. Their hearts are "an enclosed garden, a sealed fountain" (Song of Songs 4.12). Their hearts, thoughts, and senses have fortified doors that are very well guarded; no one can slip through them, for the observation of the conscience is vigilant in awareness and grace protects it. This righteous, fortified person, who is vigilant in the salvation of his soul, sings for it and sings for the Lord's protection of him, saying: "Praise the Lord, O Jerusalem ... for He has strengthened the bars of your gates; He blesses your children within you; He who grants your borders peace" (Psalm 147.1–2). Are you like this? Or are you tolerant in protecting yourself? Are you meticulous in closing the doors, or do you open them from time to time, thinking that the enemy cannot destroy your fortification?

CHAPTER 7

Do not be tolerant with sin.

Do not be tolerant with sin, relying on your strength and confident that the devil cannot overcome you, at least in this or that particular point. But take a lesson from the fallings of the saints and prophets. Know that sin has "cast down many, and all who were slain by her were strong men" (Proverbs 7.26). Whoever is not careful and does not keep away from stumbling blocks, and does not flee for his life, nor ask for God's help day and night, can fall just like the many strong men have fallen before him. Know that if you are tolerant with sin, it may drag you down, without you feeling it, step by step into falling and to destruction.

Contemplate any dangerous results which befall you whenever you are tolerant of sin. Whenever you are tolerant of sin your awareness decreases, your will weakens, and your love of God decreases. You then change, internally and externally. You are in the fullness of your strength at the beginning of the spiritual war, and in the fullness of the work of grace within you. But every time you are tolerant of sin your strength weakens, your resistance decreases, the influence of sin on you grows, and its dominance over your thoughts, feelings, and will increases. Then, the thought of sin has gained a foothold within you. Whenever you try to get out of its sphere and out of its domain, you find difficulties and enter into a struggle that you could have overcome right at the beginning.

With your tolerance, you find an enemy within you who resists you and presses upon you. With the continuation of tolerance, you become exhausted and you submit. A steel rod in a magnetic field can only be attracted to the magnet.

In your tolerance of sin, you grieve the Spirit who lives in you. You also quench the fervor of the Spirit in you (1 Thessalonians 5.19; Ephesians 4.30), and you surrender the grace given to you. With this tolerance of sin, you reject your spiritual weapon, betray the Lord, and open the door to His enemies and those who resist Him. You betray God's company and enter into the company of sin, perhaps because of negligence and slackness. Your firmness begins to shake from within. Whoever is strong cannot tolerate sin.

Your tolerance of sin means that your ideals have begun to shake. You have begun a steep descent, leaving behind God's image and likeness (Genesis 1.26), and you have agreed to negotiate with the devil and have given him a place within you. The devil then sees that you are of the type who will respond and submit to him, not the type who resists intensely and rejects his suggestions, no matter what they are.

The devil tests you, to know your type. Are you easy or difficult? Do you reject his every suggestion with firmness and without discussion? Do you accept, or negotiate? Are you tolerant with him, meeting him halfway along the path? He presents to you his thoughts and tricks. If you are tolerant, he will present them again. If you are still tolerant and become slack, he will then know your nature and will treat you according to this experience.

The demons will no longer respect you nor fear you, because of your tolerance of them. There are saints whom the demons fear and revere. There was a saint to whom the devil came to fight. The saint tied him outside the cell. A second and a third one came, and he tied them outside also. They kept screaming until he ordered them, "Go, and be ashamed." Saint Isidore, the priest of the cells, was told by the demons: "Is it not enough for you that we cannot pass by your cell, nor by the cell which is next to it? We had one brother in the desert, but you have let him attack us night and day with his prayers." The demons used to fear Saint Macarius the Great, saying, "Woe to us from you, O Macarius." The demons screamed when he entered into the island of Philae, to which he was banished by the Arians.[1]

The devil fears God's true children, who defeat him. If he sees that you accept his thoughts, tolerate him, open your doors to him, and betray the Lord because of him, then you will no longer enjoy respect in his sight, for he will see that you are neither in God's image, which he fears, nor the temple of the Holy Spirit, before whom he trembles. Therefore, the demons will play games with you; each one will hand you over to another in order to make fun of you, just like a ball in a playing field as the players pass it among

[1] Socrates, *Ecclesiastical History* IV.24.

them. Each one of them will kick it in a certain direction. Be cautious, then, and do not be a ball in the playing field.

Whoever is tolerant once will become accustomed to tolerance and continue in it. Solomon was tolerant with himself in breaking God's commandment prohibiting marriage to foreigners, and so he married Pharaoh's daughter (3 Kingdoms 9.16). The matter became easy to him, and so he continued in it. "King Solomon loved many foreign women, as well as the daughter of Pharaoh: women of the Moabites, Ammonites, Edomites, Sidonians, and Hittites, from the nations of whom the Lord had said to the children of Israel, you shall not intermarry with them, nor they with you. For surely they will turn away your hearts after their gods" (3 Kingdoms 11.1–2).

When the devil saw Solomon's tolerance, he pushed him to more dangerous things. Since he was tolerant with himself and broke the commandment by marrying these women, his tolerance increased, and he built high places for these women to worship their gods. His tolerance led him to build a high place for Chemosh, the god of the Moabites, and another for Molech, the god of the Ammonites. So, he inclined his heart toward other gods (3 Kingdoms 11.1–9). The devil might have feared Solomon at the beginning, because he was the wisest person on earth. So, when he saw him tolerating sin, he pushed him in his tolerance to the farthest limit that one can imagine.

This was clear in Solomon's tolerance of the love of women. Solomon allowed himself to be tolerant in his great number of wives. The devil did not stop him at a reasonable limit, but allowed the tolerance to continue with him until he had "seven hundred princesses and three hundred concubines" (3 Kingdoms 11.1). If tolerance can force a wise person to this level, what then can be said about ordinary people?

Therefore never be tolerant, no matter how simple the sin may seem. Merely saying that it is a simple sin will lead you to tolerance. Do not say that this is a trivial matter that does not trouble the conscience, nor that this is not a sin. Do not say, "This conduct will not cause me to stumble, and will not leave any effect in me." Many have fallen because of lack of precision. Whoever is not cautious with the small sins can fall into the great ones. Every sin is a rebellion against God and a separation from Him. It is also a defilement, a falling, and a weakness.

Do not think that the sins which destroy man are merely the great ones such as fornication, blasphemy, murder, and stealing, for the Lord said: "Whoever says, 'You fool!' shall be in danger of hell fire;" "Whoever says to his brother, 'Raca!' shall be in danger of the council" (Matthew 5.22). Many are tolerant with words, whereas the Bible considers sinful words as defilement and says: "What comes out of the mouth, this defiles a man" (Matthew 15.11). Speaking about caution with respect to the tongue and the lack of tolerance for errors of speech, Saint James the Apostle advises us to be cautious with our tongue and not to tolerate errors of speech, saying: "If anyone among you thinks he is religious, and does not bridle his tongue but deceives his own heart, this one's religion is useless" (James 1.26). Therefore, do not be cautious only of fornication, stealing, and murder, since one word might be the cause of your judgment. The Bible says: "By your words you will be justified, and by your words you will be condemned" (Matthew 12.37).

"For every idle word men may speak, they will give account of it in the day of judgment" (Matthew 12.36). The saints did not understand this phrase "the idle word" to mean an evil word, such as lying, abuse, blasphemy, and judging. They understood the idle word as any word that is not beneficial, and not for building—any word that does not build the soul of the listener, nor build up the kingdom. Therefore, they kept silent and did not talk except with consideration, when they saw that the words were for building up. Undoubtedly, whoever is not tolerant with himself when speaking a word that is not for building up will naturally not be tolerant with himself in speaking an evil word.

Whoever is not tolerant with his words will not be tolerant in actions. The precision to which he becomes accustomed includes his whole life and his every behavior, for he knows that every action leads him to the Judgment, no matter how simple it may be. The backward look taken by Lot's wife changed her into a pillar of salt (Genesis 19.26). The lie spoken by Ananias and Sapphira made them fall down dead immediately, without repentance (Acts 5.1–10). Therefore, do not divide sin into great and small in order to allow yourself to be tolerant of the small, but be strict in everything. Know that tolerance with the small thing makes it grow. The Lord Jesus did not prohibit us from fornication only, but from the lustful look as well. He did not ask us only to persevere with whoever compels us to go one mile, but to persevere with him in the second mile also (Matthew 5.28, 41).

Whoever is tolerant in the first step will fall into the second. Whoever is tolerant in the second will fall into the third, and he will continue in this way without limit. The devil has been described as a "weaver of ropes." He weaves a rope to catch us, and he is very patient. He does not mind preparing a trick over the course of ten years, to make you fall into one sin. Be cautious of him and never be tolerant with him.

The devil blames you if you are strict in your conduct and not tolerant. He describes you as radical or deluded, as one who complicates matters. Do not listen to him. Remain firm in your spirituality, and do not let these accusations infuriate you. Be like Saint Papnoute the bishop, of whom a woman once said, when she saw his great precision, "This old man is deluded." The saint answered her, "Do you know, O woman, how many years I spent in the desert in order to possess this delusion? For I have spent fifty years seeking to possess it, and should I lose it for your sake in one instant?" He then left his seat as a bishop and departed, because he considered the salvation of his soul more important. Know that sin is the breaking of God's commandment, and remoteness from His love.

Therefore, in your tolerance, you are not only tolerant with yourself, but are tolerant with God's rights. Do not be tolerant with yourself in committing sin. If you do sin, do not be tolerant in punishing yourself for this sin. Tolerance in disciplining the self for its falls, leads to carelessness, lack of fear, and contempt of God's commandments. These make it easy to commit a sin again, relying on God to be loving and forgiving, for "He did not deal with us according to our sins, nor reward us according to our transgressions" (Psalm 102.10).

Do not justify yourself, then, and do not forgive sin with ease. Know that when sin does not receive its due punishment, and when the soul is not contrite and humbled by it, then there is nothing easier than for man to return to it. Do not say that this sin I committed in the past has passed and ended, and I have received absolution and forgiveness for it. No, rebuke yourself regularly. Remember that David the Prophet drenched his couch with tears for long periods, even after he heard the verdict of forgiveness from God through Nathan. In spite of this forgiveness, his tears became his drink, day and night. He was belittled in his eyes and kept rebuking himself for a long time, saying his whole life: "My sin is ever before me" (Psalm 50). You should do likewise, and impose punishments on your sins. Be fervent in spirit (Romans 12.11). Do the work of the Lord with all eagerness and every aspiration, and do not be tolerant in this, for it has been said: "Cursed is he who does the work of the Lord deceitfully" (Jeremiah 48.10).

Be like the shepherd who is vigilant over his sheep, who guards the watches of the night, remaining awake and not being tolerant with himself in sleeping for an instant. Be fervent in your worship. If you find yourself tired, or lacking the desire to pray, do not be tolerant with yourself and sleep without praying, lest by this tolerance you become accustomed to carelessness and laxity. Rather, as Saint Isaac the Syrian said: "If you are tempted to neglect your prayers before sleeping, do not submit, but force yourself to pray at night and increase the psalms."[2] In the same way, be firm in your fasting. If you are tolerant in the time of abstaining, you will also be tolerant in the type and amount of food, and then you will be lax in controlling yourself. This lack of control will accompany you in every detail of your spiritual life. Be alert. Practice the salvation of your soul with every caution, being vigilant regularly, lest He, coming suddenly, should find you sleeping (Mark 13.36).

Do not sleep, or if you do sleep, beware the late awakening. Samson remained tolerant of his spirituality, neglecting his salvation for a long time. When did he awake? It was a late awakening, after he had lost his vow and his power, and his enemies had captured him. Lot was the same. When did he awaken? He awoke very late, after he had lost everything in the burning of Sodom. Many fell because they were tolerant of spiritual negligence, and they did not awaken to themselves until it was late, after the sin was established within them. Do not be like these people. As a person who is honest about his spiritual life, do not be tolerant of sin.

[2]Isaac the Syrian, *Ascetical Homilies*.

CHAPTER 8

Reassess your behavior and stay away from sins.

Reassess your behavior and beware of those disguised as lambs.[1] Because sin does not like to reveal itself, it disguises itself. It reveals itself to the careless who love it. However, to the children of God it always disguises itself, so that they will not be aware of it and avoid it. Nothing hinders it from disguising itself in the form of a virtue, or hiding behind any kind name which is not exposed. These sins conform to the Lord's saying: "Who come to you in sheep's clothing, but inwardly they are ravenous wolves" (Matthew 7.15).

As false teachers are misleading, so are the sins which mislead man and exploit his simplicity. The devil himself comes in sheep's clothing. As the apostle says: "Satan himself transforms himself into an angel of light. . . . His ministers transform themselves into ministers of righteousness" (2 Corinthians 11.14–15). This happens in order to achieve the deception, and so the fall is accomplished. For this reason the children of God are always in need of wisdom and discernment, in order to discern between the Lord's path and the devil's path, and to discern the Lord's will from other wrong wills.

Many people walk in the wrong path as a result of ignorance and lack of knowledge, and as a result of the deception of the demons. Therefore, the priest in the Divine Liturgy asks for forgiveness and reconciliation from God, saying: "On behalf of my sins and the ignorance of your people."[2] Why do we call them ignorant? Because the Bible says: "There is a way which seems right to a man, but its end is the way of death." This verse was mentioned in the book of Proverbs (14.12). It was repeated, because of its

[1]This is from a lecture that I delivered at the beginning of the sixties, in Damanhour [a town in the Nile Delta].

[2]*Editor's note:* From the prayer of the priest when he selects the lamb (the bread) in the offertory during the Coptic Orthodox Divine Liturgy.

importance, another time in the same book with the same wording (Proverbs 16.25). Therefore man can be deceived. The Lord said: "My people are destroyed for lack of knowledge" (Hosea 4.6). Therefore, Solomon the Wise also advised: "Lean not on your own understanding" (Proverbs 3.5). In this way we see David the Prophet crying out in his psalms and saying: "Show me Your ways, O Lord; teach me Your paths" (Psalm 24.4). If the great prophet, upon whom the Spirit of God descended, says this, then what shall we say? Not all people are wise, and the wise are not wise in everything. "The wise man's eyes are in his head, but the fool walks in darkness" (Ecclesiastes 2.14). We do not use wisdom. So, what should we do then?

We should seek advice, so that we are not deceived by the sheep's clothing. The Bible teaches: "The way of a fool is right in his own eyes, but he who heeds counsel is wise" (Proverbs 12.15). We should not listen to advice from every person, for the advice of Balaam was a deception (Jude 11). Ahithophel's advice also was not according to God's will. We can say that not every counsel comes from God, for as divine inspiration said: "O My people! Those who lead you cause you to err" (Isaiah 3.12).

There are many who perished as a result of wrong advice. This deceiving advice wore the sheep's clothing, and with it destroyed its friends. As the Bible says: "If the blind leads the blind, both will fall into a ditch" (Matthew 15.14). We saw how Rehoboam was lost as a result of the wrong advice (3 Kingdoms 12.10). The Lord rebuked the scribes and Pharisees for their wrong advice and called them "blind guides" (Matthew 23.13–16).

These, of course, are not the saintly advisors of whom the Bible says: "Remember those who rule over you, who have spoken the word of God to you, whose faith follow, considering the outcome of their conduct" (Hebrews 13.7), "for they watch out for your souls, as those who must give account" (Hebrews 13.17). Therefore, we are in need of great discernment to differentiate between correct and wrong advice, between the spirit of wisdom and the spirit of deception. As the apostle said: "Test the spirits, whether they are of God" (1 John 4.1). Whoever clings to the Spirit of God within him, will be advised by the Spirit. Isaiah the Prophet describes the Spirit of the Lord as "the Spirit of wisdom and understanding, the Spirit of counsel" (Isaiah 11.2).

We pray then that the Lord may rescue us from every deception of the demons, and from sins which are disguised in the attire of the virtues to deceive us. If anyone falls into this deception of the demons, humility will lift him up from his fall when he realizes it, or when, upon being advised by a loyal friend or a wise advisor, he then confesses his error and does not repeat it. In this way, he gains knowledge and repentance. However, it is difficult for those who are too proud of their knowledge and conduct to repent.

This is because the person who is righteous in his own eyes defends his sins, calling them something else in order not to be ashamed. This is because if he confesses it is a sin, then he must admit that he is guilty, a fact which his pride cannot accept. There is no objection, then, to clothing it in sheep's clothing and calling it by another, more acceptable name which is not embarrassing to him, so that he is not exposed before other people. He also deceives himself so that he is not exposed before himself, if possible.

Those who cover their sin with sheep's clothing will not repent. How can they repent of it and leave it, when they do not count it as sin, nor admit that it is a sin? Instead, they call it a virtue, by which they defend their conduct and hence continue in it. It becomes a habit, a firm program in their lives that they do not change, because they call sin by a false name and cover it so that it does not show.

With this naming and covering, a person's principles and standards are shaken. The sin that is revealed and known is easy to resist and avoid. It troubles the good conscience. Even if man falls into it, it is easy for him to leave it. Therefore the devil, who is wise in evil, works at changing standards at their roots.

By giving sin another name, the devil enters into a war of naming with man. The devil's deception increases if he can make of this naming a widespread misunderstanding among the people. This is more dangerous when it is spread among many people who repeat it unconsciously. This naming is an intentional deception of the devil and the instigators of evil. For the ordinary person, sin can be due to ignorance, and thus he needs spiritual awareness. Or, sin can be due to following leadership and guidance without depth. Then he needs a strengthening of personality, whether in thought or conduct, so that the whirlpool does not pull him down so that he follows the trend, whatever its direction. This is as a result of the deception of the demons and their followers who fight virtue.

We find that many values require the clarification of their meaning. That is, we enter with the demons into a war of definitions, so we must know the meaning of these virtues or values and the content or limitation of their meanings exactly, so that there is no clear error in their execution in case they have two opposing meanings with respect to one virtue.

Here are some examples of virtues that need limitation of their meaning. What is the meaning of freedom, for example? What is the meaning of power? What is the meaning of majesty and honor? In the same way, what is the meaning of victory? What is the meaning of masculinity, bravery, and courage? What is the meaning of success? What is the meaning of striving? They are all great values. People, however, assume they have good intentions, and so differ in understanding the implications and meanings. On this basis some people fall into sin, with a wrong understanding, whereas others avoid sin through correct understanding.

How many sins hide, for example, under the name of wisdom? Man falls into flattery, cowardice, and hypocrisy, and he calls these wisdom. He falls into conformity with evil and walks in the general wrong trend, and he calls this wisdom also. He uses lying, deception, detours, and evasions, and he regards these as wisdom from him—it is enough that it delivered him to his aim or kept him safe, as if the achievement in itself is the wisdom. Here he has missed the meaning of wisdom, since evil is not wise. It is unwise for man to lose the kingdom of heaven, for the sake of any perishing objective on earth. The apostle was right when he said: "For the wisdom of this world is foolishness with God" (1 Corinthians 3.19). It is not only foolishness, but it is also a reason for punishment, "for it is written, 'He catches the wise in their own craftiness'" (1 Corinthians 3.19). The "wisdom," which in this case is a type of craftiness, smartness, and trickery, is not spiritual, so keep away from it. For the serpent was "more cunning than any beast of the field" (Genesis 3.1). It was a demon.

Jacob used human wisdom, which made him fall into many sins. With this "wisdom," that is, trickery and smartness, he stole the birthright from his brother through cunning in a way that lacked brotherly love (Genesis 25.30–34). With the same "wisdom," he deceived his father and stole from him the blessing which should have been his brother's (Genesis 27). His mother Rebekah joined him in doing this. With the same wisdom, also, he took from his uncle Laban all of the newly born sheep (Genesis 30.31–43). In this point in particular he was not honest with his uncle Laban. It is the same tricky way, which is far from the innocence of simplicity.

How much is such a "wise" person in need of repentance from his wisdom? If he called matters by their true names and said that they were tricks, or smartness, he would be able to repent. However, if he calls them wisdom, then this name obscures sin and does not help him towards repentance.

Believe me, it is difficult for a person who is wise in his own eyes to repent, since he does not see any wrong in what he does. Instead, he sees that his dealings show intelligence and good conduct. Is it possible for man to repent of intelligence and good conduct? No, for instead people pursue him so that he will teach them how to reach their goal, and he then becomes an advisor leading others on wrong paths. More than this, he boasts of his wisdom and how he is able to utilize his mind to obtain whatever he wants. He exemplifies the saying in the Bible: "Whose glory is in their shame" (Philippians 3.19). The person whose soul is contrite because of shame over his own sins can repent, but the person who sees glory and pride in his shame will remain as he is, satisfied with himself. An example of this is the merchant who boasts of being able to manipulate the market and lie. Another example is the employee who is proud of hoodwinking his boss with fabricated reasons that he presented to him, so he believed the trick and believed him. It is the same way with the person who is proud of being able to act any role to any person and who wins the situation with his perfect acting; or the male youth who is proud of being able to make any young lady fall, no matter how religious she is. How can such a person repent, if he is proud of his sins?

This reminds me of the demons who were proud of making the saints fall. The Pharisees, in taking everything literally, were proud of walking in the difficult path and tightening down on themselves. Even Saint Paul, when speaking about his past, said: "According to the strictest sect of our religion I lived a Pharisee" (Acts 26.5), whereas the Lord Jesus rebuked the Pharisees for laying heavy burdens on people, for they neither go in themselves, nor do they allow those who are entering to go in (Matthew 23:13).

The Pharisees were proud of taking things literally, and therefore they did not stop being literal, but rather regarded it as precision in religious matters, as a strengthening of piety. They found another name, which covered and protected them.

In the same way, every sin can have another name that the sinner uses as his refuge. The sinner then cannot repent. Smoking, for example, does not appear to be destructive of health, the slavery of the will, or the loss of money. Rather, it takes the name of pleasure and self-relaxation, a name that does not trouble the conscience very much. Dancing takes the name of art, and the professionals in this field are called artists. Nude pictures, which make many people stumble, are also an "art." Many other things resemble this. The sin of fornication also wears sheep's clothing, and carries the name of love. Its perpetrators mix love and desire. Proclaiming good deeds in front of people in order to gain their praise is not taken as hypocrisy; when it wears the sheep's clothing, it takes the name of the good example, practical teaching, presenting God's image to the people, and not making them stumble.

Under the name of making fun and joking, many other sins are hidden. One person mocks another, hurts his feelings, and uses him as an opportunity for his fun. Others laugh at him without caring about how this will affect him. If you blame him, he will say that this is merely a joke. He therefore calls the lack of respect for people a joke. Under the name of joking, also, he lies and calls it a white lie, or making fun, or a joke. He steals and hides, or takes things which belong to others, and says that he is only joking. A male youth deals with a young lady with some unsuitable sexual dealings and considers it a joke. All types of unsuitable joking come under the name of making fun, and they extend to everyone, no matter how high his position. The person who blasphemes later apologizes for this by regarding it as making fun. All of this comes under the name of being light-hearted and friendly. You ask, is there no limit to this joking? And there is no answer.

On the other hand, harshness also wears the sheep's clothing. The harshness of the father toward his son does not appear under the name of harshness, but under the name of firmness and discipline. The harsh father finds for it a particular meaning in the saying of the Bible: "He shall rule them with a rod of iron" (Revelation 2.27). He forgets the saying of the psalm: "Nor chasten me in Your hot displeasure" (Psalm 6.1). A father might kill his sinful daughter,[3] yet does not call this matter the offence of murder but rather cleansing and elimination of disgrace, and the defending of honor. It is merely sheep's clothing, to comfort the conscience and justify the act.

The persecution of whoever disagrees with an opinion or doctrine is called holy zeal. In this way, it takes another name that makes it seem like a virtue. The Lord Jesus said about this, "The time is coming that whoever kills you will think that he offers God service" (John 16.2). Under this name, Saul of Tarsus used to comfort his conscience in every type of harshness he committed (Acts 26. 9–11). In this he said about himself, in previous boasting, "concerning zeal, persecuting the Church" (Philippians 3.6). Similarly, many shades of anger take the name of defending the truth, defending order and honor. They are all sheep's clothing that do not trouble the conscience.

The futile life hides behind the name of "freedom." Perhaps the prodigal son who left his father's house thought to practice his personal freedom, to try life and experience it. The existentialists in all of their errors make this excuse also for the practice of freedom: the feeling of their personal essence, the feeling of their existence. Under this name they perform every type of vileness and attack other people's freedom. He was right, whoever said, "How many crimes did I do in your name, O freedom?"

Similarly, many other sins wear sheep's clothing. A mother might interfere in her newlywed daughter's affairs. She calls this interference, which actually destroys that new family, "love toward her daughter," "defense and protection of her honor." A lawyer or an accountant might lie and place that under the heading of necessities for the profession, although the profession is respectable and this is not actually part of its necessities. Sin does not like to be called by its true name, because this troubles a person.

Even a heresy in religion never appears under the name of heresy. It is presented, instead, under the assumption that it is the correct understanding for religion, of which many people are ignorant. If this heresy carries a doctrine with which the people are unfamiliar, the perpetrator calls it a renewal. If the adherents to church traditions resist him, he says, "Do you hinder our thinking? We have the freedom to think as we like." He might have the freedom to think, but does he have the freedom to spread his wrong

[3]*Editor's note:* His Holiness speaks here of honor killings, which are sadly still practiced in the Middle East and other parts of the world.

thoughts among the people, and then be subjected to the judgment of Saint Paul the Apostle (Galatians 1.7–9)? Similarly, whoever causes others to stumble through his conduct does not say that he offends them, but that he is "teaching them life."

As for you, keep away from wrong meanings and the sheep's clothing of sin. In this way, you have your own firm and established principles, which are not moved by any kind of new naming or non-spiritual understandings, but rely primarily on God's word and on the faith which was once for all delivered to the saints (Jude 3). Protect your purity. Do not allow yourself to call your sins by another name to ease your conscience with a false, temporary comfort, whereas deep within you feel it is a type of escaping from responsibility. But more appropriately, reveal your sins before yourself in order to repent of them, and before God to gain forgiveness. Blessed is he who discovers his sins and regrets them, and does not cover them by another name.

If you call your sin by another name, you will not repent. Man leaves behind what he sees as wrong. If it is not wrong, why then should he leave it? It is a hindrance from the enemy, with which he prevents repentance. Using a method of false compassion, he tries to comfort the person, but he does not comfort the spirit and does not help it give importance to its eternity. As for the owners of the sheep's clothing, they must remove their cover so that they can see sin in its true light, as it is: very wrong, making the person lose his purity and need repentance.

As for those who decide on new appellations or names, they are in need of renewal of mind. The apostle advises: "Do not be conformed to this world," that is, do not look like it or resemble it, "but be transformed by the renewing of your mind" (Romans 12.2). Endeavour to renew your minds, which have been destroyed by worldly meanings and sheep's clothing, by clinging to correct spiritual understanding, "that you may prove what is that good and acceptable and perfect will of God" (Romans 12.2). With this renewing of the mind, man can repent.

CHAPTER 9

Flee from your beloved sins and treat your points of weakness.[1]

T HE SINNER IS NOT ONLY that person who falls into every sin and perishes in this complete, comprehensive fall. The sinner is also the one for whom a single sin is enough to stain his soul and become the reason for his destruction. One beloved sin represents the point of weakness in him.

His beloved sin becomes the obstacle between God and him. If he overcomes this sin in particular, he becomes victorious in his spiritual life. If he is defeated by it instead, then all his victories over the rest of his sins will be of no benefit to him. This sin represents the entrance gate of the devil into his heart and will. It is necessary for him to have victory in the same battlefield where he was defeated by the enemy. This weak point is most probably firm and recurring in all of his confessions, every time he goes to confess his sins.

This point of weakness reminds us of one hole in a ship. No matter how fabulous and magnificent the ship, this one hole can be the reason for its sinking. In the same way, one stain on a garment is enough to make it dirty, no matter how beautiful and clean the rest of it may be. One drop of ink in a cup of water makes it all undrinkable. We have to fix the hole in the ship, no matter what other improvements are being made. In the same way we should work to remove the single stain from the garment, and we should not be proud that the rest of it is clean.

A student who fails one subject in the exam is regarded as having failed, no matter how successful he is in the rest of the subjects. Even if he gains full marks in the other subjects, he repeats the year for the sake of this one subject, which he failed. He must know his point of weakness, concentrate on it, and treat it.

[1]This is from a lecture which I delivered at the Great Cathedral on Friday, December 29, 1978, in preparation for the beginning of a new year.

A sick person who suffers from a certain disease that torments him remains in pain, no matter how well the rest of the systems of his body may be. His doctor then needs to concentrate on the region of the pain in particular, in order to treat him. The same thing must be done immediately with sin, because it is a disease.

Take the example of the person who fasts. In his fast he may perhaps abstain from many foods, yet he cannot abstain from one particular food, which he desires. What does such a person gain from his fast so long as he is weak and lacks the power to control himself at the point when he is being attacked with the desire for food? Do we not say that if he abstains from this food in particular, he will be successful in his fast and in his spirituality? However, if he falls in this, then he has fallen in all. The Bible reminds us of this, saying: "For whoever shall keep the whole law, and yet stumble in one point, he is guilty of all" (James 2.10). What is the meaning of this statement by the apostle? How should we understand it? You will understand it by answering the following question: Do you love God, so that nothing can keep you away from Him? If you find anything at all, then this is the problem in your life; it is your point of weakness. It is probably your beloved sin which competes with God in your heart. God says, "My son, give me your heart" (Proverbs 23.25). If your heart is somewhere else, far from Him, then here is the obstacle that hinders you from fellowship with God.

Not many things kept Adam and Eve away from God. There was one tree, and none other. If they had been able to overcome it, their lives would have been perfect before God. However, in their defeat they lost everything. Overcome, then, the weak point in you, about which the devil already knows. He knows very well that every time he wants to defeat you, he will come to you through this door in particular.

Many people comfort themselves with the righteous deeds they have done. They remember them in order to cover this sin. The Lord, however, does not accept these coverings. An example of this is the Pharisee, whose weakness was that he thought that he was righteous while despising others for their sins. This man had many good points: he tithed from all of his possessions, he fasted twice a week, and he was standing in the temple praying. He was not an extortioner, unjust, or an adulterer. In spite of this, he did not leave the temple justified (Luke 18.9–14). Why? None of those deeds could cover his inner arrogance, which was his particular weak point. This is the one sin he must get rid of in order to be justified in front of God.

The children of Israel tried to cover their sins with sacrifices and incense, with offerings and keeping the seasons of the Sabbaths, the phases of the moon, and the rest of the rites and prayers. God, however, did not accept this from them. "'To what purpose is the multitude of your sacrifices to Me?' says the Lord. . . . 'Bring no more futile sacrifices. Incense is an abomination to Me. . . . Your new moons and your appointed feasts My soul hates; they are a trouble to Me. I am weary of bearing them. When you spread out your hands, I will hide My eyes from you. Even though you make many prayers, I will not hear. Your hands are full of blood. Wash yourselves, make yourselves clean. Put away the evil of your doings" (Isaiah 1.11–16). This is what is needed for the cure of the disease, not the covering of the rites and practices. Sin is not eliminated by righteous deeds, but by repentance.

Therefore do not lose the way. Fight your sin, wherever it is. Do not say, "I will fast two days," or "I will give my money to the poor." None of this will be accepted from you, if you sin in your heart. Instead, face the reality of yourself with honesty. Learn lessons for your life from the Bible.

Take as an example the story of the rich youth (Matthew 19.16–22). He was a person who cared about eternity, and so he asked, "What good thing shall I do that I may have eternal life?" He had kept the Lord's commandments from his youth. However, there was a point of weakness in him, which was the love of money.

The Lord concentrated on this weak point in particular. He said to him, "If you want to be perfect, go, sell what you have and give to the poor, and you will have treasure in heaven." Here, the Lord placed His hand on the wound that tormented this youth, and he went away sorrowful, for he had great possessions.

The Lord also placed His hand on the wound that troubled Job. The righteous Job was blameless and upright according to the Lord's witness: "There is none like him on the earth" (Job 1.8). He was very compassionate toward the poor and rescued the weak from their oppressors. He was "the eye of the blind, and the foot of the lame" (Job 29:15). In brief, he was a righteous man. What, then, was his point of weakness?

He was righteous, and knew himself to be righteous. So self-righteousness troubled him (Job 32.1). Therefore, the Lord dispossessed him of everything: his children and riches, his health and honor, and other people's respect for him. He had nothing left. He entered into reproof with the Lord. Finally he said: "I have uttered what I did not understand, things too wonderful for me, which I did not know. . . . I will question you, and you shall answer Me. . . . Therefore I abhor myself, and repent in dust and ashes" (Job 42.3–6). When Job reached the dust and ashes, he got rid of his self-righteousness. God then lifted up his temptation from him. He became more righteous than he had been. He was victorious over the weak point.

Balaam was a prophet who also had a weak point which destroyed him. The Lord appeared and spoke to him (Numbers 22.12). When Balaam was asked to curse the people, he said: "Whatever word God may put in my mouth, this I must speak" (Numbers 22.38). He built seven altars and offered seven sacrifices. "Then God put a word in Balaam's mouth" (Numbers 23.5). He spoke kind words and prophesied about the Lord Jesus: "The utterance of Balaam the son of Beor . . . the utterance of him who hears the words of God; who sees the vision of the Almighty; who falls down, with eyes opened wide. . . . I see Him, but not now. I behold Him, but not near. A Star shall come out of Jacob. A Sceptre shall rise out of Israel . . ." (Numbers 24.3–4, 17). Then Balaam fell through his weak point, his love of money. The Bible describes Balaam's error as a tragedy.

Solomon fell through his weak point, which was the love of women and the desire to please them. He was the wisest man on earth, with wisdom from God Himself. God appeared to him twice and spoke to him. He was the one who built the temple and blessed the people. He also wrote many of the books in the Holy Bible. In spite of this he had one weak point, which was the love of women. He married foreigners, and this one sin dragged him to his fall. He inclined his heart to the gods of his wives. With this same point of weakness, the great Solomon fell, even though he was the Lord's consecrated one, upon whom the Spirit of God fell and used to move.

We would need more time if we were to talk about the weak points that troubled the prophets. Abraham the father of fathers was perfect and righteous in everything. However, there was one weak point in him, which was the fear that made him fall into sins (Genesis 12.20). Peter, the disciple of the Lord, was a great saint. His weak point was rashness. Thomas the Apostle had a weak point of doubt. The weak point which troubled Jacob the father of fathers was reliance on human devices.

Some sinners were lost by a single weak point. The sin of envy was the one that destroyed Cain and led him to murder his brother. The sin of pride alone made many people fall, as did the sin of fornication. A person may have many virtues, and yet he falls for failing to control his tongue. In this respect, the Bible says: "By your words you will be justified, and by your words you will be condemned." Another person will fall through stubbornness.

The sin of pride by itself made the devil fall. It is the only story in which the Bible talks about the fall of the demons, as Isaiah the Prophet told it (Isaiah 14.13–14). The devil entered into the sin of envy, then lying, and his sins multiplied. All of this, however, came after the sin of pride, which made him fall from his angelic purity.

Each of the heretics also has his own fall. Do not think that every teaching of the heretics was heretical, or that their every word was an innovation in religion. Among them are those who had sermons full of spiritual depth. Tertullian fell into the heresy of the Montanists and became their leader. Eutyches, one of the most spiritual monks in Constantinople, also fell into a heresy. It was one point that destroyed each of these people. The examples are many.

A person's weak point is the reason for his fall. Contemplate your point of weakness, your beloved sin through which you fall, and against which your resistance weakens. In your repentance, concentrate all your efforts on this point—all your prayers and everything you receive from the assistance of prayer. If you overcome it, the devil will be afraid to fight you from then on. By quitting this beloved sin, you show that your love of God is what leads your life and not your love for your desires. Beware of keeping this beloved sin and saying to the Lord, "I love you, Lord, with all my heart, but relinquish to me this one point."

In this case you do not love God with all your heart, since there is a rival to Him in your heart. That rival is this sin in particular. You love this sin more than you love God. It is as if God should say to you, "Now it is clear in which battlefield you must fight, that is, this point in particular."

The devil does not fight you with every sin, but tests you first. He passes through your territory, captures it, and finds the aspects of weakness in it. Very cleverly he knows with which sin to attack you, the one into which you will fall and respond most easily. You must be honest with yourself, examine it, and know the point from which you are falling. If you cannot flee and keep away from stumbling blocks, then be cautious in this point in particular, taking every precaution. Ask for assistance from the Lord so that He can stand with you in your wars.

Do not set for yourself a long spiritual program to follow. Concentrate rather on the main battlefield, whether by escaping or by fighting. Fight the points that stain the purity of your heart and spirit, and which proved to be a battlefield of defeat for you in the past. In your struggle, learn a lesson from David the Prophet. Do not say, "I have overcome the great Goliath and defeated him, and overcome the bear and the lion and took the lamb from it. I won also when Saul was pursuing me. I tolerated him and overcame myself." Instead you should say, "My battlefield is Bathsheba, there I must be victorious." The Lord will be with you.

CHAPTER 10

Be concerned with your eternity, and calculate the cost.[1]

M Y BRETHREN, OUR SPIRITUAL ROAD IS LONG. Our entire life is not enough for it. It is necessary for us to know exactly what is expected of us. Are we walking in the way and progressing step by step each day toward our aim? Or have we not yet started? Have we walked a few steps and then stopped? In this way, from now on, we should calculate the cost, being vigilant toward our salvation. What is expected of us is not mere ordinary faith, but the life of holiness, as the apostle says: "As He who called you is holy, you also be holy" (1 Peter 1.15), "perfecting holiness in the fear of God" (2 Corinthians 1.7). Yes, we are expected to have this "holiness, without which no one will see the Lord" (Hebrews 12.14). This holiness is not the end of the road, but it is necessary, if we are to reach it, to grow in it. To what limit shall we grow? We should grow until we reach perfection, according to the Lord's commandment: "Be perfect, just as your Father in heaven is perfect" (Matthew 5.48).

Have we reached this holiness and this perfection? What we know is that relative perfection requires steps. All of the perfect among us press toward the goal (Philippians 3.14–15). To what limit do they press? To the limit the apostle describes: "that you may be filled with all the fullness of God" (Ephesians 3.19). Believe me, I paused in front of this phrase in amazement when I read it for the first time. Then I repeated the reading, wherein the apostle says: "You being rooted and grounded in love, may be able to comprehend with all the saints what is the width and length and depth and height—to know the love of Christ which passes knowledge; that you may be filled with all the fullness of God" (Ephesians 3.18–19). Here I keep silent, for what can I say?

[1]From two lectures: first, "The Long Path," which I gave at the Conference of Friends at Saint Mark's Church in Shoubra on February 24, 1963; second, "Calculating the Cost," which I gave at the Great Cathedral on October 31, 1969.

I remember, however, that the apostle did not ask us only to walk according to the Spirit (Romans 8.1) but said: "Be filled with the Spirit" (Ephesians 5.18). What is the essence of this filling with the Spirit? O Lord, I do not know. Does it mean simply that there is nothing in our substance which is void of the Spirit, or does this filling include all of our substance? If this happens to us, I wonder then, how we would walk? The apostle says that what is expected of us is to walk just as the Lord Jesus, the incarnate God, walked on earth. "He who says he abides in Him ought himself also to walk just as He walked" (1 John 2.6). Who can do this, no matter how hard he tries? Truly, how lofty are these heights to which the Spirit wants to lead us in order for us to be in "the image and likeness of God" (Genesis 1.26–27). It is a state of continual growth, which does not stop at any limit.

I said one day that it resembles the one who pursues the horizon. A man who looks at the horizon sees it there, at the end of the path. He goes to the end of the path and finds that the horizon is at the mountain, as if heaven coincides with earth. So he goes to the mountain and sees the horizon far away, at the sea. He then goes to the sea, and sees the water outstretched, without limits. The life of perfection is likewise. For this reason the saints described themselves as sinners.

We read about the Desert Fathers, who were elevated greatly in the life of the Spirit, and we see how they used to sit in their cells weeping for their own sins. Even the apostles, who were saints, also used to talk about their sins. One of the most prominent examples of this might be the saying of Saint Paul the Apostle: "Jesus Christ came into the world to save sinners, of whom I am chief" (1 Timothy 1.15). If Saint Paul the Apostle is the chief of sinners, then what shall we say about ourselves?

The example of Saint Paul the Apostle should make us feel great contrition. Saint Paul the Apostle labored more than all the apostles (1 Corinthians 15.10), preached in many countries, wrote fourteen epistles for our sake, and performed amazing wonders and miracles. By the abundance of the revelations he was given a thorn in the flesh, lest he be exalted above measure (2 Corinthians 12.7). This Paul was the one who ascended to the third heaven, and heard inexpressible words (2 Corinthians 12.4). This Paul says about himself: "Not that I have already attained.... but I press on, that I may lay hold.... I do not count myself to have apprehended; but only one thing I do" (Philippians 3.12–13). What is this that you do, Saint Paul? He answers: "Forgetting those things which are behind and reaching forward to those things which are ahead." He reaches forward to what is ahead. To where? Is there something beyond the third heaven? More than this life of his, filled with preaching, holiness, and miracles? If Saint Paul, despite all that he achieved, says: "I press toward the goal" (Philippians 3.14), then what about us, who have not apprehended anything of what this great saint apprehended, who are not walking in the love of God, nor even in His obedience? We do not act as loving children, nor even like honest, faithful servants. We have not reached even the stage of "unprofitable servants."

The Lord says: "When you have done all those things which you are commanded, say, 'We are unprofitable servants'" (Luke 17.10). For we are still within the limits of our orders and have not yet been elevated above the law to the degree of love which sacrifices everything, loses all things, and counts them as rubbish to gain Christ (Philippians 3.8). If this is the condition of whoever stops at the limits of carrying out the commandment, then what can be said of him who sins and breaks the commandment? He is definitely not a servant of God; neither a good servant, nor an unprofitable servant. Instead, he is resisting God and is a servant of the devil. I say this to you so that you know yourself, and so that you know the stage which you have reached along the path to God, in case you think that if you pray two psalms, you have attained the goal.

Know then, my brother, where you are, and be concerned with your salvation. You have one soul and none other. If you gain it, you have gained everything. If you lose it, you have lost everything. For what can you take from the world besides your soul? In the Lord's immortal words: "For what is a man profited if he gains the whole world, and loses his own soul?" (Matthew 16.26). Sit then with yourself. Examine yourself very well. Are you walking on the path or not? Are you keen about your eternity, or are you lost? Did you lose those days of your life that you should have utilized in spiritual growth and to know God and His love, to apprehend the goal for whose sake the Lord called you?

My brother, the path before you is long, and you have not started yet. The path starts with fear, since "the fear of the Lord is the beginning of wisdom" (Proverbs 9.10). Fear gradually leads to love. Up until now you have not reached the fear of God, because you still break His commandments. When, then, will you reach love? You cannot reach God unless you walk according to the Spirit. If you walk according to the Spirit, the fruits of the Spirit will appear in your life.

The fruits of the Spirit are a long program, as Saint Paul the Apostle explained. He said: "But the fruit of the Spirit is love, joy, peace, longsuffering, kindness, goodness, faithfulness, gentleness, self-control" (Galatians 5.22). Love, which is the first of these fruits, was explained in detail by the apostle in 1 Corinthians 13, and he established for it fourteen signs. So, have you reached any of them? Also, what about prayer and its details? What about contemplation and all of the other spiritual means? What about the warfare of the demons, and how to overcome them? I do not wish to burden you with the details of the spiritual life, because I will talk to you about all of it, God willing, in a large book called *The Signs of the Spiritual Path*. As for now, all that I advise you to do is to start on the first step in your relationship with God, because if you do not start with the first step, then how will you arrive?

The starting point in your relationship with God is repentance. With it you are reconciled to God and return to Him. That is, you are moved from the outer circle to the inner circle. Then grace carries you and crosses over with you every step of the way. In this way you move from the step of repentance to purity, to holiness, to relative perfection, to growth in this perfection. Do you want to start the step over to repentance? Place before your eyes the following principle: Keep God's love in order to cast out the love of sin.

Man cannot live in emotional emptiness. He either fills his heart with the love of God, or his heart is filled with the love of the world and the flesh. "Friendship with the world is enmity with God" (James 4.4). On the other hand, the love of God is stronger and deeper than any other love. Therefore, if you place it in your heart, it will definitely cast out every other desire. The saint who said that repentance is exchanging one desire for another was correct. That is, instead of desiring the world, the flesh and sin, all of your desires become spiritual, concentrated on God and life with Him. Do not let your heart be void of God's love and His kingdom, in case the love of sin comes inside to live. Keep this balance undamaged within your heart. Do not let the scale of the world dominate you with its many intrusive influences of visions, sounds, readings, and associations, but powerfully utilize every spiritual means given to you to deepen the love of God in your mind.

CHAPTER 11

Be mindful of the love of God.[1]

BE SURE THAT SIN CANNOT ENTER a heart that loves God. The person who loves God is not the person who merely practices spiritual means such as prayer, fasting, spiritual reading, going to church, Confession, and Holy Communion. Above all, it is important that these spiritual practices originate from the inner love in the heart.

Religion is love: love for God, love for doing good, and love for others. If this love is not present, the heart becomes lax and loses the spiritual flame that it received from the Spirit of God on the day that it first knew God. Laxity develops into sin, no matter how much service a person offered at church, and no matter how much activity and fervor he had.

Without the love of God within you, you cannot repent. Without the love of God, you would not leave sin because of purity of heart, but merely as the outer proceedings of a formal reconciliation with God, because of fear of His anger and punishment. A person who fears God's punishment and fears that sin might lead him into hell becomes religious. He calls this piety, that is, the fear of God and His anger. With this fear, he avoids practicing sin, but the sin does not stay away from his heart.

The heart continues swinging to the right and to the left, and will not settle except with love. Repentance, then, is the transformation of the heart's feelings into love toward God. All of the spiritual practices, such as prayer and fasting, do not stand on their own, then, but are connected to this love. So prayer, without the love of God, is not truly prayer. It is likewise with fasting, attending church, and Holy Communion. You pray and then say: "My soul shall be satisfied as with marrow and fatness" (Psalm 62.6), "Your name is loved, O Lord, it is my meditation all the day" (Psalm 118.97). You read the Bible and say: "How sweet are Thy words to my taste, sweeter than

---

[1]From a lecture on "Love and Not Religious Habits," which I gave at the Great Cathedral on Friday, November 11, 1977.

honey to my mouth." You go to church and say: "How beloved are Your dwellings, O Lord of hosts. My soul longs and faints for the courts of the Lord" (Psalm 83.2–3).

With these feelings you find pleasure in repentance, and your repentance continues and settles in. If this love is not in you, however, then even if you leave sin, it will fight you very easily so that you will return to it. Why? It is because you did not find your satisfaction in life with God. You did not find in the life of repentance what fills your heart, what fills your affections and feelings, or what protects you from asking for love from the outside. I know that you want repentance. If this were not so, this book would not be between your hands now. You may think you have actually started repentance because you practice spiritual means.

However, you pray and fast, and do not feel the love of sin has left you. Why? We all believe in the benefits of the spiritual means, but on the condition that we practice them in a spiritual way. If you pray, fast, and read the Bible, and find in this a spiritual satisfaction, pleasure, comfort, and joy, then all of this will lead you to deepen your love of God. Then you are following the practice. Whoever follows the practice arrives.

If you do not live in repentance with this love, then you are lost. You must then possess God's love, which can cast out from your heart the love of sin. You must know the Lord Jesus, in order to leave your water pot at the well (John 4). If you do not have this love, ask for it in your prayers with all persistence. It is a prayer that you say at all times, from all your heart, from all your thought, and from the depth of your depths: "Grant me, O Lord, to love you. Remove the love of sin from my heart, and give me your love."

Search for every means that will help you love God. Not every kind of reading is of benefit to you. There are, however, spiritual readings that will greatly influence your heart, touch your feelings, and motivate you to love God. Also, there are certain hymns which kindle your spiritual feelings. There are holy places that will have an influence on you and individuals who love God, who will help you to love God like them, by watching them; cling to these with all your power.

Keep away from everything that keeps God's love away from your heart. Protect this love by taking every precaution, because it casts out from you the love of sin. As the love of God increases in you, your heart rejects sin and is disgusted by it. You then regret your first days when you loved sin. Thus God grants you a new heart that loves God, and which is completely different from the old heart. In this heart that loves God you worship Him with joy, and you will not find it difficult to keep His commandments. You will then sing with John the Beloved, saying: "For this is the love of God, that we keep His commandments. And His commandments are not burdensome" (1 John 5.3). Why are they not burdensome? It is because you live in them with joy, with love, without inner struggle troubling you. You will not find another law in your members warring against the law of your mind, to bring you into captivity to the law of sin (Romans 7.23).

The person who loves God finds delight in carrying out His commandments. He finds delight in doing what pleases Him. He does not allow himself to anger Him in any way. A person who loves his parents finds pleasure in satisfying them and gaining their blessings, and does not allow himself to anger them in anything.

If you reach this feeling, you can repent with ease. Without the love of God, however, you will find repentance difficult and burdensome. You will not feel the desire, avoid walking in the paths of sin unless you find a love that is deeper to take its place. Search, then, for this deeper love. Walk in every means that will take you to it. Then you will not find repentance difficult at all, nor will you find the commandments burdensome.

When is it that you find repentance difficult and the commandment burdensome? You will find it so if the love of God is not perfected in your heart, or if you have not obtained it yet. Therefore, when you try to repent, you struggle against an opposing love from within you. You press down on your will, on your heart, and on your affections. You also try to flee from sinful, established visions in your subconscious and in your memory that pull you down, far away from God. But if you love God, then you will be unable to sin, and the wicked one cannot touch you (1 John 3.9, 5.18).

Then the commandments will not be burdensome. Instead, the sin will be burdensome. The sin will be difficult, for no matter how the enemy tries to pressure your will, you resist and refuse to sin, and you say with all your heart: "How then can I do this great wickedness, and sin against God?" (Genesis 39.9). You will find the Lord's commandments joyful and luminous, enlightening the eyes (Psalm 18.9). Repentance becomes easy for you, and from it you obtain purity of heart.

You may ask, "How can I reach this love of God that casts out from me the love of sin?" There are several means that can lead you to the love of God. Read abundantly the stories of the saints who loved God with all their hearts and sacrificed everything for His sake. They lost everything for the sake of the honor of knowing Him and being in Him. Read many books about the virtues so that the love of good will be kindled in your heart, and you will leave the state you are presently in. Read the stories of repentance and the return to God, for they are very influential and of benefit to you. Remember death, judgment, and the eternal kingdom in order to feel the insignificance of the sin which fights you, and the insignificance of the whole world. Remember also how God loved you all your life and dealt kindly with you. These pleasant memories will kindle in you feelings of love and the recognition of God's favor. You will love Him then, because He loved you first.

What more can I say? I wish you would turn the pages of this book and re-read what was written about the incentives for repentance. In addition, in order to reach repentance, you need to wrestle with God, asking Him to give you His love, or to give you a new heart that loves Him. How can this be?

CHAPTER 12

Wrestle with God and obtain power from Him to help you repent.

W RESTLE WITH GOD AND OBTAIN help from Him.[1] You want to repent and overcome your sins. You do so rightly. Remember that victory over sin is not merely a human labor.

First, because sin is strong, it has this power with which "she has cast down many wounded, and all who were slain by her were strong men" (Proverbs 7.26). Can this sin which befell Adam, Samson, David, and Solomon be fought by you alone, without divine help? Impossible! This sin had authority over you when it made you fall previously. It is not an external war alone. As soon as it finds a response within you, the war doubles.

There is the teaching of the Bible that says: "Unless the Lord guard the city, those who guard it stay awake in vain" (Psalm 126.1). This is the saying of the Lord Himself: "Without Me you can do nothing" (John 15.5). In every labor that you do on your own, without God's participating with you, you will most likely fail. Even if you succeed, you will count it for yourself and vainglory will fight you, making you think that you were victorious through your own power. It is known that humility is one of the strongest weapons that defeats the demons. It was utilized by Saint Antony, who used to say to the demons, "I am too weak to fight even with the smallest among you." Then he cried to the Lord, saying: "Rescue me, O Lord, from these who think that I am something."[2]

Your previous experiences have proven your failure to repent with your effort alone. How many times have you tried to rise, and then ended up

[1]From two lectures which were the second part of the series "The Spiritual Awakening," given on November 11, 1970, and November 20, 1970; a third lecture on "The Struggle with God," given on March 28, 1975; and a fourth lecture on "The Life of Victory and Fighting for the Lord," given on April 6, 1979. All of these lectures were delivered at the Great Cathedral.

[2]Athanasius, *Life of Antony* 9,10, 51–53.

falling later? How many times did you promise God about repentance, and said insistently that you would not do this sin another time? Sometimes you brought woes upon yourself and said, "Make me sick, O Lord, if I do this another time." You would say this as if the matter were in your own hands and capability.

My advice to you is to say, "Restore me, and I will return" (Jeremiah 31.18), instead of "I will promise You that I will repent, O Lord." Ask repentance of Him as a good gift, for He Himself promised this, saying: "I shall give you a new heart and put a new spirit within you. . . . I shall put My Spirit within you and cause you to walk in My statutes" (Ezekiel 36.26–27)[3]. Hold firm to His holy promise and ask Him to grant you this repentance. He will give you the new heart and make you follow His commandments.

This is what the Church teaches us in the prayers of the hours. We say in Psalm 50: "Purge me with hyssop, and I shall be clean, wash me, and I shall be whiter than snow." Then God washes you and you become white; you are not one who is capable of washing yourself. In many of the Psalms we say, "Save me, O Lord. Protect me. Teach me Your ways." In the prayer of the Third Hour we say, "Purify us from iniquity and save our souls."[4] Purify us from the iniquities of the body and soul, lead us to a spiritual life so that we may seek righteousness. This is also what we say during the Divine Liturgy: "Purify our souls, bodies, and spirits." We repeat this phrase more than once in the liturgy. So, we learn from the Church that repentance, cleanliness, and purity are not merely the result of our labor, but we also ask for them from God in our prayers. It is as if man says to God, "I am unable, O Lord, to purify myself. Please arise and do this work according to Your former promise. Arise, O Lord my God. Arise, my Lord, and save me, my God."

Here, the importance of prayer in attaining repentance is shown.[5] Saint Isaac concentrated on it exclusively, as is evident from his saying: "Whoever

---

[3]See the section "A New Heart" in my book *How to Start a New Year*, from page 27 to page 40 in the Arabic text.

[4]*Editor's note:* From the *Agpeya*, the petition of the Third Hour prayer, which says, "O Heavenly King, the Spirit of Truth, the Comforter, who are everywhere and fill everybody, Treasury of Goodness and Giver of Life, we ask You to come and dwell within us, purify us from iniquity, and save our souls."

[5]See my book [in Arabic] *The Return to God*, pages 53 to 56, the section whose title is "Prayer Is an Aid to Return." Also, see pages 85 and 86.

thinks that he has another path to repentance other than prayer, is deceived by the demons."[6] As for you, at least in your struggles, do not rely upon your strength, intelligence, will, or training. On your own, without help from God, you cannot arrive at repentance. Say to Him, "Lord, I am in need of You, and without You I can do nothing. 'For to will is present with me, but how to perform what is good I do not find. . . . The evil I will not to do, that I practice' (Romans 7.18–19). 'I have gone astray like a lost sheep; seek Your servant' (Psalm 118.176). Are You not the one who says: "'I shall feed My sheep and refresh them . . . ," thus says the Lord and Master. "I shall seek the lost, bring back the misled, bind up the broken, strengthen the fallen'" (Ezekiel 34.15–16). I am the lost, the broken, the sick one. Seek me. Bring me back and strengthen me. I have reached a stage of weakness and deficiency, O Lord, in which I cannot promise You that I will repent, and if I promise You, I will most likely break my promise.

"I will not promise You, but I will ask a promise from You, to save me from sin. Did You not say, 'Come to Me, all you who labor and are heavy laden, and I will give you rest' (Matthew 11.28)? Yes, I need You to give me rest, O Lord, from this heavy burden. Did You not say, 'The Son of Man has come to seek and to save that which was lost' (Luke 19.10)? I am the one who is in need of salvation from You."

"I need not only salvation from judgment, but salvation from sin itself. Your Name is Jesus, that is, the Savior, because You save Your people from their sins (Matthew 1.21). Save me then from my sins. I wish I could hear from You Your comforting words: "'Because of the oppression of the poor, for the comforting of the needy, now I will arise,' says the Lord; "I will set him in the safety for which he yearns'" (Psalm 11.6)."

Therefore, my brother, learn to wrestle with God for repentance. Wrestle like a drowning person who finds in front of him a boat that can save him. Wrestle like Jacob, who said to the Lord: "I will not let You go unless You bless me" (Genesis 32.26). Say to Him, "I have tried myself, O Lord, and have known my weakness and deficiencies in the presence of sin. It remains for You to intervene.

"Do not blame me because of my weakness, O Lord, but rescue me from this weakness. Instead of judging me, for I am defiled, purify me from

[6]Isaac the Syrian, *Ascetical Homilies* XLI.

this defilement. You have given me commandments to carry out, give me strength to carry out these commandments. Give me the resistance with which to resist the devil. Give me Your love, which will cast out from my heart the love of sin."

Stand firm, my brother, in your prayers, for it is a guaranteed route to repentance. The person who experiences powerful prayers does not experience any defeat. The person who includes the Lord in his fights and wars will never be defeated. Wrestle, then, with God. Obtain from Him the power and the spiritual weapon with which to fight. Get divine promises from Him, the new heart and the pure spirit. Take the will and determination from Him. Take the faith with which to fight and the confidence that you will win. Be sure that if you are victorious in your prayers, you will succeed in every battlefield. If you succeed in your struggle with God, no power on earth will be able to prevail against you; rather, you will enjoy the beautiful words which the Lord said to young Jeremiah: "'They will fight against you, but they shall not prevail over you, for I am with you to deliver you', says the Lord" (Jeremiah 1.19). Then "a thousand shall fall at your side and ten thousand at your right hand, yet it shall not come near you" (Psalm 90.7). It is true that "the Lord will fight for you, and you shall hold your peace" (Exodus 14.14). He will fight for you in your outer wars. He will fight for you in your inner wars, in the heart and mind. Therefore, in all of your spiritual wars, place in front of you this principle that the battle is the Lord's. "The battle is the Lord's" (1 Kingdoms 17.47). "For nothing restrains the Lord from saving by many or by few" (1 Kingdoms 14.6).

When the people were fighting against Amalek, it was the Lord who fought, for it was said: "The Lord wars with Amalek" (Exodus 17.15). In the same way the Lord will wage war with every sin that defeats you. He is the One who overcomes them in you and not you yourself, because He said: "I have overcome the world" (John 16.33). Your spiritual victory then, is only through the Lord. You will not reach repentance nor overcome any sin, except through the Lord. You will say with David: "The Lord is my strength and song, and He became my salvation" (Psalm 117.14). You will say with Saint Paul the Apostle: "We are more than conquerors through Him who loved us" (Romans 8.37).

Our victory, then, does not come through our determination, nor by reliance on ourselves, but with Him who loved us. Through His love to us, He raises us from our fall with His power and "leads us in triumph in Christ" (2 Corinthians 2.14). The Lord, as the apostle says, always "gives us the victory through our Lord Jesus Christ" (1 Corinthians 15.57). Do not turn from Him, then, concentrating all of your efforts toward repentance on yourself. Instead, take strength from Him in order to repent.

Shout out with our teacher Saint Paul: "I can do all things through Christ who strengthens me" (Philippians 4.13). In Christ, then, in His strength and with His assistance, you can do all things. Outside of Christ you can do nothing. Wrestle with Him first, before you wrestle with sin, as Jacob wrestled with God before going to meet Esau. When he won with God, Esau became light in his burden. Do you say to Jacob, go first to Esau? He will answer you, "No one can overcome this person except God. Therefore I will go to God first, and I will take Him with me when meeting Esau." Do the same thing with sin. With a very humble heart say, "I am weaker than this war." "I am too weak to fight even the littlest one," as Saint Antony said.[7]

Barak, the commander of the army, would not go to the war without Deborah the Prophetess (Judges 4.8). Nor do you overpower sin on your own, unless God fights with you. Say, "Who am I to stand in front of the demons alone? I am not qualified for this fight. You, O Lord, are my victory. Come and overcome the world in my heart, as you overcame it previously. You know everything, O Lord. You know my weakness and defeat. You know that I do not possess the will, the power, or the determination. But sometimes I do not possess even the desire for repentance. I do not know how to fight, nor do I withstand the temptations of the enemy. Briefly, I do not know how to repent. If I know, I do not succeed. If I succeed once, I am defeated several times. Pluck me like a brand from the fire, like Joshua (Zechariah 3.2)."

For the sake of Joshua's repentance, the angel of the Lord stood against the devil who opposed Joshua, and said to him: "The Lord rebukes you, O devil, even the Lord choosing for Himself Jerusalem rebukes you. Is this one not like a brand plucked from the fire?" (Zechariah 3.2). The angel plucked him from the fire and clothed him with rich robes. God loves this wrestling

[7]Athanasius, *Life of Antony* 9,10, 51–53.

with Him. Those who wrestled with Him in prayer and supplication took power from Him.

However, a person might say, "I prayed a lot, but did not repent." No, my brother, every prayer that agrees with God's will must be answered. Prayer for the sake of repentance agrees with God's will, but perhaps you have actually prayed, and yet the resulting prayer was not from the depth of the heart which wrestles with God with true desire for this repentance, and with the favor of the son with his father. Or, perhaps you have prayed, but have not stood firm in your prayers; you said some words and tired quickly, and you did not persevere in prayer. You need prayer that asks and waits for the Lord in faith, the prayer that is distinguished by struggle, persistence, and insistence. Elijah continued to ask of the Lord and repeated the prayer several times, until he received the answer the seventh time (3 Kingdoms 18.44). Look unto Jacob, who wrestled with the Lord "until the breaking of day" (Genesis 32.24)—that is, all night—and he was not bored.

Perhaps your prayers are without faith and contrition of heart. Or, perhaps the quick answer is not for your own good, as Saint Basil said: "Sometimes God delays in answering our request, so that we may know its value. Because the things which we receive with ease, we lose with ease." Sometimes God wants you to be subdued by sin, so that you may know the value of leaving it. If He grants you repentance, you feel a great joy; you will protect it with all your strength, because you received it with great difficulty and after some time. Then, you will be stricter in your repentance, being more cautious and fearful of falling.

Perhaps the delaying of repentance is caused by God's wanting to know the extent of your seriousness in requesting repentance, and the extent of your firmness in the request. The delay in the answer might be caused by you, for you are the one who wants. Truly, you ask with your mouth, but your heart does not want. You are the one who delays repentance. As the Bible says: "If you will hear His voice, do not harden your hearts" (Hebrews 3.7).

Therefore, do not ask for help while you are sleeping and lax. The labor of God for your sake is not an encouragement for you to be careless and lazy, relying on God. God wants you to work with Him. He labors for your repentance, and you participate with Him. He offers you assistance, so do not place obstacles by means of your will, nor leave your doors open to sin.

Briefly, enter with all your capabilities, no matter how few they are, in communion with the Holy Spirit (2 Corinthians 13.14). Present your desire
first, and present your submission to the labor of God in you. Present also
what labor you can.

Even then do not be upset, for God saved many who lacked the ability
to do anything. There are persons who did not do anything. The woman who
had a flow of blood touched His garment with faith. The Lord said to the
man with the withered hand, "Stretch out your hand," and so he stretched
it out. He said also to the blind man, "Go, wash in the pool of Siloam," and
so he went and washed (John 9.7). Other than these, however, there are
many who do nothing, like the paralytic who was let down through the
roof (Mark 2.4). Also the injured man, whom the Good Samaritan carried,
lay along the path between life and death (Luke 10.30), while the paralytic
of Bethesda remained thirty-eight years, unable to be healed (John 5.5). In
similar fashion were found all those who had incurable diseases.

What did these people, such as the paralytic and the like, do? Nothing.
The same applies to the dead whom the Lord Jesus raised. Could the dead
person do anything to be rescued from death? No, without a doubt. The sinner is regarded as "dead in trespasses" (Ephesians 2.5). "You have a name that
you are alive, but you are dead" (Revelation 3.1). If he cannot do anything,
then the Lord can raise him.

Therefore do not despair, nor be disturbed. All of these examples in their
symbolism give us an idea that God seeks the salvation of sinners, both those
who are able and those who are unable. He who is able is like the prodigal
son, who was able to return to his father's house. He who is not able is like
the lost sheep and the lost coin. All three were mentioned in one chapter
(Luke 15). The Lord has one condition for those who are unable, that they
do not oppose His work for their salvation. An example of those who are
unable is the barren woman who has not borne (Isaiah 54.1). This person
was a symbol of the barren soul that does not yield fruits to the Spirit, and
the Lord made her more fertile than those who have children.

There are people whom the Lord saved without their asking. The Lord
accepted Abraham's pleadings for Lot and took him out of Sodom, although
Lot himself did not ask. When the two angels informed him that Sodom
was to be burned, he was slow in leaving. The Bible says: "The angels urged

Lot to hurry." And while he lingered, "the Lord being merciful to him, the angels seized his hand, and the hands of his wife and two daughters, and brought them outside the city" (Genesis 19.15–16).

The phrase, "the Lord being merciful to him," is a comforting phrase without a doubt. God, who had compassion on all of those, will also have compassion on you, grant you repentance, and lead you to it. He will take the heart of stone out of you and give you a new heart (Ezekiel 36.26). Blessed is the Lord in all His labors of love, and in His endeavor to save everyone.

PART FOUR

THE SIGNS OF REPENTANCE

Fruits Worthy of Repentance

Saint john the baptist cried out, saying: "Repent, for the kingdom of heaven is at hand!" (Matthew 3.2). He also called out: "Bear fruits worthy of repentance" (Matthew 3.8, Luke 3.8). This is what Saint Paul the Apostle did also, for he called to all those who were in the region of Judea and then to the Gentiles, saying "that they should repent, turn to God, and do works befitting repentance" (Acts 26.20). Repentance, then, is not merely a work of the heart, but there are works and fruits that are worthy of it and show it. As the Bible said: "You will know them by their fruits" (Matthew 7.16, 20).

What are these fruits which show that a person is repentant? We wish to discuss them in these pages one by one, so that each person will examine himself by them to discover if he is repentant or not. Through them he will know the extent of the honesty of his repentance.

CHAPTER I

Confessing the Fault[1]

CONFESSING THE FAULT INCLUDES the following four important points:

1. Confessing the fault to God in prayer, because sin is originally directed toward God. As David the Prophet confessed in Psalm 50 (51): "I have sinned against You—only against You." And as in Daniel the Prophet's confession: "We have sinned and committed iniquity, we have done wickedly and rebelled, even by departing from your precepts" (Daniel 9.5). It is also like the confession of Nehemiah: "Both I and my father's house have sinned. We have departed from You, and have not kept the commandments, the statutes, nor the ordinances which You commanded Your servant Moses" (Nehemiah 1.6–7). Similarly, it is like the confession of Ezra the Scribe (Ezra 9.6).

You have sinned against God, against His compassionate heart and His majesty. You have sinned against the loving compassionate heart that took care of you with love and protection. You departed from His love and defiled His holy temple, which you are. You have loved the world more than Him. You neglected His majesty and broke His commandments. That is why Nathan said to David: "Why did you despise the word of the Lord and do evil in His sight?" (2 Kingdoms 12.9).

It is amazing that they were embarrassed before their father confessor, but not embarrassed before God. In the same way, man is embarrassed by committing sin in front of other people, but is not embarrassed by committing it before God. David was ashamed of his lack of embarrassment in committing sin before God. Therefore David said to Him: "Against you only have I sinned against and done evil in Your sight" (Psalm 50.6). Daniel also said: "We have done evil before You." In spite of this, God referred us to whoever we are embarrassed to face.

[1]From a lecture given on February 24, 1968, with other lectures.

2. Confessing to the priest, as an agent of God or as His servant, and not because of his personal attributes. Whoever confesses to a priest confesses to God in the hearing of the priest. This reminds us of the saying of Joshua the son of Nun to Achan, the son of Carmi: "Give glory to the Lord God of Israel today and make confession. Tell me what you did and hide nothing from me" (Joshua 7.19).

Confession to the priest is found in both the Old and New Testaments. All those who came out to the baptism of repentance from John the Baptist, the priest, "were baptized by him in the Jordan, confessing their sins" (Matthew 3.6). The sinner in the Old Testament, according to the law, "shall confess his sin in that thing, and he shall bring for his trespass against the Lord . . . a sin offering" (Leviticus 5.5–6). In the New Testament, "many who had believed came confessing and telling their deeds" (Acts 19.18).

The sinner confesses to the priest to receive absolution and permission to receive Holy Communion. Embarrassment in front of the priest in confession is beneficial and assists him in not repeating the sin, since the fear of the embarrassment of confession prevents him from repeating the sin. This works until he rises spiritually and becomes accustomed to embarrassment before God, who sees and hears him during his sin. Furthermore, receiving Holy Communion after the embarrassment of confession reminds us of the eating of the Passover lamb with bitter herbs (Exodus 12.8).

Confession should be mixed with repentance; it is called the sacrament of repentance. It is not the settlement of an old account in order to open a new account! It is repentance, and confession is one of its signs. Confession means a person reveals and judges himself. Therefore he needs humility and contrition, and submission also. So, the penitent should not merely tell stories to the priest. During confession the penitent should neither justify nor defend himself, nor place the responsibility for his errors on others, nor transform the confession into a complaint. If those things are done, confession loses its meaning as a sign of repentance and one of its components. We have talked about confession to God and to the priest. We will now move on to the third type.

3. Confessing to the person against whom you have sinned is to comfort his heart with regards to you and to be reconciled with him, following the saying of the Lord: "Leave your gift there before the altar, and go your way.

First, be reconciled to your brother" (Matthew 5.24). So you will say to him, "I have sinned against you in so-and-so, please, forgive me." He will forgive you, according to the saying of the Bible: "If he sins against you seven times in a day, and seven times in a day returns to you, saying 'I repent,' you shall forgive him" (Luke 17.4). There now remains only the fourth type of confession, which is:

4. The confession between you and yourself that you have sinned. This is the source of the other three confessions we have mentioned, and it precedes them in time. If you do not confess from within yourself that you have sinned, what are you going to confess to God or to the priest? How will you confess to the person against whom you sinned, if you do not feel that you have done anything wrong? You must then reckon with yourself and feel deep within you the complete conviction that you have sinned, for without this it is neither repentance nor confession. Saint Macarius the Great said: "Judge yourself, my brother, before they judge you."[2] A father of monks of the mountain of Nitria said to the saintly Pope Theophilus, "Believe me, my father, there is nothing greater than a person going back and blaming himself for everything."[3] You must then judge yourself first within your heart. This will push you to judge yourself before God and the priest.

Whoever does not judge himself cannot repent. The tax collector judged himself a sinner. Therefore, he was able to stand in the temple with humility and offer repentance, asking forgiveness and walking out justified (Luke 18.13). As for the Pharisee, who judged himself in nothing, he found no error in his life for which to offer repentance or ask forgiveness. Whoever feels that he is completely healthy finds it impossible to search for a doctor, or to ask for healing. Similarly, from the spiritual aspect, only the person who confesses his sins asks for repentance.

When David did not feel his sin, he did not offer repentance. David sinned, and within the whirlpool of sin, he scarcely thought about what he had done. Therefore he offered no regret, nor any repentance. It was then necessary for God to send Nathan the Prophet, who revealed to him the burden of his sin and its ugliness. David then confessed that he had sinned (2 Kingdoms 12.13). Only at this time did the story of his repentance begin.

---

[2]Macarius the Great, *Bustān al-Ruhbān* (*Paradise of the Fathers*, Arabic).
[3]Theophilus the Archbishop 1, *Sayings of the Desert Fathers*.

Job likewise did not know that he was being attacked by self-righteousness. He therefore entered into a long discussion with his three friends, and his complaints to God Himself increased. He said to Him: "You know that I am not wicked, and there is no one who can deliver from Your hand" (Job 10.7). "But He knows the way that I take; when He has tested me, I shall come forth as gold" (Job 23.10). "He was righteous in his own eyes" (Job 32.1). The matter required God to send Elihu, the son of Barachel the Buzite, to reveal to Job himself, for God to talk and explain to him, until Job finally reached contrition and said to the Lord: "Behold, I am vile; what shall I answer You? I lay my hand over my mouth" (Job 40.4). He also said. "I have uttered what I did not understand, things too wonderful for me, which I did not know" (Job 42.3).

The two greatest matters that prevent confession and repentance are excuses and self-righteousness. Man excuses himself on the grounds of his weakness, or the weakness of human nature generally, or the severity of the outer warfare, or that he committed the sin through ignorance or forgetfulness, or that he was the victim of someone else. He may also place the responsibility on someone else, and so he accuses the Church of not caring for him, or accuses his father confessor of not being concerned for him, or reproves God for not sending assistance. The true penitent, however, accuses only himself, carrying the disgrace of his sin by himself. He stands before God as a sinner, not justifying himself, but like the thief on the right who confessed: "And we indeed justly, for we receive the due reward of our deeds" (Luke 23.41).

We may use excuses try to cover up sin, or to lighten its burden. Self-righteousness, however, is more dangerous, because it denies the existence of sin. It is more dangerous than excuses, which confess the existence of sin but try to escape its responsibility or at least reduce it. As for self-righteousness, it does not see that it has done anything wrong. That is why the Lord rebuked the Pharisees, "who trusted in themselves that they were righteous" (Luke 18.9). He said that He "did not come to call the righteous, but sinners, to repentance" (Matthew 9.13). Truly, those who see themselves as righteous and beautiful in their own eyes are perhaps described by this saying of the Bible: "There is a righteous man who perishes in his righteousness" (Ecclesiastes 7.15). These people are completely far from repentance. If you confront them with their sins, they will argue a lot and will not confess. Heaven will not rejoice over the ninety-nine (just persons) such as these, who consider that they "need no repentance" (Luke 15.7); it rejoices over one sinner who is contrite in his repentance, confessing his sins.

The sins that a sinner confesses are the ones of which he repents and asks forgiveness. We regret only the sins we know and confess. However, we also need to regret the sins we discover in our past, which God will reveal to us, or which will be revealed through our spiritual reading, through sermons, or through the mouths of our advisors and spiritual fathers. So we begin to repent of them. In this way, we grow in our repentance and in the confession of our sins.

Our spiritual measures become more sensitive, and our balance becomes more precise. So we know not only our sins, but feel even more the burden of these sins and their ugliness. David the Prophet, when he knew the depth of his sin, had a similar depth of repentance and contrition of heart, and humility before God. It is therefore up to us to deepen our spiritual understanding, to know our exact condition.

The virtues we are proud of now may cause us to cry in the future. We will cry over their triviality, insignificance, and the weakness of their levels. When our spiritual horizons and spiritual vision expand, we will also weep for taking pride in these virtues. Most importantly, we must have true knowledge of both our sins and our shortcomings.

With confession, man is worthy of forgiveness. According to Saint John the Apostle: "If we say that we have no sin, we deceive ourselves, and the truth is not in us. If we confess our sins, He is faithful and just to forgive us our sins and to cleanse us from all unrighteousness" (1 John 1.8–9).

Confession is not merely the words, "I have sinned." Achan the son of Carmi said this word after missing the opportunity to repent (Joshua 7.20). He remained far away from confession until God pointed to him by name. So he was obliged to confess. He did not receive forgiveness, but was stoned by the people. Judas Iscariot said, "I have sinned" (Matthew 27.4), and died perishing. Out of diplomacy and not through repentance, Pharaoh said, "I have sinned" (Exodus 9.27). He repeated it another time and said to Moses and Aaron: "I have sinned against the Lord your God and against you. Now therefore, pardon my sin yet this time" (Exodus 10.16). In spite of this, Pharaoh perished, because his heart was unrepentant.

The confession that we refer to is the one that springs from repentance. Confession is one of several signs of repentance, and one of its components. Confession without repentance, however, does not benefit you in any way. As long as we are in the flesh, and as long as the opportunity for repentance is before us, before the door is closed, we should examine ourselves, realize our sins, confess them, and offer repentance for them. In this way our sins are covered by the blood of Christ, and we receive absolution for them. We will also receive absolution through the spiritual path of advice, to walk in the correct path. Confession that is mixed with repentance includes leaving sin and regretting it. The signs of repentance also include embarrassment and shame.

CHAPTER 2

Embarrassment and Shame[1]

EMBARRASSMENT AND SHAME accompany repentance, when the penitent feels the ugliness of sin. It is as if he were to say to himself, "How did I fall to this level? Where was my mind? Where was my conscience when I did this? How did I become so weak? How did I submit? How did I forget my divine image and my spiritual position?"

He is embarrassed by his sin, which stands before him always (Psalm 50). The visions of sin pursue him as if they were whips of fire that enflame his conscience, so he feels ashamed of himself. He hides his face and places his hands over his eyes, as if he does not want to see. He is, before himself, a person who was caught in the act.

He cannot lift his face up to God because of the severity of his embarrassment, like the tax collector of whom it was said that he, "standing afar off, would not so much as raise his eyes to heaven" (Luke 18.13). Rather, he beat his breast, confessing his sin and asking for mercy. He is also like the prodigal son, who because of his great embarrassment said to his father, "I am no longer worthy to be called your son" (Luke 15.19).

Every time he remembers his sin, he says with the psalmist: "All day long my disgrace is before me, and the shame of my face covers me" (Psalm 43.16). It is as if he says with Daniel the Prophet: "O Lord, righteousness belongs to You, but shame of face belongs to us" (Daniel 9.7). He is embarrassed by the disgrace of his sin and its exposure. He is embarrassed by the defilement of sin and its impurity. He is embarrassed by his defeat before sin, as if he were a soldier who surrendered his weapon to the enemy and was taken captive.

---

[1]See my book *The Spiritual Awakening*, which has a section on embarrassment and humiliation, as one of the feelings which accompany the spiritual awakening (from pages 65 to 74 in the Arabic edition).

He is embarrassed by God's love for him, and by God's holiness. He is embarrassed every time he compares his treatment of God to God's treatment of him, and how he met God's love with rejection and denial, and also with betrayal. Also, he is embarrassed by how God saw him when he fell—God, who is all-Holy and perfect. He is embarrassed by God's perseverance, how God remained patient with him until he repented.

He is embarrassed by the spirits of the saints and angels, who saw him fall and were amazed, and prayed for his sake that he would be raised up again. He is also embarrassed by the spirits of his relatives and friends who have passed away, and how without a doubt they were amazed when they saw his condition. How shall he face them in the future?

He is embarrassed by his enemies who would rejoice over him if they knew of his falls. He is embarrassed before all these people. He is also embarrassed before the Church and its holiness, by the sanctuary and the altar, by proceeding to Holy Communion. He is embarrassed by his prayers, which contain statements of God's love and adherence to Him, for he is the one who separated himself from this love.

He is embarrassed by the promises he made to God previously: how he broke all his oaths, even those that he spoke to God with great seriousness, whether before the altar, with his hand placed on the Bible, or on spiritual occasions. He is also embarrassed in his confession, every time he mentions the ugliness of his sins. He is belittled in his own eyes. He despises himself in this state of fallen weakness, as if he wished to get rid of his entire past. He is ashamed of this part of his past, in particular.

On the whole, shame over sin is a healthy sign. It shows that the person is rejecting sin and is disgusted by it. This is a sign of purity of heart. It differs from the state of his fall, in which he accepted sin and was satisfied with it or enjoyed it. If this shame of sin remains with him, it will help him not to fall in the future.

There are types of people who try to escape from shame and embarrassment through sinful deeds that push them to continue in sin. The devil utilizes their embarrassment over their previous sins and pushes them to change the religious surroundings in which they live, where they are embarrassed by comparing their falls with its purity. Or, the devil calls them to change their father confessor, so that they will be too embarrassed to say their sins in front of him. Or, he invites them to leave confession completely, or to leave the Church and religious life. Or, they escape from their embarrassment by drowning in the life of entertainment, amusement, and laughter.

All of these examples are actions of despair, against the life of repentance. Therefore, we bless the penitent ones who feel ashamed of their sins. Accompanying this shame also is regret, tears, and the torment of the conscience.

CHAPTER 3

Regret, Suffering, and Tears[1]

SUFFERING BECAUSE OF SIN is one of the signs of true repentance. David
the Prophet said of this suffering: "For my bones are troubled; and my soul
is greatly troubled" (Psalm 6.3–4). Truly, the Lord Jesus suffered for our
sins, but we must enter with Him into "the fellowship of His sufferings"
(Philippians 3.10).

The penitent's suffering due to sin is balanced by his previous enjoyment
of it. The enjoyment he received previously he returns in repentance fourfold, by bearing the suffering of the torments and rebukes of his conscience.
He literally suffers the "weeping and gnashing of teeth" in his repentance
by any measure, in a hell he passes through here on earth, like the burnt
offering made by fire which is a sweet aroma to the Lord (Leviticus 1). He
reprimands himself severely, disciplines and punishes himself: He asks for
spiritual penances from his father confessor, in case his conscience should
rest for even a little while. With penances he declares his objection to his
sins.

Whoever repents, bearing his disgrace, accepts two types of punishment.
The first type is the punishment he inflicts on himself, whether by bitter reprimand or by forbidding himself from things he loves, so that he renounces
this world he previously loved. The second type is all of the punishments
that come to him from the outside, whether from God or from other people.
He accepts all of these punishments with satisfaction, without grumbling
or complaining. He is convicted by them and feels that they are less than
what he deserves.

Even those punishments which afflict him unjustly he also accepts
with satisfaction, like what happened to Saint Ephraim the Syrian. He was
imprisoned once unjustly, so he accepted this and said that he deserved it for

[1]The lecture about tears dates to 1964. I added to it a lecture called "He Carries His
Disgrace," which I gave at the Great Cathedral on April 7, 1974.

233

an old sin, which had no relation to this matter. Also, it is like the acceptance of David the Prophet of the scorn and abuse from Shimei the son of Gera (2 Kingdoms 16.5–10). Similarly, it is like Saint Moses the Black's acceptance of his eviction on the day of his ordination as a priest, when he said to himself, "Rightly they have done to you, you black man whose skin is grey."[2]

Those who do not withstand discipline and punishment are far from repentance, for the penitent feels that he deserves everything he faces. He does not reject any bitterness that sin brings, but accepts it with thanks, bearing his disgrace. Suffering is a clear result of sin, as happened to Adam and Eve (Genesis 3.16–17). You cannot escape from it.

Whenever the punishment continues for a longer period, the heart becomes more purified, like clothes that continue boiling for a longer period and become cleaner. The heart becomes purified like gold that remains in the fire for a longer period, becoming cleansed of impurities. Contrary to this, whoever gains forgiveness with ease, escaping from any suffering that sin brings, finds it easy for him to return to sin another time, since he does not feel the ugliness of the results of sin.

Do not say, "The Lord has borne all the suffering for me, and I will rest." Do not look at the Lord's sufferings with this carelessness, thinking only about yourself. Remember that those who partook of the Passover ate with bitter herbs (Exodus 12.8). What is the position of the bitter herbs in your life? What is the extent of your entering into the fellowship of the Lord's sufferings? If you see the Lord carrying the cross as a ransom for your sins, run behind Him and say to Him, "Let me carry it with you, like the Cyrenian" (Luke 23.26).

Or say to Him in suffering, "I am your cross, O Lord, you carried me all this long time. I am the thorns which they placed around Your head, O Lord. I am the nails with which they pierced Your hands and feet, O Lord. I wish I were crucified with You like the thief on the right. Or I wish I could say with Saint Paul the Apostle: 'I have been crucified with Christ'" (Galatians 2.20).

Do not put the sufferings of Christ out of your thoughts, since this will make you careless and you will look to your sins without suffering. If we should go forth to Him outside the camp, bearing His reproach (Hebrews

[2]Moses 4, *Saying of the Desert Fathers.*

13.13), then we should at least bear our own reproach with humility and tears.

There are many types of tears. Here we will talk about one type: the tears of repentance, which man weeps over his sins. Do not think that weeping over the sins is a step for beginners. Many of the great saints wept for their sins. This was a known spiritual program for the fathers of the desert.

The most prominent example of weeping over sin might be David the Prophet. He was the one who said: "All night I make my bed swim; I drench my couch with my tears" (Psalm 6.7). What was the amount of weeping of this penitent prophet, who used to drench his couch with his tears? Did he only weep for his sins in the evening, when he returned to his house? No, for he says: "My tears were my bread day and night" (Psalm 41.4). Even while eating and drinking, he says: "I ate ashes like bread, and mingled my drink with weeping" (Psalm 101.10). That means that while drinking his tears fell into his cup, so he mingled his drink with tears.

His tears were abundant, despite the majesty that surrounded him. He was a king, a leader of the army, a judge to the people, and the father of a large family. In spite of this, he did not give importance to any of this majesty and luxury, but said to the Lord: "Give ear to my supplication" (Psalm 38.13). He also says to God: "Put my tears into Your bottle" (Psalm 55.9).

If someone asks, "Why should I cry when my sin has been forgiven?" we say to him, "David wept for his sin after it was forgiven, and not before. Before his forgiveness he did not feel the danger and the ugliness of his fall, until Nathan the Prophet alerted him to this, so he confessed his sin, and God forgave him through the words of Nathan the Prophet who said to him, 'The Lord also has put away your sin. You shall not die' (2 Kingdoms 12.13). After that, David wept all of those tears." Why did he weep? Was this because of fear of punishment or a plea for forgiveness? Not at all.

The servant weeps for fear of punishment, but the son weeps from the sensitivity of his heart toward his father. Who among us has wept as David wept? Who among us has drenched his couch with his tears for one night, let alone every night, as he did? David kept weeping for his sin all of his life. He did not rest from his weeping until his death. When he came closer to death, he said: "Return, O my soul, to your rest, for the Lord has dealt bountifully with you. For He delivered my soul from death, my eyes from tears" (Psalm 114:7–8). He rescued him from eternal death by accepting his repentance. He rescued his eyes from tears, because He moved him to "the place where grief, sorrow, and groaning have fled away."[3] The Lord rescued him there from tears, because he wept enough here.

This reminds us of the story of Saint Arsenius, who wept greatly. He wept while he was in the state of holiness, while he was a pillar in the desert. He wept until his eyelashes fell from the abundance of his weeping. In the summer, he drenched his palm leaves with tears. He used to place a towel on his lap to collect his tears. At the time of his death he wept greatly. His disciples said to him, "'Truly, Father, are you also afraid?' 'Indeed' he answered them, 'the fear which is mine at this hour has been with me ever since I became a monk.'"[4]

If this saint wept, in spite of his many virtues and in spite of his meekness, wisdom, silence, and his vigilance all night in prayer, and despite the fact that the Pope himself asked him to visit him to receive a word of benefit, then what shall we say about ourselves? When Saint Poemen heard about the departure of Saint Arsenius, he said, "Blessed are you, our Father Arsenius, because you wept for your soul in this world." He continued, "For the one who does not weep for his soul in this world, inevitably will weep forever in the other world. As for his weeping here, this is by his own choice. There, however, he will weep because of the punishments that he will receive. It is impossible for man to flee from weeping here and there."[5]

Such weeping was the advice of Saint Macarius before his departure. "I heard that the elders who are in Nitria have sent to Abba Macarius the Great who lived in Scetis and pleaded with him, saying: 'We plead with you, our father, to come to us so that we may see you before you depart to the Lord, so that not all the people will go to you.' When he came to them, they all gathered together with him, and the elders asked him to say a word of benefit to the brethren. The saint wept and said to them, 'Let us weep, my brothers, and may our eyes overflow with tears, before we go to that place in which our tears will burn our bodies.' They all wept and fell on their faces, saying, 'Pray for us, O father.'"

[3] *Editor's note:* From the Coptic Orthodox Litany for the Departed.
[4] Arsenius 40, *Sayings of the Desert Fathers.*
[5] Bemen 41, *Sayings of the Desert Fathers.*

What sins did the saints commit for them to weep like this? The customary advice that the elder would give to anyone who came to him seeking advice was, "Sit in your cell and weep for your sins." If this is the program of the saints, then what should we do, who have innumerable sins? Look also to the weeping of an elder such as Peter the Apostle, who when he felt his denial of the Lord, "went out and wept bitterly" (Matthew 26.75). The weeping of the elders has more influence on the soul than the weeping of the little ones and the youth.

Among those famous for weeping was Saint Isidore. He was the great priest of The Cells, under whose spiritual advice were 3,000 monks. He was the father confessor of Saint Moses the Black. He was a man of revelations and wonders; the demons feared and revered him greatly, and fled from him. In spite of all that, this saint used to weep with abundant tears and loud sobs, to the extent that when his disciple, who lived next to him, heard him weeping, went and asked him, "Why are you weeping, my father?" he answered, "My son, I am weeping for my sins." The disciple said, "Even you, our father, have sins to weep for?" The saint answered him, "Believe me, my son, if God revealed all of my sins to me, three or four people would not be enough to weep with me for them."

Here is a sensitivity in the delicate heart and the strict conscience. He wept because he angered the loving God, because he fell from his suitable spiritual level as God's image, because he fell when he should not have fallen. He wept in embarrassment over his condition. Although the sin was forgiven, forgiveness does not erase what occurred. God forgave Peter's denial, but history still talks about that denial. God forgave Rahab, but the Holy Bible still uses the title "the harlot Rahab" (Hebrews 11.31).

The Church teaches us to weep every day. Every one of us should stand to pray the second part of the Midnight Prayer every day and say, "Give me, Lord, fountains of tears as You did in the past to the sinful woman. . . ." The Church gives us the Bible reading specific to this woman, who washed the Lord's feet with her tears and wiped them with the hair of her head (Luke 7.36–50), so that we may read it and take her as an example in weeping for sins, "so that we may gain for ourselves a pure life with repentance."[6] If you pray this prayer at midnight, say, "Give me, Lord, many fountains of tears to

[6]*Editor's note:* Prayers quoted from the petitions of the Midnight Prayer in the *Agpeya.*

weep for this and that," and mention before God all your sins, weaknesses, shortcomings, and falls. I wish that you would mention them with tears before Him.

You may ask, "Why should I mention them, when Christ has forgiven them?" Here, it is very suitable for us to remember the saying of the great Saint Antony: "If we remember our sins, God will forget them, and if we forget our sins, God will remember them." Yes, mention your sins so that you may know your weaknesses, be cautious, and become strict in your life. Mention them so that you know how much God has forgiven you, and how much He bore for your sake on the cross, so you will love Him. Your tears will become a sign of love, as were the tears of the sinful woman.

It is the gentle heart that weeps. The harsh heart, however, does not weep. Your heart must be gentle in your repentance. Your weeping must beg for pardon before the Lord against whom you sinned, and also be proof of your embarrassment for what you have done. Be aware that whoever weeps for his sins will not return to them easily another time, for he tasted the extent of the pain that sin brings to the heart and conscience.

God invites us to this weeping for repentance. He says in the book of Joel the Prophet: "Turn to Me with all your heart, with fasting and wailing, and with mourning; rend your heart and not your garments. Return to the Lord your God" (Joel 2.12–13). He says in the book of Malachi the Prophet: "You cover the altar of the Lord with tears, with weeping and moaning" (Malachi 2.13). He also says: "Blessed are you who weep now" (Luke 6.21), "blessed are those who mourn, for they shall be comforted" (Matthew 5.4). Weep for your sins, and then the saying of the psalmist will comfort you: "The Lord heard the voice of my weeping . . . the Lord received my prayer" (Psalm 6: 9–10). David said this after saying: "I drench my couch with my tears." Tears are a sign of repentance, and God responds to them. They have a sound that God hears, and His heart sympathizes with you.

How beautiful is the saying of the psalmist, "Those who sow in tears shall reap with exceeding joy" (Psalm 125.5). This joy is the comfort that man reaps from his tears. Beware if your tears are fake; they might be the reason for self-righteousness instead of being the reason for contrition of heart, or a result of it, or a sign for repentance. According to the opinion of one of the saints, "If tears come to you, then remember the reason for which they came." That is, remember your sins that caused these tears. Then do not be puffed up by your tears, but be contrite. One may ask, "Where do these tears come from? Am I unrepentant, then, if I do not weep, or will God not accept my repentance?" No, God will accept you, but search for why tears have escaped you.

There are reasons why tears come, and reasons why they are held back. The first reason might be the type of heart. The naturally gentle heart is easily influenced and weeps readily, like the heart of Jeremiah the Prophet, and David. Other hearts do not weep with ease. If they weep, then there is surely a reason why they were pushed to weeping, a reason which was stronger than the resistance of their nature, and whose influence was greater.

Gentleness of heart, then, brings tears. Harshness and severity prevent them. Proceed then, toward this gentleness in your life, and avoid severity. Know that harshness does not agree at all with the life of repentance. The penitent is a person who implores God's mercies. The Bible says: "Blessed are the merciful, for they shall obtain mercy" (Matthew 5.7). He must be merciful so that God will treat him with this same mercy, since He says: "With the measure you use, it will be measured back to you" (Matthew 7.2).

The judgment of others also prevents tears. Whoever judges another is not preoccupied with his sins, but with the sins of others. He forgets his weaknesses and failures, and concentrates on the weaknesses of others. How can he weep like them, and for whom? Such a person moves further away than others from tears, especially if his judgment of others involved harshness, severity, or accusation, or harsh reprimand of their sins.

Anger is another factor that prevents tears. The repentant person should be angry with himself, and not with another person. If he is angry with others, his emotions and thoughts will be concentrated on the sins of others, and the tears will leave him even if he had them previously. Anger also includes harshness and severity.

Enjoyment and pleasure also prevent tears. Whoever lives in luxury and enjoyment, in the different types of worldly pleasure, finds it difficult for tears to come to him. Generally, these matters do not agree with the life of repentance in which man restricts and punishes himself, forbids himself many enjoyments, and imposes fasts on himself. Therefore, many peoples' repentance was accompanied by fasting, sackcloth, humiliation, and the like, as in the fast in the days of Joel, and in the fast of Nineveh. This agrees with repentance and tears.

Naturally, whoever keeps away from tears finds laughter and jollity. Truly, for everything under heaven there is a time: "A time to weep and a time to laugh" (Ecclesiastes 3.4). Laughter and joking, however, belong neither in the season nor during the time of repentance. The life of amusement, mockery, hilarity, and the different delights of the world do not agree with tears, but rather hinder them, because whoever weeps for his sins is a person who is seized by grief over his falls.

Among the things that bring tears is the feeling of alienation from the world, the feeling in man that he is a stranger on earth, and that it is not right for him to place his hopes in it. On the contrary, it is his job to renounce the world and all that is in it, and prepare for eternity. All of this assists in tears.

Similarly, there is the remembrance of death, judgment, and the other world. All of this brings tears. Therefore the Church arranged for us to remember death in the prayer before sleeping; to remember the Second Coming of Christ in the midnight prayer; and to remember in all of them, and in the prayer of the *Settar* (Veil) also, how the great Judgment will be.[7] This happens every day. Since these remembrances are of benefit to us, helping us in repentance and preparation, they also bring tears. Similarly, the visiting of graves also brings about tears, for during this time the penitent says with David the Prophet: "O Lord, make me to know my end, and what is the measure of my days, that I may know how frail I am" (Psalm 38.5).

Similarly, the life of meekness and contrition assists in tears, whereas pride, majesty, and the love of praise do not agree with feelings of repentance, nor do they agree with tears. Therefore it is better that we move on to this point from the signs of repentance.

---

[7] *Editor's note:* The Prayer of the Veil is in the *Agpeya*.

CHAPTER 4

Contrition and Humility

T HE TRUE PENITENT LIVES WITH this same contrition, being pressed by embarrassment and regret, and he feels the humiliation of sin. He walks with this humiliation within himself and before God. This appears in his treatment of other people.

While he is contrite, he rebukes himself regularly for what he did. He rebukes himself for the days of his life that were lost and without fruits, for his weaknesses, failures, and betrayal of the Lord. He says to himself, "Many others have passed me long ago and arrived at relationships of deep love with God, while I am still struggling to repent. How long will this carelessness and laziness last?" This penitent mourns over himself and his fall, remembering the saying of Saint Isaac: "The penitent who does not mourn everyday as a result of his sins, should know that he has lost that day, even if he did every good deed in it."[1]

His self-rebuke makes him humble, no matter how his life changes through repentance. No matter what good deeds he does in his repentance, he is not proud, because his sins are before him always. Man should remind himself of his falls in order not to be proud, so that the fruits of repentance do not push him to vainglory. As Saint Isaac also said: "If you are attacked by thoughts of vainglory, do not accept them, but remember Mary [of Egypt] with her fornication and Israel with his defeat." By blaming yourself and knowing your weaknesses, you will possess humility of thought.

The humble penitent sees himself as deserving of the grief that afflicts him. This is because he accepts everything that comes to him with quietness and satisfaction, with neither grumbling nor toil nor complaint, feeling deep within himself that he deserves much worse than this. He sings with David, saying: "It is good for me that I have been afflicted, that I may learn Your statutes" (Psalm 118).

[1] Isaac the Syrian, *Ascetical Homilies* XXXVII.

Whenever the penitent's period of contrition lengthens, his repentance increases in depth, because he realizes the humiliation of sin, its ugliness, and its results within himself. He also realizes his weakness and becomes accustomed in his life to being cautious and strict. Unfortunate is the person who in repentance sees that his life has changed and, believing that he is no longer in need of struggle and caution, forgets his previous weakness.

It is dangerous for the penitent to leave contrition too quickly for joy. Nothing is easier for man than to return to the sin that did not take its full term of contrition and humiliation, because its danger and ugliness were not implanted long enough within his soul. David did not rush in his repentance toward joy, but remained contrite; his psalms witness to his contrition. Saint Mary of Egypt remained many long years in the life of repentance. Jacob the struggler remained about eighteen years in weeping for his sins.

In the life of repentance, nothing is more dangerous than the person who moves quickly from sin into church service or the desire for talents. A person who is new in repentance might stand at the pulpit of the church to tell of his spiritual experiences, and say in simplicity, "When I was a sinner," or "When I used to live in sin," as if presently he had no relationship with sin, which concerns the past only. You might ask such a person, "And now, do you not sin?" When he answers you, "Now, thanks be to the Lord," he means that he is thankful for the righteousness in which he now lives. He speaks with great courage about the light shining presently in his heart, and the love toward God that fills his heart.

The phrase "when I used to sin" is very dangerous. It is devoid of humility. It shows a lack of true knowledge of the soul. It does not conform to the repentance of the tax collector and his prayer in the sanctuary, nor with Saint Paul the Apostle's expression "to save sinners, of whom I am chief" (I Timothy 1.15). It does not agree with the many stories of repentance in the lives of the saints.

You, my brother, were a sinner, and you are still a sinner. The difference between your previous condition and your present one is that you were a sinner who continued in sin, and perhaps you were not aware of yourself. Now, you are a sinner, you feel you are a sinner, and you struggle with the grace of the Lord to repent. Repentance will remain with you all of your life, until you reach purity.[2] The person who does not feel that he is a sinner, in this sense, commits the greater sin.

There is no one without sin, not even if his life were one day.[3] We all sin, every day. We all stand at every hour in front of God as sinners. In the Lord's Prayer, which we pray regularly, we say, "Forgive us our sins. . . ." We repeat this theme in the rest of the prayers; even if you are a righteous man, the Bible says: "For a righteous man may fall seven times and rise again" (Proverbs 24.16). Perhaps you are now repentant. You are not infallible, however. You will only reach purity of heart through the contrition of your soul.

Whoever does not possess contrition is not truly repentant. He, without a doubt, does not know himself. He is building on a sinful foundation, which will lead him to arrogance. What is more beautiful than the hymn in which we say to the Lord, "This sin is characteristic of me. Forgiveness is characteristic of you"?[4]

Read about the saints who repented and remained poor in heart. They also preserved their humility. If the thought came to them that they had already repented, they attributed any virtue to God: "He raises the poor man from the earth, and lifts up the poor from the dunghill" (Psalm 112.7). They insisted on considering themselves sinners all the days of their lives, like the great Saint Sisoes, who was seen at the hour of his death asking for a chance to repent.[5]

Therefore, no matter how much you grow in grace, it is better for you to say, "I want to remain in the feelings of repentance all of my life." Live in contrition of the heart because, "the Lord is near those who are broken-hearted" (Psalm 33.19). If the devil invites you to ascend to the heights, to sit in the heavens and attain virtues, then say, "I have not yet reached any of this. All that I know about myself is that I am a sinner who wants to repent."

If you enter into service in the Church, do not let that make you forget your sins. Do not let your success in any spiritual work make you forget your tears and contrition. On the contrary, rebuke yourself and say, "Who am I to

---

[2] See Part Five, which concerns the life of purity, in this book.

[3] *Editor's note:* From the Coptic Orthodox Litany for the Departed.

[4] *Editor's note:* From the Midnight Psalmody of the Advent Season (Coptic Month of Kiahk), the Sunday Psali.

[5] Sisoes 14, *Sayings of the Desert Fathers.*

serve? I have not reached the spirituality of the servant, no matter how much knowledge I have." Knowledge is not what saves the soul.

Saint Paul the Apostle remained contrite even after his apostleship. His sin remained before him even after revelations, signs, and wonders, even after he ascended to the third heaven, and even after he labored more abundantly than all the apostles (1 Corinthians 15.10). In his discussion about the appearance of the Lord to His disciples after the Resurrection, he says: "Then last of all He was seen by me also, as by one born out of due time. For I am the least of the apostles, who am not worthy to be called an apostle, because I persecuted the Church of God" (1 Corinthians 15.8–9). In his first epistle to his disciple Timothy, he says: "I was formerly a blasphemer, a persecutor, and an insolent man; but I obtained mercy because I did it ignorantly in unbelief" (1 Timothy 1.13). We might say to him, "It was not you, O great Saint Paul the Apostle, but Saul of Tarsus. You, however, are a new person in the Lord Jesus, a preacher, a missionary, an apostle, and a builder of the heavenly kingdom." Yet this saint maintains his contrition and says: "I am not worthy to be called an apostle . . ." (1 Corinthians 15.9).

His old sin has ended with respect to his punishment, but not with respect to his memory. It lingers in his memory, granting him contrition and the feelings of unworthiness. In spite of his long years in apostolic service, he lived as a beginner, as the least of the apostles and the first of the sinners.

You, too, will live as a beginner all the days of your life, as if you were still a child in the life of the spirit. It is enough for you that "The Lord preserves the simple" (Psalm 114.6). Do not ever think that you have reached your spiritual goal. For the great Saint Paul the Apostle says: "I do not count myself to have apprehended or attained anything: but I press on, that I may lay hold" [of the prize] (Philippians 3.12–13). The great Saint Arsenius used to pray: "O God . . . let me now make a beginning of good,"[6] as if he had not yet started. Contrition is one of the signs of repentance.

---

[6] Arsenius 3, *Sayings of the Desert Fathers.*

CHAPTER 5

Repairing the Results of the Fault

It is not enough by any means for you to leave sin, to repent of it, confess, and receive absolution for it. You must repair the results of your sin as much as you can. We will give some examples of this.

Let us assume that someone has stolen. Is it enough for him to confess the stealing? Is his confession enough for forgiveness, when he still has the unlawful money he obtained by theft? By no means, for to the extent that he is able, he must return the stolen thing to its owners, even if it is done in a discreet way.

If he has done injustice to anyone, he should try to redress this injustice. There is a clear example for our instruction before us, in the form of Zacchaeus the chief tax collector. When he repented, he said to the Lord publicly: "Look, Lord, I give half of my goods to the poor; and if I have taken anything from anyone by false accusation, I restore fourfold" (Luke 19.8). If you cannot do what Zacchaeus did and restore fourfold, then at least restore the stolen thing itself, or redress and remedy the injustice, without multiplying.

You will feel the beauty of repentance if, as part of it, you restore the right to its owners. If you feel embarrassment in doing this, in practically confessing that you did an injustice and stole, this embarrassment is good for you; it will be like a fortress for you, preventing you from committing this sin another time. You will also feel from within that your repentance is built upon principles which command respect, so your heart will rejoice and be comforted.

Similarly, if you defame someone and hurt his reputation, is it not right for you, in your repentance, to restore his reputation? Especially since you did him injustice and hurt him, for the wrong words spread about someone else can cause bad results in his life.

What if repairing of the results of sin is impossible? If it is truly not possible, then at least you should be contrite for this reason: you have committed sins that are difficult to redress.

CHAPTER 6

Compassion for the Sinners

SAINT ISAAC SAID: "Whoever mourns for himself will not know the faults of others, and will not blame anyone for any offense."[1] If a person repents with feelings of contrition and lack of worthiness, he will by no means think about the sins of others; he will not judge anyone if he himself falls under judgment as a result of his sins. As the Lord said to those who wished to stone the sinful woman: "He who is without sin among you, let him throw a stone at her first" (John 8.7). Truly, he who is occupied with removing the plank from his own eye, cannot judge the speck which is in his brother's eye (Matthew 7.5). Every time the thought of judging someone comes to him, he says, "I have fallen in this and that, and this person is more righteous than I am, because my sins are more numerous than his."

Contrition removes all harshness from the heart of the penitent and gives him mercy toward everyone, no matter how sinful they may be. His remembrance of his sins makes him compassionate toward sinners; he does not judge them, but weeps for their sakes, as Saint John the Dwarf did in the meekness of his heart. Whenever he saw someone in sin, he wept and said, "If the devil made my brother fall today, he will make me fall tomorrow. The Lord will forgive my brother and he will repent, and I may fall and not repent," and he wept. How magnificent are the words that Saint Paul the Apostle said about this: "Remember the prisoners as if chained with them—those who are mistreated—since you yourselves are in the body also" (Hebrews 13.3). The person who does not sin judges sinners from a position of pride. As for the person who has sinned and tried the weakness of human nature, he has compassion on them.

We have a clear example in the life of Saint Moses the Black. He was invited to a monastic council to judge a brother who had sinned, but went there carrying on his back a sack filled with sand, in which there was a hole.

---

[1] Isaac the Syrian, *Ascetical Homilies* LVII.

When they asked him about this, he answered, "These are my sins which run behind my back and I cannot see them, and I have come here to judge my brother."[2]

The penitent does not mention the sins of others, even if they were against him. Saint Amos mentioned that one of the signs of repentance is "forgiveness of your neighbor's sins, leaving the judgment of others, and humility of heart." Saint Isaac said that the penitent should have perfect patience over insult and blame. The great Saint Antony said: "If someone blames you from the outside, it is your responsibility to blame yourself from within, so that there is a balance between your outside and your inside."[3]

The penitent forgives others, as the Lord forgave him—or so that the Lord will forgive him, according to His divine saying: "Forgive, and you will be forgiven" (Luke 6.37). When the Lord taught us the Lord's Prayer, He stressed only one of its requests, which concerned forgiveness. He said: "For if you forgive men their trespasses, your heavenly Father will also forgive you. But if you do not forgive men their trespasses, neither will your Father forgive your trespasses" (Matthew 6.14–15). Let this forgiveness be in love; it must agree with the commandment to "love your enemies" (Luke 6.27), and it must agree with the life of humility, which is worthy of repentance.

[2]Moses 2, *Sayings of the Desert Fathers.*
[3]Antony 4, *Sayings of the Desert Fathers.*

CHAPTER 7

Other Feelings

THE REPENTANT PERSON who weeps for his sins is always gentle and peaceful. He neither argues nor raises his voice, nor causes his voice to be heard in the street (Isaiah 42.2). The penitent feels the desire to be silent when he sees that he is not worthy to speak. It is better for him to listen, for hearing is better than speaking. In this way the penitent keeps away from teaching, remembering the saying of James the Apostle: "My brethren, let not many of you become teachers, knowing that we shall receive a stricter judgment. For we all stumble in many things" (James 3.1–2). He says to himself, "Who am I to teach others? Teaching is a level above my standard. What are my spiritual experiences, that I may teach others also?" The penitent feels a spiritual greatness that God opens before him, and that he has begun to enter into the taste of the kingdom. That is why we mostly see penitents characterized by spiritual fervor.

CHAPTER 8

Spiritual Fervor

Repentance is a fervor that runs through a person, inflaming him with the desire to change his life for the better. Saint John Saba [of Dalyatha] was right when he said about repentance: "Everyone who is born of it develops wings of fire, and he flies high with the spiritual people."[1]

Repentance gives birth within the heart to great love toward God. For every time we meditate on the heavy burden that He lifted and carried for us, every time we meditate on the ugliness of the many bitter sins for which He forgave us, then our love for Him greatly increases. It is like the sinful woman who washed His feet with her tears, of whom He said that she loved much, because He forgave her much (Luke 7). The sinners who feel the burden of their sins and the Lord's forgiveness are the ones who love God most, and they understand the depths of the cross and of redemption.

In this love the sinner is ready to sacrifice himself for the sake of God. An amazing fervor possesses him and greatly pushes him forward. This push is the same one that changed sinners such as Pelagia, Mary of Egypt, and Augustine into saints. They are the ones who repented, felt the delight of this life of repentance, and grew in it.

The problem for many people is that they have lost the initial fervor of their repentance: the fervor that once inflamed their hearts with love and pushed them to compensate for all that they had lost in their past lives. If the penitent does not preserve this fervor and kindle it regularly, what could be easier than for him to lose it? He then devolves to laxity, and perhaps his feelings cool down after he forgets his sins or avoids them for a certain time.

The penitent feels that his eyes are opened to a new life, as if the door of paradise has been opened in front of him, and he sees there what he had not seen before. This new life attracts him strongly, to the point that some

[1] John of Dalyatha, *Letters*.

father confessors even fear for their confessing children during their extreme rush into this period.

There are many who consecrate themselves to God in the fervor of their repentance, like Saint Pelagia, Saint Mary of Egypt, and others. These, in their repentance and regret for their sins, felt drawn to the renunciation of the world, for there was nothing in it any more to entice them after they had tasted the love of God.

In the spiritual fervor that accompanies repentance, the penitent feels a power within him which he did not have before. He was weak in his sin before the devil and his wars, but in his repentance the Spirit of God gives him a special grace, and power for the life of repentance. This reminds us of the sick person who, because of his weakness, was given a blood transfusion and was strengthened by this new blood. God has given the penitent new hearts, from which runs new, strong blood, filled with the love of God. So the prophecy of Isaiah applies to them: they "shall renew their strength; they shall mount up with wings like eagles" (Isaiah 40.31).

"They shall run and not be weary, they shall walk and not faint," he also says. "He gives power to the weak, and to those who have no might he increases strength" (Isaiah 40.29). I wonder, my brother, if you have touched this power in your repentance and felt how the right hand of the Lord carried you to the life of light, and how God "renewed your youth like the eagle's" (Psalm 102.5). If you feel it, you will sing with David, saying: "The right hand of the Lord exalted me; the right hand of the Lord worked its power. I shall not die, but live" (Psalm 117.16–17). With this power you will live a virtuous life.

CHAPTER 9

Walking in the Virtuous Life

T HERE IS NO REPENTANCE without a change in life. Repentance is not merely confession and Holy Communion; it is leaving sin to walk positively in the life of righteousness. With this the penitent receives forgiveness, according to the saying of Saint John the Apostle: "If we walk in the light as He is in the light, we have fellowship with one another, and the blood of Jesus Christ His Son cleanses us from all sin" (1 John 1.7). Our walking in the light is a fundamental condition for our purification from sin. It is one of the signs of repentance. Saint Paul the Apostle expresses this walking, which purifies from sin and lifts judgment, when he says that "there is therefore now no condemnation to those who are in Christ Jesus, who do not walk according to the flesh, but according to the Spirit" (Romans 8.1).

Thus, among the conditions of this new life is to walk in the light, according to the Spirit, or, as Saint Paul said: "Walk worthy of the calling with which you were called" (Ephesians 4.1). He also said: "That you may walk worthy of the Lord . . . being fruitful in every good work" (Colossians 1.10). "Walk in love. . . . Walk as children of light" (Ephesians 5.2,8).

Repentance, then, is not merely falling down at the feet of Christ, as some say. It is distinguished by a particular spiritual behavior and by keeping the commandments of the Lord. Saint John the Apostle said: "He who says he abides in Him ought himself also to walk just as He walked" (1 John 2.6). He also said: "He who says 'I know Him,' and does not keep His commandments, is a liar, and the truth is not in him" (1 John 2.4).

We throw ourselves at the feet of Christ, to obtain from Him assistance and grace. Grace does not mean that we should be lazy or continue in the life of sin, but that we should keep His commandments and walk as He walked, walking in the light just as He is in the light. This leads us to the final sign of repentance.

CHAPTER 10

Purity

PURITY IS THE POSITIVE COMPONENT in the life of repentance, the fruit of the change of life. In it disappear the desire for the world, the body, and sin; the desire of the heart becomes holy in the life of righteousness and the love of God. The penitent is not influenced any more by the love of sin. One of the signs of purity is that man practices virtue without struggle, without labor, without wrestling. There is nothing within him to resist it. If you find yourself wrestling between good and evil, then you have not yet reached purity but are struggling to attain it. If you labor to reach the life of righteousness, then you are still in the virtue of struggle and have not reached purity yet.

With purity, peace reigns over your heart, and the wrestling is stopped by the victory of good. With purity you find rest in God, and also your desire and happiness. Purity covers your entire life, your expressions, senses, body, heart, and thoughts. You become a dwelling for the Holy Spirit, from which the fruits of the Spirit appear. Purity is an involved topic, and we do it injustice if we make it only one part of this book, as one of the signs of repentance.

Therefore, I will, with your permission, set aside a special section for it. We will speak to you in it about purity, how it should be, and how it should be examined. What are its components? What limit does purity reach on earth? What is the purity we will receive in eternity?

PART FIVE

Purity of Heart[1]

S<small>O LONG AS THE PERFECTION</small> of repentance is hatred of sin—that is, the heart completely purified from every love for sin or conformity to it—then purity of heart is one of the signs of perfect repentance. What is the measure that we use to measure the purity of heart from sin? How does man know that he has reached perfection of repentance, that is, the hatred of sin? We will examine this point together.

---

[1]The source of this part is as follows: A lecture I gave at the Angel Mikhail Church in Damanhour in 1996, during a series on the life of repentance and purity; a lecture I gave in the hall of Saint Mark's at Anba Rewais, May 28, 1966; two lectures which I gave in the Great Cathedral in Cairo, the first on February 16, 1973, and the second on July 6, 1973 on the life of purity; and a lecture on knowing sin, which I gave at the Cathedral on March 11, 1977.

CHAPTER I

Purity from Sin

A PERSON MAY THINK THAT HE IS repentant because he has left behind the major sin that had troubled his conscience, and he has not returned to it nor fallen into it again. He has not returned to committing adultery, for example, or to stealing, cheating, or getting drunk. He has not resumed committing sins of this level. Therefore his conscience has rested, and he thinks he has repented. This is because the revelation of those great sins on which he once concentrated covered up the other sins that he did not commit. Perhaps, at the same time, he was in the midst of many sins he regarded as insignificant, and which did not enter into his personal measure of repentance. These sins might include talking about the self, enjoyment of praise, self-justifications, abundant arguing, walking according to personal desire, or the adherence to opinions that leads to stubbornness. Along with these go neglecting prayer and laxity in spiritual readings. Perhaps also he does not tolerate insults, and does not keep holy the Lord's day. In all of this his conscience does not rebuke him, because he has not yet reached the level at which he feels rebuke for such matters. Do we consider such a person a penitent?

He, without a doubt, needs to raise his standards so that he can repent of sins he considers insignificant. When, then, shall we consider him a penitent? Will it not be when he departs from all sins, even the ones that seem small in his sight? He leaves them in practice and also dismisses them from his heart and thoughts. Here, man ascends one step in repentance every time he matures spiritually. His conscience becomes very sensitive, overlooking nothing. With this he enters into true repentance. If he reaches this stage, do we judge him to have reached purity of heart?

Here we mention an important observation, so that we may have precision of judgment: perhaps he is not sinning because the devil has left him for a while. The devil is wise in doing evil. He knows when to fight, how to fight, and on which sin he should concentrate his warfare. If he finds a person very zealous and prepared, he leaves him for a while until this person is confident of himself with a confidence that might push him to carelessness, laxity, and lack of precision. The devil then returns to him at a time when he is less prepared and cautious, and so his fall becomes easier. This period is not a period of victory over sin, but a period without fighting. It is a period of rest from spiritual wars, not victory and purity.

There is a big difference between victory and lack of fighting. If you find yourself not falling into a certain sin, this does not mean that you have been purified from it completely; your lack of falling into it means that the devil is not presently fighting you with it. Or perhaps you are not falling in it now because circumstances are not favorable. So you do not find war, nor stumbling, nor will you find whatever stimulates you to sin.

The devil does not fight you now, not because he wants you to rest, but because he is preparing for you another type of trap. In addition to this other trap, perhaps the demon of vainglory will come to you and say, "Woe to you, for you have slipped from me. You have been renewed and sanctified, you have become a new creation, and the old things have passed." Do not listen to him, do not repeat in your mind what he says to you, for you are under weakness as long as you are in the flesh. The devil will not stop his fighting. It is more suitable for you to reply to these thoughts and say, "I know my weakness, and all that is in the matter is that the Lord through His compassion has covered this weakness." Do not say, then, that you have reached purity and no longer fall, but rather say, "If the Lord had not been with us ... then they would have swallowed us alive" (Psalm 123.2–3). I am actually weaker in fighting than their littlest one, as Saint Antony said.[1] Thanks be to the Lord, however, for He has protected us.

We note that some sins have their seasons and are not continual. They are like the cycles of suffering or pain; they conduct their cycle with severity and harshness, then ease and start a new cycle, and so on. Or they are like a plant, which sometimes has a season of stagnation and at another time a season of fruits and flowering.

Perhaps God wants to give you a period of rest from the burden of sin, so that your soul is not swallowed up by despair. A continual succession of falls

[1]Athanasius, *Life of Antony* 9,10, 51–53.

drags the sinner into despair. That is why God's mercies reach out to him, giving him rest, if even for a short while, and lifting the war from him. Grace protects and supports him, even if it is only for a time. So he passes through a period of calmness, in which sin does not trouble him—not because he has been purified, but because he is not fighting.

Perhaps you are peaceful now because prayers have been offered for your sake (whether by saints in heaven or by your beloved on earth) that the Lord has answered, and ordered the lifting of the war from you. You thus rest from sin and its pressures for this reason, and not because you have reached purity. You are in a period of calmness and peace, without fighting with the devil. This is not the level of purity. With regard to the difference between purity and lack of fighting, we offer the following important observation.

There is a difference between the purity of children and the purity of those mature in age and spirit. Truly, a child has a pure, simple heart, which does not yet know sin. However, there is a big difference between this purity and the purity of the mature in age. The difference is that children have not entered into spiritual warfare, and their will has not yet been tested. That is, they have not reached the age at which their will is tested. They are different from older, mature people who have entered into the wars of the enemy, who fought and overcame as their free will rejected the enticements of sin. These people have the reward of the "victorious," which is not for children. How great are those who reach the purity of children after suffering wars which children do not know. Their purity is the result of wrestling and wars, out of which they came victorious. Purity of heart is a very high level. Even if a person is attacked by a certain sin and purified from it, this is not perfect purity.

Perfect purity is purity from every sin, in all its images and types, whether by deed, or by thought, or by senses, or by feelings of the heart, or by falls of the tongue; whether in the relationship with God, or with people, or with the self. It is a comprehensive purity, not merely liberation from a certain sin which used to afflict you. The Pharisee who prayed in the sanctuary at the time of prayer of the tax collector thought that he had become one of the purified, because he was not like the "extortioners, unjust, adulterers," nor negligent in fasting and paying tithes (Luke 18.11–12). But he had not been purified from pride, nor from judging others, nor from vainglory and self-righteousness. Therefore he did not leave justified. Do not think, then, that you have reached the level of purity, merely because you have been liberated from some sins which had authority over you.

Your true measure of your attaining purity is that no sin among the sins has authority over you. Look at the question of the Lord Jesus: "Which of you convicts Me of sin?" (John 8.46). Which sin, He asked, without exception. Therefore He could say about the devil: "The ruler of this world is coming, and he has nothing in Me" (John 14.30). Have you reached this purity from all sin, so that the devil has nothing in you, whether large or small? Not even from the little foxes which destroy the vines, or from the sins which disguise themselves in sheep's clothing?

True purity starts with complete hatred of sin, by knowledge, true insight, and sound understanding of the Holy Spirit of what is good and what is evil, "to those who are of full age, that is, those who by reason of use have their senses exercised" (Hebrews 5.14), such that the conscience is completely sound in its judgments, not being deceived by the devil in anything, and the person's deeds are pure.

There is something more important than man's visible deeds. Purity must spring from the heart, not from the outside. We say this because many people are concerned with the appearance of purity and not with its essence. As an example, many preachers who talk about a woman's decency will concentrate on her clothing and decorum, without being concerned for the heart's motive or the reason the young lady has abandoned modesty. If they were concerned with treating the heart from within to achieve purity, then a spontaneous result would be modesty in clothing and decorum. The same words can be applied to young men who grow their hair long.

We do not want by means of purity to cleanse the outside of the cup only (Matthew 23). In treating the sins of the tongue, the matter does not end with an exercise of silence, for sinful speech has its origins from within the heart. The Bible says: "Out of the abundance of the heart the mouth speaks" (Matthew 12.34). We should be concerned, then, with purity of heart, so that its expressions are spontaneously pure. Take lying, for example. It is not enough to merely avoid it from the outside, but we must treat the reason for it within the heart, whether it is fear, pride, or reaching a certain goal, since lying is the result of these inner sins which need purifying. Be concerned, then, with the inside.

Here some people ask, "Should I delay external purity until I reach inner purity?" Of course not. What this means, however, is that you are not satisfied just with outer purity. God wants the heart before everything. Be cautious of the outer sin with all your power, because it likely includes others also. At the same time, treat the inside with every power, every patience, and every assistance from grace. In this way your pure deeds originate from a pure heart.

A condition of a deed's purity is that it must be pure, and its goals and means pure also. Every deed that you do must be pure in itself: pure in the incentives which lead to it, and pure in the way in which it is carried out. Is this, then, the perfect purity? Perfect purity is a long topic, but this topic is purity from sin.

CHAPTER 2

Testing Purity

A LACK OF FALLING INTO SIN is not purity of heart. There are other reasons for not falling besides the inner condition of the heart, and we have explained some of them. It is as if man at some point is not being attacked by sin, or perhaps grace has intervened, without any call from us, and it came over us. We therefore say, in this respect, that man is considered completely pure if he enters into war with sin in its depths and severity, and is not shaken. Not only does he not fall, but he is also not shaken. Many people fight sin from their own desires and thoughts, and not from the devil, since the wars of the demons are very difficult. An example of this is the story of the young man who complained to Saint Bishoy that "'the wars of the devil have increased toward me,' while the devil said: 'I have not yet sensed that this young man has become a monk.'" The devil was very harsh in fighting him. If he were able to take his freedom completely, he would have struggled so as to deceive, if possible, even the elect (Matthew 24.24).

If you overcome in a spiritual war, say, "Perhaps it is a simple war," since God in His compassion does not permit us to be attacked beyond the potential of our tolerance. Perhaps we pass through light wars and are victorious in them—not because of our power or the purity of our hearts, but because of the weakness of the war. If the war had increased its burden, we would have fallen. Therefore we thank God for the greatness of His mercy, instead of vainly taking pride in claiming purity.

Your purity, then, is tested by a severe, harsh war. Will you withstand it, or fall? It is good for you to shout with humility and say, "I am not stronger than Solomon, the wisest on earth; I am not stronger than David, the Lord's anointed, the man of the flute and harp. I am not stronger than Peter the Apostle in his zeal, as long as sin 'has cast down many wounded, and all who were slain by her were strong men' (Proverbs 7.26). The best position, then,

is for me to know my weakness, and say that I have not yet reached purity."
I pray every day, "Lead us not into temptation, but deliver us from evil."

Have you entered into the severe wars and obtained victory? Know then
this truth: the severe war tests the person with its continuance and persistence. Man may triumph one time in a severe war, but if it continues for a
long time he may weaken before it, and be unable to overcome the resistance.
It is like Samson who, when the persistence increased toward him, weakened finally and submitted (Judges 16.16–17).

The severe war also tests man through its types and surprises. A person
might be victorious in a certain war, but in another type of war his resistance
lessens and he cannot withstand. The devil tests every person, studies the
points of weakness in him, and pushes harshly on them. His wars increase
in harshness whenever he attacks suddenly, without a man' being prepared
to face him. Here purity is tested.

What is the correct definition, then, of the person who possesses purity
of heart? He is the person who has been purified from every type of sin, in
thought, heart, sense, tongue, body, and in deed. He has entered into the
wars of the enemy, with all its types, severity, persistence, and continuance,
and struggled; grace supported him, and he overcame and remained victorious. This is a very high level. It is not the beginning of the spiritual life, but
the end of the trip, so that you will be worthy of the blessing of the Lord,
who said: "Blessed are the pure in heart, for they shall see God" (Matthew
5.8). Some measures of this purity follow.

CHAPTER 3

Purity of Thoughts and Dreams

In ADDITION TO PURITY FROM SIN, there is purity of thoughts and assumptions. One of the saints said: "It is not only your external deeds which show your reality, but more often your thoughts and assumptions." He gave an example of this: "A person is standing in a dark place, and seen by three people. One of them thinks that he is a robber, hiding and waiting for the opportunity to steal. The second thinks that he is an evil person waiting for a woman, whereas the third person thinks that the man is standing in the dark, in a place where nobody can see him, to pray."

In this way, our thoughts and assumptions will accord with the condition of the heart. Of this, the Bible says: "A good man out of the good treasure of his heart brings forth good; and an evil man out of the evil treasure of his heart brings forth evil" (Luke 6.45). As the saying goes, every vessel brings forth what it contains.

Therefore, if your assumptions are evil, your heart has not yet been purified. The person who has a pure heart always has pure thoughts and thinks no evil. As much as he can, he perceives matters in innocence and purity. In this way nothing makes him stumble, nor does he judge any work except the obvious sin, which carries its judgment within itself. He also takes the brighter side of any matter that has two sides. Because of this he is on good terms with other people, for he never links any sin to anyone and excuses every person for his actions.

You may ask if this means that the pure heart is never attacked by assumptions and evil thoughts. Yes, he is still attacked from the outside, without these thoughts coming forth from within him. On the contrary, he rejects them from the inside. He does not accept them, but dismisses them quickly. The deception to which some people are subjected is that they allow the evil thought to remain, even using the excuse of examining or attacking it, or hoping with a certain curiosity to see where it will end. The result is that the thought defiles a man and makes him lose his purity. The correct attitude is to dismiss the thought quickly, because the pure heart is disgusted with sinful thoughts and does not accept even their examination. Among the measures of purity, then, is the purity of assumptions and thoughts.

The second measure of purity is the purity of dreams. There is a person whose conscience may be cautious, guarding the purity of his thoughts, but his dreams contain many sins because his subconscious, which has not yet been purified from its visions, stories, and memories, contains remnants of old sins. His memory is either still defiled by its evil storage, or there are feelings in the heart hidden deep inside him that have not yet been purified. They are the source of his sinful dreams, which stain the purity of his mind. This person needs to be purified from his past, to match his present purity.

Whatever the condition, purity of dreams requires the passage of time before a person reaches a state far from evil dreams. With time and lack of repetition, the sources of these dreams will disappear from memory. The subconscious will store instead pure and sanctified matters suitable to the life of repentance and purity which he now lives, and they will be the source of perfectly pure dreams. Among the measures of purity of heart, then, is purity of thoughts, assumptions, and dreams.

CHAPTER 4

Purity from Vanities

T HERE REMAINS ANOTHER LEVEL for the perfect or the mature, which is purity from vanities, that is, purity from transient or futile matters. For example, a person concerned with transient or futile matters spends much time speaking about insignificant things that are considered neither sin nor righteousness. Or, he spends time thinking about such matters or is preoccupied with them. He demonstrates by this the fact that his mind or heart can be readily occupied with these trivialities, and as a result he wastes time he could have spent with God in prayer, meditation, spiritual reading, praise, or other pursuits which suit the condition of the pure heart.

Transient matters are neither good nor evil in themselves, but are trivialities that delay the positive spiritual work. These vanities are the ones of which the Apostle Paul warned us, saying: "We do not look at the things which are seen, but at the things which are not seen. For the things which are seen are temporary, but the things which are not seen are eternal" (2 Corinthians 4.18). The person who does not look at things which are seen is the one who says with David the Prophet: "But as for me, it is good to cling to God" (Psalm 72.28). This perfect clinging to the Lord does not come except by purity of heart.

Purity from sin is a holy condition, but the fathers do not call it purity of heart; they call it sanctity. Sanctity is less than purity in its level. Sanctity, in many of its concepts, is negative in its holiness, meaning it is departure from defilement and sin. Purity, however, is positive in its holiness. It is the continual attachment to God in mind, heart, and deed. It proceeds as a stage after sanctity. Among its advantages is purity from vanities. What are these vanities? We live in a world full of transient images. Must we close our eyes so that they do not see, if we are to follow the apostle's saying: "We do not look at the things which are seen"?

No, we shall not close our eyes, but we should not be concerned with what we see and hear. That is, if our eye falls on something to see, we refrain from meeting it. This also applies to the rest of our senses. It is said that the senses are the "doors of thought." What our senses gather is then considered by our mind, or at least becomes one of the thoughts entering our mind. Here we are faced with a choice between two actions. Our thoughts about these matters either pass and fade away like smoke—and this is one of the conditions of purity of heart—or the thoughts remain in us for a shorter or longer period and work within us at levels that surpass a limit or time, according to our purity.

These images bring thoughts of sin to the person who has not yet been purified, and are transformed in him into desires and lusts. I am not talking about this, for this is related to the first point about purity from sin. I say, however, that such images bring to the man of God not thoughts of sin, but some preoccupations and concerns that differ according to the purity of his heart and his death to worldly things, or the death of worldly things in his heart.

These transient thoughts, at the least, waste time. Time is part of your life. God has not given it to you to waste, but to benefit from for the salvation of your soul, for the purification of your heart and mind, and for binding your feelings to God. So do not waste it in trivialities. The mind that is occupied with trivialities demonstrates its lack of love for God. One's heart is not tied to God in a complete and permanent unity, and there are also trivial matters which divert the mind from God, even chattering, which has no benefit. When will you be purified from all of this, so that all that remains in your heart is God alone?

The perfectly pure heart is the heart that has entirely died to all vanities of the world, so as to live entirely to the Lord. Its mind becomes unoccupied with things which can be seen, because of its constant occupation with the unseen. The mind works tirelessly and thinks continuously. Its thinking differs, however, according to the matter with which it is occupied. It is one of two things, either images or unseen matters. The occupation with divine matters which are unseen is the ideal condition of purity.

Thinking about transient matters is an intermediate condition between thoughts of sin and divine thoughts. To the normal person it is not a sin, but it is a condition of deficiency in him. It develops and is transformed into sin. Saints flee from this deficiency, which demonstrates that the heart has not been completely purified from worldly things. Saint Paul the Apostle, in talking about the married man, said he "cares about the things of the world" (1 Corinthians 7.32–33). There are matters other than marriage which also cause concern with worldly things: money, or the desires of the flesh in general. Each of us should examine himself to know the doors through which the world enters into him with its vanities and finds a place in his mind or heart.

Here I would like to distinguish between two words: work and concern. Man works in the visible things, without the visible things working in him. His heart is with God. Like the fathers, the saints used to work with palm leaves in the desert, and their hearts did their divine work in singing, praying, and praising God. They used to work in these things without looking at them, that is, they were not preoccupied with them. The Lord did not direct blame to Martha because she was working, but because in working she was in a condition of concern and distress (Luke 10.41). The work was not done with her hands only, but reached the mind and heart, and thus she was preoccupied with it. In her preoccupation she was unable to devote time to the Lord. "He will be loyal to the one and despise the other," for no one can serve two masters at the same time (Matthew 6.24). Is it possible, then, for us to work without being preoccupied, distressed, and concerned? This is what is required of a pure heart. "I want you to be without care" (1 Corinthians 7.32).

How can this be? It requires us to keep our relationship with visible things superficial, not entering into their depths. This in turn depends upon the extent of our evaluation of matters. Every time the importance of a matter increases in our sight, its depth and concern increases in us. That is why our fathers, for whom the world had died in their sight, counted them as rubbish that they might gain Christ (Philippians 3.8). Every worldly matter ceased to have value with these saints, no matter how great its value in the eyes of those who look to what can be seen. Hence, those matters no longer preoccupied them; they were not distressed by them, but lived in peace. The saying of Saint Paul the Apostle applies to them: "And those who use this world as not misusing it" (1 Corinthians 7.31).

Many times, however, we forget ourselves and our spirituality. We hear a specific story, for example, or read about a certain incident, or enter into a discussion, and forget that both our heart and mind are for the Lord. We continue talking, commenting, discussing, giving opinions, and zealously reply to those who oppose us. The matter is not worthy of any of this attention. However, despite this it reigns not only on our tongues and in our thoughts, but also our nerves and affections. Here, the waters have entered into our souls. We then become concerned and distressed over many matters. However, we are not occupied with the person who is needed, but we think that "when we have a convenient time we will call for him" (Acts 24.25). We return to our homes, the matter being still in our minds, and we pour it into the minds of others and occupy them with it as well.

Thoughts are not barren, but give birth to other thoughts. A thought deepens within our subconscious and gives birth to dreams and assumptions. We stand and pray while our minds become confused with many thoughts. This is because we have the thoughts deep within us, and so they assume authority over us. Be careful, and do not let the matters of the world enter deeply into your thought, feelings, and time. If old habits come to you, wake up quickly and say to the Lord with the psalmist: "Turn away my eyes that I may not see vanity" (Psalm 118.37).

The awakening of the mind and the struggle with thoughts precede purity of mind and heart. Saint Or used to say to his disciple, "Be cautious, my son, that no irrelevant word enter this cell."[1] He means by this any word which is foreign to God and His kingdom. Saint John the Dwarf used to shake out his ears before entering his cell, so that no discussions he had heard from others would enter into it.[2]

This is a negative struggle. On the positive side, however, we need to be removed from the world if we are to be stirred by the thought of divine things. Man's feeling of alienation from the world causes him to avoid pressing himself into worldly matters, incidents, news, conversations, and upheavals. If any of these things reaches him, he does not interact with it or respond to it, but says to himself, "I am a stranger. What have I to do with this matter?" Similarly, the occupation of the thoughts with divine things

[1]Or 3, *Sayings of the Desert Fathers.*
[2]John the Dwarf 23, *Sayings of the Desert Fathers.*

makes him unoccupied with worldly matters, and he avoids them because they delay him from his divine ecstasy, of which he says: "How I love Your law, O Lord. It is my meditation the whole day long" (Psalm 118.97).

When will the heart and mind then reach purity? When man is liberated from sin, when he is purified from dreams, thoughts, and assumptions, and when he is purified from vanities. All of these are from the negative side. What about the positive side?

CHAPTER 5

The Positive Side of Purity

THE LOVE OF GOD POSSESSES the pure heart in place of the love of the world. It does everything for the sake of its love for God, and not merely out of obedience to His orders or to execute His commandments. Even the departure from sin occurs because a much deeper love has taken its place, which makes the heart feel the insignificance of the love of sin and as well as its defilement. With the love of God, purity enters into a new positive role.

The fruits of the Holy Spirit appear in the life of this repentant person, of whom the apostle said: "But the fruit of the Spirit is love, joy, peace, long suffering, kindness, goodness, faithfulness, gentleness, self-control. Against such there is no law" (Galatians 5.22). That is, he has moved from the stage of laws and commandments to the stage of love.

Your relationship with God is transformed into love, like the relationship of a friend with his friend, a son with his father, or one who loves with his beloved. You find every delight in the presence of God. Your prayers will be transformed into refuges of love; no longer a duty, nor a church deed, nor one of the characteristics of the spiritual person, they will become merely an expression of the great love present in your heart toward God. The rest of your spiritual deeds will be done in the same way. Love is the first of the fruits of the Spirit. There are other fruits, and these will inevitably appear in your heart with the life of purity.

You might ask, "Are all the fruits of the Spirit necessary in the life of purity?" Yes, because He said: "Therefore bear fruits worthy of repentance" (Luke 3.8), and also: "Every branch in Me that does not bear fruit He takes away; and every branch that bears fruit He prunes, that it may bear more fruit" (John 15.2). Struggle, then, with all your power to attain these fruits. If you want me to talk about purity of heart, I will talk to you about each and every component of these fruits and about all of them as one homogeneous unit. This matter needs a separate book or set of books, but now is not the time for it. As for now, I will continue with purity of heart and talk about its peak: the purity that we will receive in eternity.

CHAPTER 6

The Purification of Heart from Knowing Sin

W ITH THIS WE NOW DIVIDE purity of heart into two types. The first is a type we can receive here on earth, which we have already mentioned. The other type we will not receive except in eternity, in the other world. We mention it here so that we can desire it and ask for it, and so that we know the extent of the depth of the purity that will be for us there.

Our eating from the tree of knowledge is what made us lose our original purity. We knew only good. But when we ate from the tree of knowing good and evil, we then knew evil also. We entered into the duality of good and evil, righteousness and sin, choosing good and walking in iniquity. As for totally not knowing evil, this is a high level which we will not reach on earth. We will be given it, however, in eternity, when we eject the fruit that we ate. Then we will know nothing but good. We will be liberated from the duality of good and evil. We will then have the characteristics of simplicity and innocence, which do not know evil.

We will be like the innocent child who knows nothing about the deceptions, contriving, tricks, and evils which society presents to him later on, making him lose his innocence. We will have purity like that of Adam and Eve before they ate from the fruit of the tree, which put thoughts into their minds that were not there previously. They lost their simplicity, and their eyes were opened to matters that perhaps made them say, "We wish we did not know that." Man then progressed from knowing evil to exploring it.

If you have known things about sin, then do not proceed to the end of the road. As long as the knowledge of sin harms you, then do not add any new thing to it. Try to forget what you have known by neither using it nor speaking about it. Do not think about this knowledge. If you remember it, try to interchange it with another thought. Do not let the knowledge of sin be transformed from a superficial knowledge to a deep knowledge. Do not let sin be transformed from fact to exploration, then to tasting, then to acceptance or wrestling with it. As much as you can, stop this knowledge at a set limit. Ask God to purify your thoughts and sanctify your subconscious and memory from all that has precipitated and been recorded there.

Roam in the crown of the Lord, which He will grant us on that Day (2 Timothy 4.8), when all knowledge of sin will be removed from us, and sin will no longer exist. All our experiences with sin in this world will be like a bad dream from which we have awakened in eternity, and have completely forgotten. Truly, how beautiful this is! However, as long as here in this world we do not have purity from the knowledge of sin, then what shall we do?

Train yourself in the life of spiritual simplicity. Do not let your mind work alone, in the complications of thought and arguments, but add to it the simplicity of spirit. You will then have the simple, luminous eye. Do not mix with sin, nor with its thoughts and stories, so that your mind is not defiled with the remembrance of evil that entails death. Be patient with purity, no matter how late its arrival. Ask for it as a gift from God to you. Let evil always be outside of you, even if its wars increase, and the Lord will be with you.

"I drenched my couch with my bitter tears"

I drenched my couch with my bitter tears.
I promised my Lord, my Lord, this is the last time.

I'll be firm in your love, as firm as a rock.
From all my heart, my heart, I'm not returning.

I'm not returning, I'm not returning,
From all my heart, my heart, I'm not returning

It came to me, the war strongly.
I returned again, again to the depth of sin.

I wept from my heart with a pure repentance.
But for a while, a while, then returned again.

Returned again, returned again,
But for a while, a while, then returned again.

I strengthened my will, I increased my promises.
From my great conceit, conceit, I increased my promises.

Being sure of my determination, being sure of my struggle
I deceived myself, myself, and I returned again.

Returned again, returned again,
I deceived myself, myself, and I returned again.

I cried intensely and said, have mercy.
I know my weakness, my weakness, O Lord, assist me.

Power is from you from above, not from me.
As long as You are with me, with me, I'm not returning.

I'm not returning, I'm not returning.
As long as You are with me, with me, I'm not returning.

PART SIX

PROTECTING REPENTANCE

CHAPTER I

The Possibility of Backsliding

IT IS EASY FOR A PERSON TO REPENT for one day, but it is important that he repent continuously—that is, to live the life of repentance, to live in repentance all his life and not return to sin again. It is very easy for a person to train himself and be successful in spiritual exercises for a day or two, or a week. But can he continue in these spiritual exercises throughout his life? Similarly, with repentance what is important is its protection, that is, its continuation, for it is very easy to return to sin. The devil who watches a person's life does not rest in the least if this person slips from his hands by repentance. He therefore tries with his every means and trick to turn him from repentance, even after a long time.

The time of the book of Judges offers a very clear example of this return to sin. The Israelites walked in the worship of idols and were defiled by the Gentiles who mixed with them. The Lord delivered them by raising up a judge for them, and so they repented. However, "when the judge was dead, they went back to their former ways and behaved more corruptly than their fathers, by following other gods" (Judges 2.19).

Sometimes the periods of repentance lasted for tens of years before they returned to sin. We read in the book of Judges, "Then the land remained at peace for forty years. Then Othniel the son of Kenaz died. And the sons of Israel again did evil before the Lord" (Judges 3.11–12). "The land remained at peace for eighty years. . . . The sons of Israel continued to do evil before the Lord" (Judges 3.30, 4.1). "Let the land be at peace for forty years. Then the sons of Israel did evil before of the Lord" (Judges 5.31, 6.1).

It is a story that has been repeated in the life of this nation and in the lives of others, whether nations or individuals, as a result of hearts which are not firm in the love of the Lord, nor serious in the life of repentance. They have not finished with the life of sin. They leave it and then return to it.

The Apostle Peter describes them with a harsh metaphor: "A dog returns to his own vomit," and "a sow, having washed, to her wallowing in the mire" (2 Peter 2:22).

> For if, after they have escaped the pollutions of the world through the knowledge of the Lord and Savior Jesus Christ, they are again entangled in them and are overcome, the latter end is worse for them than the beginning. For it would have been better for them not to have known the way of righteousness, than having known it, to turn from the holy commandment delivered to them. But it has happened to them according to the true proverb: "A dog returns to his own vomit . . ." (2 Peter 2.20–22).

Yes, many have walked with the Lord one stage, and yet did not complete the way. They felt the difficulty of the way, so they left it and left the Lord behind with it. They were not able to carry their cross till the end. Or, they betrayed the Lord when they returned and preferred sin rather than Him. What Saint Paul the Apostle said about the foolish Galatians applies to these people: "Having started with the Spirit, are you now ending with the flesh?" (Galatians 3.3, NRSV).

CHAPTER 2

They Started in the Spirit and Ended in the Flesh[1]

Saint paul the apostle presented Demas as another example. He was one of Saint Paul's assistants in preaching and serving, that is, he was one of the pillars of the Church. The apostle once put him on par with Luke the Physician (Colossians 4.14), declaring that he was one of the people working with him: "Mark, Aristarchus, Demas, Luke" (Philemon 24). The story of the preacher Demas ended on a painful note, for Saint Paul the Apostle said: "Demas has forsaken me, having loved this present world" (2 Timothy 4.10).

It is truly painful that the love of this present world should return to conquer the heart of a great preacher among Saint Paul's assistants. If this is so, then every person should be cautious of the world and its love, no matter how much he has repented. Saint Paul mentions other examples besides Demas who came to the same painful end. He wrote about them to the Philippians: "For many . . . of whom I have told you often, and now tell you even weeping, that they are the enemies of the cross of Christ" (Philippians 3.18).

He completes his account of them by saying: "Whose end is destruction, whose god is their belly, and whose glory is in their shame—who set their mind on earthly things" (Philippians 3.19). These people were not normal believers. It is enough that Saint Paul the Apostle mentioned them in his epistles. It is painful when he says "for many," indicating that they were not just one or two. What is even more painful is his saying, "whose end is destruction." So long as the return to the life of sin is possible to whoever is not cautious, then they permit the love of the world to enter into their hearts.

---

[1]From a lecture I gave at the Great Cathedral on Friday, August 9, 1974.

Do not be proud, then, if you repent and start on a spiritual life. What is important is that you continue. You continue walking in the spiritual path till the end of the goal, till the end of the days of your pilgrimage on earth. The apostle said: "Whose faith follow, considering the outcome of their conduct" (Hebrews 13.7). What is important, then, is for repentance to continue until the outcome of the conduct. The penitent must not be like those who started in the Spirit and ended in the flesh. If you repent and walk with the Lord for a beautiful spiritual period, and then return to sin, will the spiritual days save you? Or is where you end up that for which you will be judged?

King Saul is another clear example. Samuel the Prophet anointed him as king, the Spirit of the Lord descended upon him, the Lord gave him another heart, and he prophesied until some were amazed, saying: "Is Saul also among the prophets?" (1 Kingdoms 10.9–11). In spite of all of this, Saul returned and sinned; his sins increased, and the Lord rejected him. It was said of him: "But the Spirit of the Lord departed from Saul, and an evil spirit from the Lord tormented him" (1 Kingdoms 16.14). He started with God—or God started with him—but Saul did not finish.

It was the same with the people of Israel who passed through the sea and followed the Lord in the wilderness. They were delivered from Pharaoh's slavery. They lived under God's direct leadership. The cloud overshadowed them by day, the pillar of light guided them by night, and they ate manna and quails. They were the first people to whom God sent a written law, and they promised, saying: "All that the Lord has said, we will do, and be obedient" (Exodus 24.7). In spite of this, they returned and sinned many times against the Lord; they complained, and worshipped the golden calf (Exodus 32). The Lord was angered by this complaining generation. He refused to let them enter into the promised land, and they all died in the wilderness.

Do you think that all those who are perishing started on their path with destruction? Of course not, for the devil himself started his life as a pure luminous angel, but he did not continue. We are not concerned with the starting point, then, but with the end of the journey.

The heretics did not start out as heretics. Some of them had a very good start. Eutyches was one of the most virtuous monks of Constantinople. He was a spiritual person and an abbot. He did not continue, however, but ended up in heresy. Arius was one of the most virtuous and powerful priests of Alexandria. Nestorius was one of the most powerful teachers of his time; he even became Patriarch of Constantinople. All of these men ended up lost. Origen was the greatest scholar of his time. He was an ascetic who suffered much for the sake of Christ, and defended the faith. Yet finally this painful saying applied to him: "O great tower, how did you fall?"

Each of us, then, should be cautious. If you have repented, then listen to this advice: It is not enough to come out of Sodom, if you do not continue to Zoar. Lot's wife came out of Sodom, with her hand in the hand of the angel. She was not burned with the burning city. She did not, however, continue walking with God, but looked back (Genesis 19.16). She perished by one look. How terrifying!

Be cautious, then, about looking behind you. Think no longer about the world you left for the sake of the Lord. Do not try to remember the pleasures of sin from which you repented. Do not in any way look back, but rather "stretch forward." Try to grow in your repentance without returning to sin.

Whoever goes back is like the person who destroys what he has built. I do not wish to frighten you by this saying of the apostle: "For the earth which drinks in the rain that often comes upon it, and bears herbs useful for those by whom it is cultivated, receives blessing from God; but if it bears thorns and briars, it is rejected and near to being cursed, whose end is to be burned" (Hebrew 6.7–8). Nor do I wish to repeat what the apostle said elsewhere in the same epistle: "For if we sin willfully after we have received the knowledge of the truth, there no longer remains a sacrifice for sins, but a certain fearful expectation of judgment" (Hebrews 10.26–27). The apostle might not mean just sin, since every person is subjected to it, but he means the condition of continuance in sin. All that I wish to say, however, is that you should be cautious in your repentance.

If you repent, do not be proud of yourself. Do not be haughty, but fear (Romans 11.20). Do not think that repentance gives you a state of infallibility. There is no one without sin but God Himself (Matthew 19.17). How easy it is for the enemy to fight you and make you fall. Therefore hold firm to the Lord, and let your heart be contrite before Him, so that He will give you the life of continual victory. Remember the words of Saint Paul the Apostle: "Work out your own salvation with fear and trembling" (Philippians

2.12). This matches what Saint Peter the Apostle said: " Conduct yourselves throughout the time of your sojourning here in fear" (1 Peter 1.17). The fear mentioned here does not mean being terrified; what is meant is caution, care, and diligence in the spiritual life. It means the departure from the arrogance in which the penitent thinks that he has been delivered from sin forever and raised above his level.

In such fear or caution there is a shade of humility. Many are saved by this humility, in which man feels his weakness and knows that he is still subject to errors, still in need of caution to avoid even the simplest sins. He who feels his weakness will be surrounded by God's power, which will help and save him. How beautiful is the humility in Saint Paul the Apostle's saying: "I discipline my body and bring it into subjection, lest, when I have preached to others, I myself should become disqualified" (1 Corinthians 9.27). If Saint Paul the Apostle says this about himself, then what shall we say about ourselves, when we are the people best informed about our own weakness? When the apostle says, "I discipline my body and bring it into subjection," is it not to give us a lesson in being cautious continually throughout life?

Caution demonstrates that the penitent is serious in his repentance. It shows that he is honest in the pledges he promised God when he started his repentance. Be cautious continuously: "Remember therefore from where you have fallen; [and] repent" (Revelation 2.4). Search for the reasons why sin made you fall previously, and avoid these things with all your power. It is better if we set this point aside as a special separate topic.

The Canaanites on the Land [1]

MANY PEOPLE, AFTER REPENTING, returned to their sins. The reason was that they left the causes of sin to remain as they were, while leaving the doors of sin open. Therefore sin returned to them, or they returned to it, because the source of sin was still present. This reminds us of the story of the Canaanites on earth. What is this story and its significance? The Canaanites were some Gentiles who worshipped idols. The order was issued to expel them from the land, so that they did not become a stumbling block to attract God's people to their worship. The Canaanites were very powerful. It happened that Joshua did not drive them out of some regions, and they remained as forced laborers (Joshua 16.10). Their thorn increased. When the children of God grew strong: "They put the Canaanites under forced labor, but did not drive them out completely" (Judges 1.28). So the Canaanites dwelt in the land (Judges 1.27, 30, 32, 33).

The Canaanites became partners to God's people and were upsetting to them (Judges 2.3). They mixed with them, they married with them, and worshipped their gods (Judges 3.5–7). The Canaanites here represent the remainder of evil present on earth that had not been removed from its roots, so it became a reason for forgetting God, departing from Him and returning to sin again. Here we ask: When you repented, and God allowed you to eat milk and honey in your new life, did you keep some Canaanites on the land, even as servants to serve you as forced labor? You think that they are submitting to you, whereas in the end you will fall into their defilements and worship like them.

Have you kept some of your old habits while living the life of repentance? I ask this because sometimes we find servants in the Church who are perhaps devoted to the service; these people naturally see themselves as not only living the life of repentance, but perhaps even more the life of

[1]From a lecture I gave at the Great Cathedral on Friday, October 13, 1978.

righteousness. In spite of this, they have habits that resemble the people of the world exactly. Their behaviors are earthly and not spiritual. How did this happen? How did they combine both the service and these old habits? We will give examples.

Before he knew the Lord, a person had been angry. He then repented, but he kept the anger within him. Before repenting and entering the life of serving God, he would get angry, become provoked, raise his voice, curse, and quarrel. After he repented, he kept the "Canaanites on the land." He kept those habits with him. You can see him during the service getting enraged and shouting, despite his great responsibility in it. If provoked, he gives orders with a loud voice and kindles the atmosphere with fire. When you rebuke him for his anger, he says to you: "That is holy anger. I am angry for the sake of God and His honor. I am enraged for the sake of correcting the wrong situation, for the sake of the commandments, and so that I can teach others how it should be."

Actually, he is enraged because he is incapable of resisting anger from within himself. This is not a holy anger, because it is against the commandment that says: "Love suffers long and is kind, is not provoked" (1 Corinthians 13.4–5). It is against the commandment that says: "The wrath of man does not produce the righteousness of God" (James 1.20). It is also against the commandment that says: "Let all bitterness, wrath, anger, clamor, and evil speaking be put away from you . . . and be kind to one another" (Ephesians 4.31–32).

Holy anger should be holy in its means, and not in its goals and objectives alone. Whoever is enraged like this shows that his nerves are not in good order. He offers a bad example, giving a dishonorable appearance to the church service, and shows lack of purity in conduct and in his method of dealing with people. The fact is that this person has kept with him some bad habits and, wishing to bestow upon them a holy veneer, has put those same errors to use within the Church. His repentance and service become a stumbling block, like the person who puts a piece of new cloth onto an old garment (Matthew 9.16). It would have been better for him to leave behind all the old anger with its many manifestations. When he asks, "Should I not defend the truth?" we answer him as follows.

If God wishes to give you a holy anger to defend the truth, then it will be another kind of anger, which is different in substance, image, execution, and expression. It will be a spiritual anger, different from your worldly anger. You will be angry in it and not sin (Psalm 4.5). Abigail defended the truth when she talked to David, but in a kind, wise, and well-mannered way (1 Kingdoms 25). The Lord Jesus revealed to the Samaritan woman her sins, but in a spiritual and gentle way (John 4). God's children always express their objection toward sin in a spiritual way, without loudness, noise, or nervousness. All of these matters originate from the remnant of "the Canaanites on the land."

The problem here is that the spiritual measures used are unsound. Those measures which permit this sinful anger and consider it holy for the sake of God, are unsound measures without a doubt. They merely justify the presence of an old sin from which the heart has not been purified yet. It does not agree with the life of repentance, nor with what is suitable for repentance, such as humility and contrition. It can develop and destroy all of a person's spirituality. It would then be as if he had not repented.

Another example is confusing cursing and spiritual reproach. This is the same situation. A person used to curse before repentance and then repented, or thought that he repented, whereas in actuality he kept some of his old sins. Among them were cursing and some hurtful expressions. He considered them beneficial to use when rebuking sinners. He forgot that the penitent should only rebuke himself and not forget his own sins, in order to avoid being concerned with the sins of another and rebuking him for them. Instead, he still holds firm to the saying of Saint Paul the Apostle: "Convince, rebuke, exhort" (2 Timothy 4.2).

He forgot the spiritual method for rebuking. Saint Paul, who gave this advice to his disciple Timothy, a bishop, is the one who also said to the priests of Ephesus: "For three years I did not cease to warn everyone night and day with tears" (Acts 20.31). Do you warn people with love and tears or with pride and authority, despising them and their feelings?

The penitent does not rebuke anyone. If he does rebuke, he never forgets the spirit of gentleness. The apostle spoke about this: "Brethren, if a man is overtaken in any trespass, you who are spiritual restore such a one in a spirit of gentleness, considering yourself lest you also be tempted" (Galatians 6.1).

Yes, we all make mistakes. The penitent who remembers his sins, if he must correct someone else, does not by any means forget that he sinned like this person previously. If he forgets, he subjects himself to the loss of his repentance, and the spirit of pride enters him. As for the person who in his rebuke is insolent and curses others, he has not repented yet. He should remember the saying of the apostle, "Nor [will] revilers . . . inherit the kingdom of God" (1 Corinthians 6.10).

Whoever keeps cursing keeps in his character the "Canaanites on the land" for its destruction. The use of cursing is not suitable during the service, because such means of service are impure. It is not suitable for the penitent to cover his sins with verses he misunderstands or misuses deliberately. It is better for him to confess that some of his weaknesses are still present—such as anger, nervousness, violent nature, and cursing—and that he has not yet been liberated from them. Rather, he has carried them into his new life, where they stain that life and prevent him from guarding his repentance. Do not say, "The Holy Spirit rebukes people through my tongue." The Holy Spirit has His own particular method and pure expressions.

Another person may think he has repented, whereas he is keeping another sin. In his repentance, he has kept whatever stubbornness is in his nature. Stubbornness is always tied to pride. It is the result of wrongly placed confidence in oneself, resulting in adherence to personal opinion, despising the opinions of others, and a lack of concern for the results of one's rigid opinions. This stubbornness and rigidity is then used in the environs of the church service and Sunday School. Everyone says, "So-and-so is very difficult to reason with." And yet he is not merely a penitent but also a servant, perhaps with great responsibility in the services, active in preaching and talking about spirituality, theology, doctrine, and the stories of the saints. He has knowledge, but the Canaanites still remain on the land.

He tries to call his stubbornness by the name of "defending the truth," whereas in fact truth calls him to be meek, understanding, and respectful of the opinions of others. Some sins wear sheep's clothing. The truth of the matter is that the ego is still present. This person in his repentance may have been delivered from many sins, but he has not been delivered from the ego: he has carried it with him in his repentance. How many fail in their repentance because of the ego? Perhaps it makes them fall into many sins, and returns them to their condition before repentance. Many of those who have repented do not sense this war of the ego, however, and perhaps do not see that it is their greatest sin.

There is a person who repents, but holds onto the sin of judgment and criticism. A person may have fallen into this sin to a great extent, and then entered into the life of repentance. The great sins which he left occupied him for a while. The sin of judgment he had lingered on, until it appeared another time. The amazing thing is that every time this person feels that he has matured in repentance, become closer to God, and kept away from sin, the sin of judgment by the same measure increases its appearances in his life.

He becomes critical of everything and everyone, and does not like anything. The spiritual insight given to him in repentance he directs toward the deeds of others, and not to his own deeds. The ideal that he loved in repentance he uses to measure other people's dealings and not his own, and with it he criticizes everyone. The actual issue is not the protection of the ideal, but rather the lack of ability to forgo the sin of judgment and criticism that he brought with him from his past, for the Canaanites are still on the land.

This spirit enters even into service and teaching. So one branch of the service rejects the general syllabus and keeps criticizing, "This syllabus has errors such and such, and lacks this and that. The syllabus of our branch is better." This branch is transformed into a "private sector" on the outskirts of the service. He is not concerned with the unity of education in the Church. The ego still remains; it did not die when repentance started.

The spirit of criticism creates closed groups. It is as if there were islands within the Church not connected to any other land. Ships leave them to go to this or that land, and ships come to them from another land. In spite of this, there are islands that stand on their own within the self, that still remain after repentance. They are not satisfied with this individuality, but severely criticize every other situation. If you ask one of them, "Why all of this?" he answers you with the words of Jeremiah the Prophet: "Who will give water to my head and a fountain of tears to my eyes, that I might weep day and night . . . for the wounded daughter of my people?" (Jeremiah 8.21).

My brother, weep for your sins before you weep for other people. This type, unfortunately, does not see that they have sins which require weeping. After they started repenting, they were occupied only with the sins of others; therefore they live continuously in an atmosphere filled with judgment and criticism of others, without mercy. As for them, however, they place themselves under the category of those "who need no repentance" (Luke 15.7). Therefore they live by the syllabus of the Pharisee rather than the tax collector (Luke 18.9–14)—the Pharisee who fasts, gives tithes of his possessions, and is not like the extortioners, unjust, adulterers, but who keeps the Canaanites on the land.

Another person repents, but keeps the laziness in his character. Perhaps he is a lazy person who, when he repents, leaves his other sins but keeps his laziness. You see this laziness clearly in his service, worship, exercises, readings, attendance at meetings, and in his regularity at confession. If someone were to ask him why he allowed himself to remain in this laziness, he would answer, "It is enough that I love Jesus."

We are amazed: is his love of the Lord of glory the reason for his laziness? The apostle invites us to be "fervent in spirit, not lagging in diligence, continuing steadfastly in prayer" (Romans 12.11–12). It seems, however, that the attempt to cover up sins becomes a habit with some people. The reply to the claim that the Lord's love is sufficient is simple, for the Lord Himself said: "Whoever loves Me keeps My commandments" (John 15.10). So, where is the keeping of the commandments with respect to this laziness?

A person might repent and keep with him the sin of trickery. Before he repented, he had this character flaw. He knew how to reach his goal by twisted methods, detours, and evasions, by human tricks, cunning, and his own methods. After he repented, he kept this character within him. He sometimes resorted to it, as Jacob resorted to deceiving his father in order to take the blessing. The Church or the service might encounter a problem, leaving everyone at a loss in how to solve the problem. This person intervenes and says, "Leave this problem for me to solve." How will he solve it? "I will solve it in my own way, I know this game very well." Naturally, he knows it because he used to play the game previously, before he repented. There is nothing hindering him from playing it again now. Some will ask how he reached this solution. The answer is clear: the Canaanites that are still on the land gave him "good" advice.

You discern from his solution to the problem that he has not yet repented. In spite of this, his conscience does not trouble him. Formerly, he resorted to detours, evasions, and twisted methods for the sake of worldly matters. Now, he resorts to these for the sake of God. There is no need, then, for his conscience to rebuke him. In this way he declines to repent. He does not feel that he has changed in his repentance. The old personality remains as it was, without changing its methods. His reliance on human strength remains with him even in repentance. This matter affects every aspect of his spirituality, and ends with his failure in the life of repentance. He was not aware of this point, for he thought that repentance merely meant leaving the great sins such as fornication, stealing, drunkenness, gambling, etc.

A person may have repented, but has kept self-righteousness. He considers defending himself as something normal. He defends himself in everything, as if he did not sin in anything. He even keeps from himself every kind of advice or reproof. He may fall into innumerable sins through self-righteousness, no matter what level he reaches in the service.

There is yet another type other than these. This type of person struggles with pessimism. This person repents, but keeps his pessimism with the remainder of its wars. You find him troubled in his spiritual life by any problem. He breaks down, he is disturbed and loses his peace. He says, "There is no use in me. I have lost hope. I have been thrown into confusion by such-and-such a matter." Pessimism is a war from the devil, or weariness from the nerves. It is not one of the attributes of the children of God, because the fruits of the Spirit include joy and peace (Galatians 5.22). With this pessimism a person can digress from his spiritual path and lose the way to God.

We must examine ourselves very well, to see what we have kept from our previous lives before repentance, in order to be rid of it. We might think we have actually entered Canaan, whereas we are still lost in the wilderness. Whoever purifies himself from every remnant of the old life can open his path to God with ease, and does not turn back in his repentance; and especially he does not turn back to the sins that take other forms.

There is the example of the love of money or possessions. One might assume that the matter is clear: how can a person in repentance be deceived by it? I will tell you how the deception occurs. A person used to love money, or he was greedy, not wanting to spend what he had. He then repented, or thought that he had repented, and lived the new life with God. Perhaps he became a known servant, or a monk in the monastery. You then find this old sin taking on an ecclesiastical appearance.

The love of money returns, but it is expressed for the sake of the church or monastery. This occurs by a method that does not agree with the life of repentance nor with spiritualty in general. The penitent makes an excuse, saying, "I am not taking anything for myself. I am collecting for God." This is true, but he is collecting in an earthly way that is not spiritual; it does not agree with the lack of love of money, nor with asceticism and renunciation. You can see amazing things from some of those who are responsible for the finances of churches and societies. You may well ask, "Where is the life of repentance?" Such people, however, have kept some Canaanites on the land.

This also applies to rich churches that do not assist the poor churches. Is not all money God's money? With God it is the same whether the money is spent on this church or that one, but the love of money requires it to be collected in one location or another. There are many treasurers. The love of money, however, invites its collection here and not there (in heaven), and how many are the treasurers!

CHAPTER 4

Do Not Falter Between Two Opinions[1]

Eᴌɪᴊᴀʜ ᴛʜᴇ ᴘʀᴏᴘʜᴇᴛ sᴀɪᴅ ᴛᴏ ᴛʜᴇ ᴘᴇᴏᴘʟᴇ: "How long will you be undecided between two opinions? If the Lord is God, follow Him, but if Baal, follow him" (3 Kingdoms 18.21). Faltering between two opinions demonstrates that the heart is not firm in its love of God, and that its repentance is neither true nor perfect. If repentance reaches perfection, man will not waver between two opinions, between God and the world. But if his eyes begin to look here and there, this demonstrates that he has begun to reconsider his repentance. When does this happen? It happens sometimes when man presents his will to God, for the sake of obedience, but not his heart, the whole heart. He surrenders his hand to the angel who will lead him out of Sodom, but his heart is still inside it.

His repentance is merely an attempt to satisfy God, and not out of love of righteousness. Or, he may have left sin for the sake of the fear of God alone—out of fear of punishment, merely to protect his eternity—without the love of God or righteousness being firm in his heart. Therefore, any tremor from the enemy that troubles him will either return him to sin or incline his heart to it.

This also happens when the aim of repentance is not sound. Ananias and Sapphira sold their possessions and presented the proceeds to the apostles, not for the sake of the renunciation of money and love for God, but to follow the spiritual atmosphere that prevailed in the apostolic era. It was an act of mere conformity, with a lack of faith in their hearts concerning the insignificance of money. Therefore they did not present all of their money, but kept part of it back, because the love of the world was still in their hearts (Acts 5).

Are you the same? Has repentance entered as a kind of conformity with the spiritual atmosphere? What I mean by this is mere conformity or tradition, without the heart being purified from within from the love of sin,

[1]From a lecture that I gave in the Great Cathedral on Friday, February 7, 1975.

and without its being convinced entirely of sin's defilement and ugliness. Repentance for the reason of conformity invites faltering between the two opinions. Rachel left her father Laban's house and went with Jacob, perhaps out of love for Jacob and to agree with him in leaving that troublesome environment. However, the main aim, which was to leave the place where idols were worshipped, was not present. Therefore Rachel was able to leave her father Laban's house and take her father's idols with her. In this way she faltered between two opinions (Genesis 31.34).

And you, did you enter the new life for the sake of a person like Jacob, or for the love of God? Perhaps the love of a spiritual person lead you to the spiritual path. This, however, must only be the starting point, to be then transformed into the love of God. For if this incentive alone remains, then the spiritual life remains attached to the love of that spiritual person, and the penitent is liable to return to sin.

The children of Israel left Egypt and followed Moses. They did not, however, form a firm relationship with God. That is why they were restless and returned to sin. The mere absence of Moses from them for forty days, while he was with God on the mountain, made these people rethink their relationship with God, and they ended up worshipping a golden calf (Exodus 32). Any afflictions they underwent in the wilderness made them complain and desire to return again to Egypt. They desired meat, melons, and leeks (Numbers 11.4–5).

It is impossible, then, to form a firm relationship with God, for fear of a relapse. It is not right for the starting point in repentance to remain as it is. The penitent must mature in his spirituality, incentives, and relationship with God, so that his heart does not desire to return to the previous life in sin. As long as the relationship with God is firm, the penitent is no longer subjected to the feeling of faltering between two opinions, and the desire for return to sin.

How easy it is for him to struggle with combining the two matters (God and the world) despite the Bible's clarity: "Friendship with the world is enmity with God" (James 4.4). Samson tried to combine being the Lord's consecrated one and a friend to Delilah at the same time, and so he failed in his vow to God. Lot tried to combine the love of the abundant land with being a man of God, so he lost all of what he had in Sodom. Truly, there is no communion between light and darkness (2 Corinthians 6.14). In the same way, the angel of the Church of Sardis tried to combine service and negligence. The angel of the Church of Laodicea tried to combine service and laxity. Each of them was sent a warning from God (Revelation 3.3–16). It is amazing that King Saul resorted to a medium and to Samuel the Prophet at the same time (1 Kingdoms 28.11).

The penitent must be strict in avoiding worldly things. The Lord clearly said that no one can serve two masters (Luke 16.13). In keeping away from worldly things, beware of opposing influences that draw man far away from repentance. He may truly have repented, but worldly matters still have wars and pressures, and a person is not immune in dealing with them. That is why caution and diligence are necessary.

The enemy fights the penitent with what is called the intermediate path. There is a well-known saying: "The intermediate path has saved many." Some spiritual fathers utilize it to advise anyone who rushes into an extreme spirituality that troubles him. We say, however, that departure from extremism does not mean departure from diligence. It is contrary to the commandment to depart from diligence and try to reach God through the wide door and the broad path (Matthew 7.13). What we fear from this matter is that the penitent may become accustomed to leniency in his life. This leniency pushes him down until he loses the fervor of repentance, then repentance itself, and falls into sin.

The penitent also struggles with the external appearance of worship and spirituality. A repentant person is urged by the fervor of his repentance to grow in worship. This growth may be measured in length rather than depth, however. So he increases his prayers, even if they are without spirit; he increases his readings, even if they are without understanding; he increases his reception of Holy Communion, even if he does so without preparation; he increases the tiring of his body, even if it is without benefit. Slowly, slowly, he is transformed into the guise of worship. This outward appearance will not benefit him. He will realize this and abandon it. Then he will tire of the spiritual life and desire his original life.

The penitent here is in need of leadership and spiritual guidance in order to understand the spirituality of worship and how to proceed in it. He also needs guidance in order to know that God rejects superficial worship, for He wants the heart first. Every image of worship, such as prayer, contemplation, reading, fasting, Holy Communion, and confession, must originate from a heart that loves God. These must be practiced with understanding, spiritual depth, and love toward God. They must originate from the heart. The penitent should place in front of him the Lord's reproof of erroneous worship: "These people draw near to Me with their mouth, and honor Me with their lips, but their heart is far from Me" (Matthew 15.8).

The external appearance of spiritual life is far removed from the life of repentance. Piety is not appearance and outward manifestations. These do not demonstrate a relationship with God. The Lord rebuked the scribes and Pharisees despite their great diligence in keeping the commandments. Their diligence led them to literal meanings and a departure from the Spirit. God did not accept this from them, saying that they were only concerned with the cleanliness of the outside of the cup. Certainly, the scribes and Pharisees were not repentant. Although they were proud of their diligence in executing the law, they were far away from repentance.

Do not abide by the letter of the law in your repentance, nor be concerned with appearances. For if you do this you will retreat, and lose your repentance. Be concerned with the spirit before everything. Be concerned with the love of God, so that your piety will originate from this love. In this way you will guard your repentance and guarantee that you do not falter between two opinions. Balaam was concerned that his external appearance was sound, without any sin or bad word being attributed to him, whereas his heart within was not with God (Numbers 24–25, Jude 11). He wanted to enjoy sin, without manifesting the appearance of sin. However, God is the One who examines hearts. Balaam's heart was not sound before God. He faltered between two opinions. He loved Balak's possessions, and he wanted to satisfy him. At the same time he did not say with his tongue one word to anger the Lord, and Balaam perished. Whoever falters between two opinions reaches this state.

He commits sin if he finds a door to escape from responsibility. What occupies him, then, is the responsibility, not purity of heart nor the love of God. That is why he is far from the life of repentance. Do not let yourself be the same, but let your heart be firm in God's love, not faltering on the path of sin. For your heart to be firm in God's love, also be concerned with the nourishment of your spirit.

CHAPTER 5

The Separation of Light and Darkness[1]

If you have repented and the light of God has entered your heart, then to preserve your repentance separate yourself from every work of darkness. It is a principle that God set for us from the beginning, which the book of Genesis narrates: "And God saw the light, that it was good; and God divided the light from the darkness" (Genesis 1.4). The principle continued in the New Testament, where it says: "What communion has light with darkness?" (2 Corinthians 6.14). It is not possible for a spiritual person to combine the two in his life.

That is why everyone who walks in the path of God must separate himself from everything that leads to sin and stumbling. This is what God wanted from the beginning of creation. However, the principle was broken and caused sin. The first breaking of this principle occurred when Eve sat with the serpent (Genesis 3), and we saw how darkness suppressed the light. The Bible talks to us about another dangerous infraction of this principle when it tells that preceding the flood "the sons of God saw the daughters of men were beautiful, [and] took wives for themselves of all they chose" (Genesis 6.2). The result was that man's evil increased and God was compelled to purify the earth from corruption by the flood. So, darkness for a second time suppressed the light.

God returned and separated light from darkness by means of the ark. He chose a holy group—Noah and his family—and he separated them from the evil world so that He would have a righteous group remaining, unaffected by the corruption of the world. Over time, as corruption entered into Noah's children, God chose Abram and separated him from the evil world, saying to him: "Get out of your country, from your kindred and from your father's house, to a land that I will show you. I will make you a great nation; I will bless you ... and you shall be a blessing" (Genesis 12.1–2).

---

[1]From a lecture that I gave at the Great Cathedral on Friday, January 31, 1976.

It is as if God says to Abram His servant, "Leave the place of sin, to preserve the purity of your heart, far away from evil. The light that is in you must be separated from the darkness that is in them." In the same way, the Lord ordered His people not to make a covenant with the people of the earth, and not to be married to them (Exodus 34.15–16). He also prohibited them from strange foreign women (Proverbs 2.16). God wants His children to keep away from every evil company (Psalm 1).

The apostle ordered the believers neither to eat nor keep company with sinners, and to put away from themselves any wicked person (1 Corinthians 5.11). In the same way, Saint John the Beloved said: "If anyone comes to you and does not bring this doctrine, do not receive him into your house nor greet him; for he who greets him shares in his evil deeds" (2 John 10–11).

Separation must take place from sin and sinners, both in conduct and knowledge. If external influences made Samson, David, and Solomon fall, then the weak should be even more cautious and keep away, for this is better for them. Similarly, the Church in the apostolic era—and in the first four centuries of Christianity in particular—cast sinners out of the Church. All the believers remained as a holy group, separated from evil and the ungodly, as happened in the story of Ananias and Sapphira (Acts 5), and with the sinner of Corinth (1 Corinthians 5.5).

The first instance in which man is isolated from evil is baptism, wherein he repudiates the devil with all his wicked works and repulsive evils, and all his soldiers, tricks, and authority. As he is isolated from the devil, he is also isolated from the old man, who is buried in baptism so that a new man may be born in the image of God. He places before him all his life the intention to live separate from sin and sinners.

How can we do this? If you cannot be separated from sinners by location, then be separated from them in practical terms. Be separated from them in your thought, conduct, and way of life. You are not capable of keeping away from the company of every sinner in the world, or else you would have to go out of the world, as Saint Paul the Apostle said (1 Corinthians 5.10). Let your dealings with them be within the limits of necessity only. Let your thoughts be separated from their thoughts, your conduct different from their conduct, your life different from their lives, and your expressions also different from their expressions, for as the Bible says: "Your speech betrays you" (Matthew 26.73).

That is why Saint John the Apostle said: "The children of God ... are manifest" (1 John 3.10). If they sit with the people of the world, the separation fully appears: a separation not by location, but in the type of life, in conduct, even in their appearance, features, looks, and actions. Their spirit distinguishes them. Here you see practically how God has separated light from darkness.

I hope that this separation is without pride. We do not want the man of God, who lives the life of repentance separated from sinners, to be separated because of arrogance, loftiness, and pride, as if he were better than they are, just as the Pharisees and scribes, who blamed Christ for sitting with tax collectors and sinners, used to do. What is meant instead is that there should be no communion with them in any wrongful deed.

There should be no conformity to sinners, nor imitating their habits, nor courtesy on account of truth. The apostle says: "Do not be conformed to this world" (Romans 12.2), that is, do not look like them. The penitent does not follow sinners in their sins. At the same time, neither does he judge them, but he has compassion on them and prays for the sake of their salvation. He attributes his refusal to mix with them in this way, "For the sake of my weakness, I cannot endure this mingling. I keep away because I am easily influenced and attracted. External factors can overcome my will. That is why keeping away is safer for me and escaping more suitable. It is not a matter of arrogance, because I do not forget my recent sins."

In this way, his approach differs from that of the pastors, who visit sinners and check up on them. They do this in order to attract them to repentance and reconcile them with God. The pastors do this provided that they at such moments are alert, not losing their spiritual reverence, nor merging with sinners in their amusements and indulgences. Instead, they are witnesses to the truth, ambassadors of the Lord, and a good example before these people. The Lord Jesus used to sit at the tables of tax collectors and enter their homes, in order to attract them to repentance and to raise their self-esteem, so that they would realize they had a share in Him, and that He was not there only for the righteous.

The penitent, however, says, "I am not at the same level as the pastors, nor do I have the same power as Christ. I am weaker than this company, so I will avoid it. I have not yet reached the level of those who can guide another and lead him to repentance, for I am still in need of someone to guide me and confirm me in my repentance." For these reasons he isolates himself from sinners, preserving the contrition of his heart. He does not despise any of them. He does not see himself as a light separated from darkness, for such a distinction in his mind would not agree with the feelings of repentance.

In his heart, he knows those of whom it was said that they were "light." The righteous person is light, of whom the Lord said: "You are the light of the world" (Matthew 5.14). If such a person is in any place, darkness disappears because of his light. It is as if a lamp were placed in a dark place, so that darkness is dispersed and the place becomes luminous. The same thing happens with the presence of the righteous in any place they stay; light spreads and darkness disappears.

Similarly, with the saints, because of their spiritual reverence, darkness can find no opportunity for itself in their presence. Sinners are embarrassed to be around them on account of their dignity and holiness. No one dares in their presence to act in a degrading way, or say a bad word, but rather he is ashamed of himself and his conduct. The people present feel that a spiritual atmosphere has prevailed in that place as a result of the presence of one of these righteous people. If there was sinful talk before their entrance, it stops, and everyone is quiet and the darkness disappears when they enter. No one can sin in their presence.

Are you the same? Have you become light after your repentance? Have you become even a small candle, giving dim light but in any case dispersing darkness? If you have not become such a light, then be very cautious of darkness. Remember at all times the saying of the Lord: "Let your waist be girded and your lamps burning" (Luke 12.35).

Let your light first of all be for your sake, in order to see well and have the spiritual insight to distinguish God's path and will, like one of the wise virgins (Matthew 25) who had oil in their lamps, so they were luminous and worthy to enter with the bridegroom. With these burning lamps, reveal the darkness and keep away from it.

In order to preserve your meekness, take darkness in its subjective meaning rather than its personal meaning. Take it to mean sin with all its images, and separate yourself from it. Separate yourself from every evil thought and desire. Do this in order to be able in your repentance to love the Lord your God with all your heart and with all your thoughts, according to the commandment (Deuteronomy 6.5).

How can love be with all the heart, if the heart is not separated from every sinful feeling, and if it mixes with worldly thoughts and desires? Every time you are attacked in your repentance by a worldly thought with its love and pleasures, remember the saying of the apostle: "Do not love the world or the things in the world" (1 John 2.15). And this saying: "If anyone loves the world, the love of the Father is not in him," for "the world is passing away, and the lust of it" (1 John 2.15–17). In order to keep away from the love of the world, avoid thinking about it and its desires. It is not possible for you presently to be disconnected from it by location, so separate yourself in thought and feeling. Say to the Lord, as we say in the Fraction Prayer in the Divine Liturgy, "Every thought that does not please Your goodness, let it be taken away from us."[2]

Be very strict and quick to separate yourself from sinful thoughts. For sin can enter into the heart of man even through a tiny hole, and keep widening a place inside until it destroys the heart. Sit with yourself, examine your heart and ask, "Is there still within me any mixing with the causes of sin, or with its thoughts and feelings?" If you find any of these things in you, reject and dismiss them, saying to them, "God has separated light from darkness."

[2]*Editor's note:* From the Fraction Prayer of the Coptic Orthodox Liturgy of Saint Basil the Great.

CHAPTER 6

Caring for the Spirit.[1]

Caring for the spirit is the necessary positive side of guarding repentance. Our discussion of removing the Canaanites from the land, not faltering between two opinions, and the separation of light from darkness represents the negative side of caution, whereas caring for the spirit represents the positive work, since the powerful spirit can keep man pure.

That is why it is necessary for man to care for his spirit, as he cares for his body. He should care for both together, and keep order and balance between them. He should observe this principle: the care that sacrifices for the sake of one must not harm the other. I say this because some people might care for the body and its health by prohibiting it from fasting, although this harms their spirit. Many parents fall into this error in bringing up their children, as if they were bringing up bodies without spirits. In our upbringing of animals, we either care for their bodies and work toward strengthening them for labor, or we work toward fattening them for the sake of slaughter. However, do we do the same thing with respect to man, bringing up his body for the worms to eat? It is shameful for us to care for the human body alone. Therefore care for your children's bodily health, and care also for their spiritual health. Do the same for your own health.

The health of the spirit is of benefit to the spirit and body also. If the spirit is sick, the body can become sick with it, and some diseases of the body are related to spiritual diseases. While the disease of the spirit harms the body, it is not necessarily true that the disease of the body harms the spirit. On the contrary, the spirit most likely benefits from it. The severest diseases of the body can benefit the spirit, leading man to repentance and prayer, awakening him and the people around him and teaching them renunciation

---

[1]From two lectures I gave on this topic in Saint Mark's hall in the Monastery of Anba Rewais on Friday October 15, 1965 and on Friday, October 22, 1965.

in life. Care for the health of your spirit, then, more than you care for the health of your body.

Do not show compassion toward your body while your spirit perishes. The Lord asked for the opposite when He said: "If your right eye causes you to sin, pluck it out and cast it from you . . . and if your right hand causes you to sin, cut it off and cast it from you" (Matthew 5.29–30). He showed us by this word that the spirit is more important. For its sake, you sacrifice the body.

Your spirit is God's image and likeness. It is very precious to Him. He became incarnate for its sake and sacrificed His pure blood on the cross. So the price of your spirit is the blood of Christ and every suffering that Christ endured for your sake. Further, you have only one spirit; you do not have another. If you lose it, you have lost everything; and if you gain it, you have gained everything. It is more precious than the world. That is why the Lord said: "For what is a man profited if he gains the whole world and loses his own soul? Or what will a man give in exchange for his soul?" (Matthew 16.26).

No one can harm your spirit except you. A person may detain your body, but he cannot detain your spirit. It remains free, even in prison. A person may kill your body, but he cannot kill your spirit.

Your spirit is a heavenly element. It is what gives life to the body. If you take care of it, you can elevate the body to a high spiritual condition. You will then resemble an earthly angel. You must take care of it, then, even if your body is weakened in the process. The apostle says: "Even though our outward man is perishing, yet the inward man is being renewed day by day" (2 Corinthians 4.16). Our outward man is this body, while the inward one is the spirit. The apostle likened this body to a tent in which we live (2 Corinthians 5.1). More importantly, God lives within. I wish then that you would take care of your spirit, so that it would not sin and the body sin with it.

You feed your body every day. You should feed your spirit, also. The spirit is nourished just as the body is nourished. The Lord says: "My food is to do the will of Him who sent Me" (John 4.34). The spirit is nourished "by every word that proceeds from the mouth of God" (Matthew 4.4). Is your spirit nourished by the words of God and by doing His will? Does it take this nourishment every day?

The body is nourished by three meals every day: at the beginning of the day, in the evening, and in between. Are you careful in giving your spirit its nourishment a few times every day, or do you neglect it so that it weakens?

The body requires many types of nourishment to satisfy all the necessary elements. You give it complete nourishment from fats, sugars, carbohydrates, proteins, vitamins, and iron. You are careful that it lacks nothing it needs. Do you give your spirit, like your body, all that it needs? Do you give it the nourishment of prayer, praise, meditation, spiritual reading, and *metanoia*? Do you give it what it needs from God's love? Does it receive this nourishment every day, a few times a day, along with other types of nourishment?

Do not be satisfied with giving nourishment to your body every day, several times a day, from different integrated components. For its nourishment you also give it food in sufficient amounts, as many calories as it needs. Do you treat your spirit in the same manner? Do you give it enough prayer to satisfy it, or do you pray for a few minutes and then get bored? Do you give it enough spiritual reading from the Holy Bible, the lives of saints, and spiritual topics to satisfy it? Or are you neither diligent nor concerned that your spirit receive its nourishment, while it hungers and thirsts for righteousness (Matthew 5.6)?

The body is not satisfied merely with certain amounts and types of food, but requires that the food be well cooked, palatable, and acceptable to its appetite. Do you present to your spirit good, tasty food, or do you offer it quick, unfocused prayers lacking in understanding, affection, or fervor? Do you think that such prayers are beneficial to the spirit? Do you offer your spirit reading without contemplation, depth, or understanding, and without application? Can the spirit digest this nourishment and benefit from it for its growth? This applies to the rest of the spiritual means.

Take care of your spirit, then, and know that just as the body weakens from lack of food, so does the spirit. The body loses weight from lack of food, while the spirit becomes lax and loses its fervor. Many are those who are afflicted by spiritual anemia, or weak spirituality. As the body becomes sick from malnutrition or indigestion, in the same way the spirit is sickened by all of these. It needs protection and immunity, exactly like the body.

If the body becomes sick, it needs a physician. It is the same for the spirit. The physicians of the spirit are the father confessors and spiritual advisors.

Spiritual remedies are numerous and well known, and everyone who feels deficient in a certain direction needs to take them. We say to the Lord in the Gregorian Liturgy, "Bind me with all the medications which bring me to life."[2] We also say to Him, "O true physician of our souls and bodies."[3] There is no doubt that the body receives greater attention from man than the spirit.

For this reason, one of the fathers explained this verse from the saying of the wise Solomon: "I saw servants on horses and princes walking on the ground like servants" (Ecclesiastes 10.7). This father indicated that the servants riding on the horses are our bodies, which we honor more than is necessary. The princes who walk on the ground like servants are our spirits, which do not find honor, like our bodies, but rather negligence in every aspect. We neglect the spirit, which has dominion by nature, to the point that it loses its authority and submits to the body, walking on the ground like a servant. We care for the body, however, and so we give it nourishment and beautify it with adornment.

Just as the body is adorned, the spirit also must be adorned. The spirit is adorned with virtues, the ornament of a gentle and quiet spirit, as the apostle says (1 Peter 3.4). It will wear "the wedding garment" (Matthew 22.11–12). Whoever wears it is worthy to enter with the Lord into His kingdom. It will wear fine linen, which means the righteous acts of the saints (Revelation 19.8). It will stand before God in white clothing. Do you adorn your spirit with all the fruits of the Spirit (Galatians 5.22)? Or do you stand naked before God, like the angel of the Church of Laodicea (Revelation 3.17)?

Know that every ornament of the body from the outside is of no use, for as the Psalmist says: "All her glory as the King's daughter is within" (Psalm 44.14), while her clothing is "interwoven with gold" (Psalm 44.10). Your spirit will stand on the Last Day with all its ornaments before God "as a bride adorned for her husband" (Revelation 21.2). With respect to the attire of the spirit, how beautiful is the phrase spoken about baptism: "For as many of you as were baptized into Christ have put on Christ" (Galatians 3.27)—a day in which the spirit proceeded from baptism in perfect splendor.

[2] *Editor's note:* From the Coptic Orthodox Liturgy of Saint Gregory the Theologian.

[3] *Editor's note:* From the Coptic Orthodox Litany for the Sick, prayed during evening raising of incense prayers.

To this attire is added whatever crown the spirit wears as a result of its struggles and victories. What does your spirit wear as a result of these? Are you like the Ark of the Covenant, which was covered with gold inside and out? (Exodus 25.11)? In caring for the spirit, place in front of you these commandments:

1. Walk in the Spirit, and you shall not fulfill the lust of the flesh (Galatians 5.16).
2. Be filled with the Spirit (Ephesians 5.18).
3. Be fervent in spirit (Romans 12.11).

In this way you worship God in the Spirit (Philippians 3.3). You will pray with the Spirit and sing with the Spirit (1 Corinthians 14.15). You will bring forth the fruits of the Spirit (Galatians 5.22), knowing that "He who sows to the Spirit will of the Spirit reap everlasting life" (Galatians 6.8). If you walk like this in life, you will be able to preserve your repentance and not turn back. Give your spirit its nourishment. As for your body, give it enough to sustain it, and not as much as it desires.

Your sustaining of your spirit preserves you from falling. Everyone is subject to temptations, enticements, and spiritual warfare. However, the strong in spirit will be as firm as the house built on the rock (Matthew 7.24–25). Those whose spirits were nourished with the word of God and strengthened by spiritual practices have experience with the wars of the demons. They have the ability to fight them, having become strong from within like fortified cities.

Why do some fall, however? They fall because they have no resistance from within, nor any immunity. As when a disease attacks an entire town, the strong are able to withstand while the weak fall. If the matter is so, then try to be strengthened in spirit, so that if sin comes to you it will find neither acceptance nor submission. It will pass and go away. Form for yourself spiritual reserves that will benefit you in the lean years.

The majority of those who fall, and of those who suffer relapse after their repentance, are satisfied with leaving sin at the beginning of repentance. At the same time they left their spirits without nourishment, strengthening, or care, so that they became weak, which made them fall easily. As for you, do not be like this. Have spiritual means that tie you to God, and which you follow in order and regularity. Attend spiritual meetings, have spiritual friends, read spiritual readings, and have a spiritual atmosphere that surrounds you on every side, along with your spiritual father and his advice and guidance.

CHAPTER 7

Other Means

AMONG THE THINGS THAT ASSIST in preserving repentance is the full measure of contrition. This is so one can realize the ugliness of sin and its bitter consequences, and experience the torment of the conscience so that he will not return to sin again. We have discussed in a previous chapter the feelings of shame, the grief and the tears, that accompany repentance, as in the stories of the saints. In the same way, contrition is accompanied by abandoning the "best seat" and avoiding opportunities for leadership that can make man forget sin. If this is not done, some people regrettably try, at the beginning of their repentance, to jump quickly to joy. They do so without passing through the stage of contrition, regret, and grief, and forget that joy is a later stage that they cannot claim for themselves; rather, it is granted by the Lord to those who have proven that their contrition is genuine and their repentance firm.

The penitent who rushes toward joy can easily return to his old sins. Contrition is a strong wall that guards repentance and keeps the heart awake. It calls for caution and diligence, and confirms the fear of God in him. Contrition keeps the penitent in humility of heart. Grace works within the meek and protects them from falling. As long as the penitent is contrite, he will remember his weakness and failures, and this will make him continuously cautious.

The devil, however, provokes that quick joy in you to lead you to carelessness. He makes you feel that you have come out entirely from the circle of sin having been sanctified and renewed. Sin no longer has authority over you, because you are protected and preserved by grace, which causes you not to care. Truly, grace protects us, but it does not cancel our will, and it does not make us walk toward good. What will happen if we do not cooperate with the work of grace in us? Therefore, if you are called to joy, say, "I do not deserve it." If God grants you the joy of His salvation (Psalm 50), let this joy be a reason for an increase in contrition, along with self-reproof.

The canons of the early church fathers included laws of severe punishment. As a result of these punishments, every penitent used to feel the measure of the sin into which he fell, so that his heart was contrite and he felt unworthy even to enter the church. At that time the Church was holier, and believers were more serious and strict in their lives. When these punishments stopped, negligence entered into the souls of many. I wish that every penitent would place in front of him the saying of Saint Macarius the Great: "Judge yourself my brother, before they judge you."[1] If we regret our sins as we should, then this regret will help us in not returning to sin. For how can we return to what we regret?

One of the reasons for spiritual relapse and the return to sin is a wrong concept of spiritualty and of the love of God. Some people concentrate greatly on God's love and forgiveness, which makes them forget God's goodness and holiness. It makes them forget the fear of God as well. So they lack the fear which would push them to caution. If they fall, they do not regret it for very long, relying on God's love. In this way, sin becomes easy in their eyes.

One of these erroneous concepts is thinking that confession is merely mentioning your sins to the priest, receiving absolution for them, and that's the end of the matter. They do not combine confession with true repentance, great regret, reproof of the self, and a true determination to leave sin and avoid its causes. The ease of confession might be one reason for a person to return to sin. Another erroneous concept is thinking that repentance is merely the exchange of one behavior for another, going from wrongful actions to a virtuous life without concentrating on the relationship with God.

You, however, should say, "If I am given all the virtues without You, O Lord, I do not want them. In my repentance, I want You. Virtue is an expression of my connection with You. Shall I say, 'I will give You my heart,' merely as a form of energy with which to look at my feelings? No, but I will rather give You all the love in my heart, to live with You and be confirmed in You. Repentance is not about attaining virtue, but reaching You."

[1]Macarius the Great, *Bustān al-Ruhbān* (*Paradise of the Fathers*, Arabic).

In this manner, repentance can be confirmed and established on the love of God and adherence to Him. For love, as the apostle said, "never fails" (1 Corinthians 13.8). As was also said in the Song of Songs: "Much water will not be able to quench love" (Song of Songs 8.7).

Among the reasons for spiritual relapse is forgetting the promises made to God—those promises that you made to the Lord on the day of your repentance. You may have promised God in certain details. That is why, if you are attacked by sin, you should reject it and remember your promises. Say, "I have an agreement with God. I cannot go back on my promises to Him, because I have promised, and I want to be a man according to the commandment of the Bible: 'Be strong and become a man'" (3 Kingdoms 2.2). Do not be like the ground wherein the seeds were sown, and the birds came and devoured them, or thorns sprang up and choked what had sprouted.

Among the reasons for spiritual relapse, also, is the lax conscience: the conscience that accommodates everything, justifies everything, and swallows the camel (Matthew 23.24). It is sometimes assisted by a mind that stands at the service of every distraction that attacks the soul. It presents proofs and examples, and perhaps verses and stories of the saints, in order to serve ignorantly every evil desire of the soul. This is why you need continual spiritual guidance so that you are not distracted.

Place yourself under the leadership of wise guidance. Remember that "those who are without an advisor fall like the leaves of trees." One of the saints said that the greatest fall for a youth is that "he walks as he pleases." The wise man said: "Lean not on your own understanding" (Proverbs 3.5). The advisor preserves balance in the life of the penitent. He does not let the penitent grieve excessively, which may make him lose hope. Nor does he let him ask for the joy and delight that would lead him to carelessness.

"Do not labor for the food which perishes, but for the food which endures to everlasting life" (John 6.27).

CHAPTER 8

Some Questions on Repentance

1. I am always conscious of my sins.

Question: To what extent should we apply the phrase, "I am always conscious of my sins?" Does this mean we should remember our sins regularly?

Answer: We should remember regularly that we are sinners and always be conscious of our sins, in order to attain meekness and contrition of heart, and to feel our weakness so that we increase in caution and ask for God's help through prayer.

If remembrance, however, brings sin back to us, we should refrain from it. Remember what we say in the Divine Liturgy, "The remembrance of evil entailing death."[1] According to the teachings of the fathers, it is better for us to avoid the remembrance of lustful and provocative sins, because this remembrance brings back the wars of sin.

If we remember a lustful sin, let us not enter into its details, because it is a cause of stumbling. With the sin of fornication, for example, the penitent is not permitted to remember the details and steps of committing it, in case the desire for the sin comes back to him again. Even if the desire does not trouble him the first time he remembers these details, it might trouble him later.

Similar to the desire of fornication is the desire for majesty and position, the desire for the best seat, and other daydreams. If the penitent enters into the details of his hopes and dreams—whatever positions, lusts, precedence over others, or the love of praise and honor that he desires—it is easy for these feelings to come back and entice him as he delights in them. He indulges in these, and perhaps this is the cause of the daydreams that may trouble his thoughts in time of prayer. It is better for him to flee from all of this.

---

[1] *Editor's note:* From the Coptic Orthodox Liturgy of Saint Basil the Great.

The same goes for the sin of envy. Entering into its details is not permitted. This is where the penitent remembers the person who was better at something than he was, or enjoyed a pleasure he wanted but could not obtain. Such remembrances bring back to him the wars with his old lusts, along with feelings of a lack of love toward that envied person.

This is also the case with the sin of anger over people's wrongdoings, whether they are visible or suppressed. This goes along with the memory of the causes for these wrongdoings and their outward appearances, and the feelings of rage or hatred, or the desire to seek revenge, which they arouse. If the penitent remembers these details, he might feel that he has begun to warm up and become agitated from within, instead of being remorseful over his anger. This happens if he enters into the details.

In any case, a man should watch his feelings. The sins or details that he mentions in a painful way will take him back to the feelings of sin, so he should avoid them. However, he should relive the memory that brings regret, tears, and contrition of heart to him, as long as it is within the feelings of repentance.

2. The penitent's readings

Question: I am a person who is new to repentance. What readings do you advise for my spiritual benefit in this period? What should I refrain from reading?

Answer: Keep away from any readings that cause stumbling, or bring laxity and judgment of others. Also avoid readings that arouse argument or love of teaching in you, or feelings of superiority and intelligence. Also avoid readings that cool your spiritual fervor, dry your tears, and introduce you into an atmosphere of pleasure and comedy.

Among the readings which would be very beneficial to you are the lives of the saints and the persons of the Holy Bible. Since these readings present practical ideas to you, and you desire to live like them, this will give you energy and spiritual fervor.

In the same way, the reading of spiritual and ascetical books will benefit you. It will enlighten your path, and will also protect your thoughts in a pure spiritual atmosphere. It is important that you choose the books that have depth, by which you are influenced, which push you to be connected to God, reproach you over your sins, open before you high horizons, and make you humble, no matter what your attainment in repentance may be.

The stories of the saints who repented are also beneficial to you. Some examples are the life of Saint Augustine and his *Confessions*, the life of Saint Jacob the Struggler, Saint Moses the Black, and others. There are also the lives of female saints who repented, such as Saint Mary of Egypt, Saint Pelagia, Saint Martha, Saint Evdokia, and Saint Mary, the niece of Saint Abraham the solitary.

From the Holy Bible, choose for yourself certain sections which influence you, such as the books of Ecclesiastes, Proverbs, Jonah, Joel, and Deuteronomy; from the New Testament, the epistles to the Philippians, Ephesians, the two epistles to the Corinthians, and Timothy. In a notebook, write down the verses which influenced you in order to learn them.

3. Spiritual practices and the love of God

Question: Which is better for me in the period of repentance: spiritual exercises or a vigorous love for God that would make the path short?

Answer: In this respect, not all people are of the same type. Some people are granted in their repentance a burning love in their hearts that removes every previous weakness, sin, and deficiency. Yet there are other people who carve a path amidst rock, and need great struggle to resist every sin with harsh exercises and a great vigilance which is very keen on their salvation, as Saint Paul warned the Hebrews: "You have not yet resisted to bloodshed, striving against sin" (Hebrews 12.4).

Here the person must train himself and examines how he did each exercise. The saints also practiced exercises in matters pertaining to their spiritual lives and growth. Saint Paul the Apostle says: "This being so, I myself always strive to have a conscience without offence toward God and men" (Acts 24.16). He also said: "In all things I have learned both to be full and to be hungry, both to abound and to suffer need" (Philippians 4.12).

Therefore, the answer depends on what path the Lord grants you to follow. If He kindles you with love, walk in the path of love. If He leads you step by step through struggle and toil, you struggle and toil in order to reach your goal.

4. Old friends

Question: Do you think it is necessary to get rid of the friends whom I lived with for many years before repentance, in a close association of heart and a deep relationship? I trusted them, and they knew my secrets. How can I leave them?

Answer: Your true friend is your companion in the way to the kingdom. He shares with you the spiritual life and encourages you toward it, and you encourage him also.

Every relationship or association outside God's love should be discarded. For the Lord says: "He who loves father or mother more than Me is not worthy of Me" (Matthew 10.37). If your old friends make you stumble, or lead you away from the life of repentance, avoid them with conviction and firmness.

There is no objection to having old friends if you can attract them to repentance with you. If you cannot, then let your relationship with them be superficial. If they are dangerous to you, then you should prefer your relationship to God over your relationship with them. Even if you encounter difficulty, bear it for the sake of the Lord. Remember what Abram the father of fathers did when the Lord called him. He left his family, kindred, and country to walk behind God (Genesis 12.1). Likewise, in order to preserve your repentance for the sake of God, you leave all who hinder you.